JUMP Math 7.2

Book 7 Part 2 of 2

Contents

jump math™

MULTIPLYING POTENTIAL.

JUMP Math
Toronto, Canada
www.jumpmath.org

Writers: Dr. John Mighton, Dr. Sindi Sabourin, Dr. Anna Klebanov
Contributing Writer: Margaret McClintock
Cover Design: Blakeley Words+Pictures
Text Design: Pam Lostracco
Layout: Laura Brady, Rita Camacho, Nuria Gonzalez, Pam Lostracco, Ilyana Martinez, Craig Wing-King
Cover Photograph: © Gary Blakeley, Blakeley Words+Pictures

ISBN: 978-1-897120-58-3

Eleventh printing July 2018

Printed and bound in Canada

Welcome to JUMP Math

Entering the world of JUMP Math means believing that every child has the capacity to be fully numerate and to love math. Founder and mathematician John Mighton has used this premise to develop his innovative teaching method. The resulting materials isolate and describe concepts so clearly and incrementally that everyone can understand them.

JUMP Math is comprised of workbooks, teacher's guides, evaluation materials, outreach programs, tutoring support through schools and community organizations, and provincial curriculum correlations. All of this is presented on the JUMP Math website: **www.jumpmath.org**.

Teacher's guides are available on the website for free use. Read the introduction to the teacher's guides before you begin using these materials. This will ensure that you understand both the philosophy and the methodology of JUMP Math. The workbooks are designed for use by students, with adult guidance. Each student will have unique needs and it is important to provide the student with the appropriate support and encouragement as he or she works through the material.

Allow students to discover the concepts on the worksheets by themselves as much as possible. Mathematical discoveries can be made in small, incremental steps. The discovery of a new step is like untangling the parts of a puzzle. It is exciting and rewarding.

Students will need to answer the shaded questions using a notebook. Grid paper and notebooks should always be on hand for answering extra questions or when additional room for calculation is needed. Grid paper is also available in the BLM section of the Teacher's Guide.

Contents

Unit 3: Probability and Data Management

Unit 4: Patterns and Algebra

Unit 5: Geometry

Unit 6: Number Sense

Unit 7: Geometry

Unit 8: Probability and Data Management

1. Match the fractions and decimals.

A $\dfrac{4}{10}$ B $\dfrac{4}{1000}$ C $\dfrac{44}{100}$ D $\dfrac{4}{100}$ E $\dfrac{44}{1000}$

0.04 ____   0.4 ____   0.004 ____   0.44 ____   0.044 ____

> **REMINDER ▶** A **decimal fraction** has a power of 10 (10, 100, 1000, …) in the denominator.

2. Write the fraction as an equivalent decimal fraction and as a decimal.

a) $\dfrac{1}{2} = \dfrac{1 \times 5}{2 \times 5} = \dfrac{}{10} = 0.$ ____   b) $\dfrac{1}{5} =$ c) $\dfrac{1}{4} =$

d) $\dfrac{3}{4} =$ e) $\dfrac{6}{25} =$ f) $\dfrac{17}{50} =$

3. Write three different fractions that are equivalent to the decimal.

a) 0.5   b) 0.2   c) 0.25   d) 0.60

4. Write the decimal as a fraction in lowest terms.

a) $0.35 = \dfrac{}{100} = \dfrac{}{20}$ b) $0.25 =$ c) $0.6 =$ d) $0.40 =$ e) $0.48 =$

5. a) Describe the patterns in the numerator and in the denominator of the equivalent fractions.

i) $\dfrac{1}{5} = \dfrac{2}{10} = \dfrac{3}{15} = \dfrac{4}{20} = \dfrac{5}{25} = \dfrac{6}{30}$ ii) $\dfrac{3}{4} = \dfrac{6}{8} = \dfrac{9}{12} = \dfrac{12}{16} = \dfrac{15}{20} = \dfrac{18}{24}$

b) What decimal do the equivalent fractions equal?

6. a) Circle the fractions in which the numerator and denominator have at least one common factor.

$\dfrac{3}{5}$ $\dfrac{2}{10}$ $\dfrac{3}{10}$ $\dfrac{5}{12}$ $\dfrac{12}{15}$ $\dfrac{8}{20}$ $\dfrac{13}{40}$ $\dfrac{2}{100}$ $\dfrac{7}{100}$ $\dfrac{15}{100}$ $\dfrac{17}{100}$ $\dfrac{125}{1000}$

b) Which fractions in part a) can be written in lower terms (e.g., $\dfrac{6}{8} = \dfrac{3}{4}$)? Explain.

c) Use your explanation in part b). Circle the decimals that can be written as a fraction with a denominator smaller than 100.

Example: $0.16 = \dfrac{16}{100} = \dfrac{4}{25}$

0.12   0.33   0.24   0.07   0.13   0.06   0.29   0.55   0.99   0.01

7. Would you use a fraction or a decimal in each case? Explain.

a) $\dfrac{1}{4}$ h or 0.25 h   b) 0.25 m or $\dfrac{1}{4}$ m   c) $\dfrac{1}{8}$ kg or 0.125 kg   d) $\dfrac{3}{4}$ cup or 0.75 cup

A **unit fraction** has 1 in the numerator. Examples: $\dfrac{1}{2}, \dfrac{1}{3}, \dfrac{1}{7}$

1. Write the fraction as a sum of unit fractions and as a product of a fraction and a whole number.

   a) $\dfrac{3}{8} = \dfrac{1}{8} + \dfrac{1}{8} + \dfrac{1}{8} = \underline{\quad} \times \dfrac{1}{8}$

   b) $\dfrac{3}{4} =$

   c) $\dfrac{4}{5} =$

2. Write the fraction as a sum of unit fractions. Then write the unit fractions as decimals and add.

   a) $\dfrac{3}{5} = \dfrac{1}{5} + \dfrac{1}{5} + \dfrac{1}{5} = 0.2 + 0.2 + 0.2 = 0.6$

   b) $\dfrac{4}{5} =$

   c) $\dfrac{3}{4} =$

   d) $\dfrac{3}{2} =$

3. Write the fraction as the product of a unit fraction and a whole number. Then write the unit fraction as a decimal and multiply.

   a) $\dfrac{4}{5} = 4 \times \dfrac{1}{5} = 4 \times 0.2 = 0.8$

   b) $\dfrac{3}{4} =$

   c) $\dfrac{3}{5} =$

   d) $\dfrac{5}{4} =$

4. a) What is the rule for the pattern 0.05, 0.10, 0.15, 0.20, … ?

   b) $\dfrac{1}{20} = 0.05$, $\dfrac{2}{20} = 0.10$, $\dfrac{3}{20} = 0.15$, … Continue the pattern to write $\dfrac{11}{20}$ as a decimal.

   c) If you know $\dfrac{1}{20} = 0.05$, how can you use multiplication to find $\dfrac{11}{20}$ as a decimal?

5. a) $\dfrac{1}{4} = 0.25$, so $\dfrac{7}{4} = \underline{7} \times \underline{0.25}$

   $= \underline{1.75}$

   b) $\dfrac{1}{5} = 0.\underline{\quad}$, so $\dfrac{21}{5} = \underline{\quad} \times \underline{\quad}$

   $= \underline{\quad}$

   c) $\dfrac{1}{2} = 0.\underline{\quad}$, so $\dfrac{13}{2} = \underline{\quad} \times \underline{\quad}$

   $= \underline{\quad}$

6. Write the fractions as decimals. Add the decimals. Write the sum as a fraction in lowest terms. Check your answer by adding the fractions.

   a) $\dfrac{1}{4} + \dfrac{2}{5} = 0.25 + 0.4 = 0.65 = \dfrac{65}{100} = \dfrac{13}{20}$

   Check: $\dfrac{5 \times 1}{5 \times 4} + \dfrac{2 \times 4}{5 \times 4} = \dfrac{5}{20} + \dfrac{8}{20} = \dfrac{13}{20}$

   b) $\dfrac{1}{2} + \dfrac{1}{5}$

   c) $\dfrac{1}{2} + \dfrac{4}{5}$

   d) $\dfrac{3}{2} + \dfrac{3}{4}$

NS7-57 Relating Fractions and Division

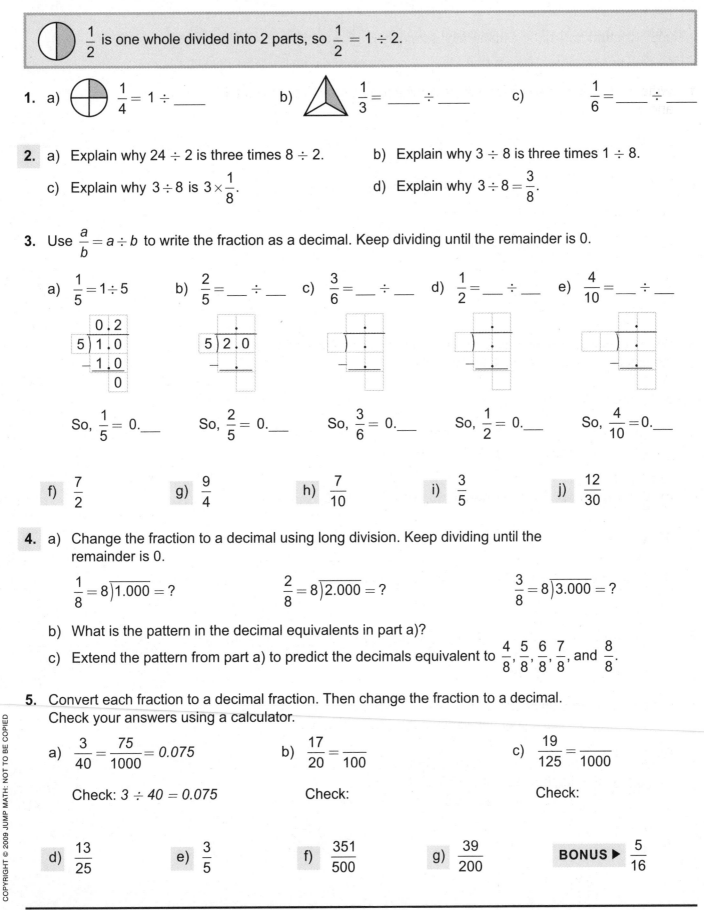

$\dfrac{1}{2}$ is one whole divided into 2 parts, so $\dfrac{1}{2} = 1 \div 2$.

1. a) $\dfrac{1}{4} = 1 \div$ ____   b) $\dfrac{1}{3} =$ ____ $\div$ ____   c) $\dfrac{1}{6} =$ ____ $\div$ ____

2. a) Explain why $24 \div 2$ is three times $8 \div 2$.   b) Explain why $3 \div 8$ is three times $1 \div 8$.

c) Explain why $3 \div 8$ is $3 \times \dfrac{1}{8}$.   d) Explain why $3 \div 8 = \dfrac{3}{8}$.

3. Use $\dfrac{a}{b} = a \div b$ to write the fraction as a decimal. Keep dividing until the remainder is 0.

a) $\dfrac{1}{5} = 1 \div 5$ b) $\dfrac{2}{5} =$ ___ $\div$ ___   c) $\dfrac{3}{6} =$ ___ $\div$ ___   d) $\dfrac{1}{2} =$ ___ $\div$ ___   e) $\dfrac{4}{10} =$ ___ $\div$ ___

$$5\overline{)\begin{array}{l}0.2\\1.0\end{array}}$$
$$-1.0$$
$$0$$

$$5\overline{)2.0}$$

So, $\dfrac{1}{5} = 0.$___   So, $\dfrac{2}{5} = 0.$___   So, $\dfrac{3}{6} = 0.$___   So, $\dfrac{1}{2} = 0.$___   So, $\dfrac{4}{10} = 0.$___

f) $\dfrac{7}{2}$ g) $\dfrac{9}{4}$ h) $\dfrac{7}{10}$ i) $\dfrac{3}{5}$ j) $\dfrac{12}{30}$

4. a) Change the fraction to a decimal using long division. Keep dividing until the remainder is 0.

$\dfrac{1}{8} = 8\overline{)1.000} = ?$ $\dfrac{2}{8} = 8\overline{)2.000} = ?$ $\dfrac{3}{8} = 8\overline{)3.000} = ?$

b) What is the pattern in the decimal equivalents in part a)?

c) Extend the pattern from part a) to predict the decimals equivalent to $\dfrac{4}{8}, \dfrac{5}{8}, \dfrac{6}{8}, \dfrac{7}{8}$, and $\dfrac{8}{8}$.

5. Convert each fraction to a decimal fraction. Then change the fraction to a decimal. Check your answers using a calculator.

a) $\dfrac{3}{40} = \dfrac{75}{1000} = 0.075$ b) $\dfrac{17}{20} = \dfrac{}{100}$ c) $\dfrac{19}{125} = \dfrac{}{1000}$

Check: $3 \div 40 = 0.075$ Check: Check:

d) $\dfrac{13}{25}$ e) $\dfrac{3}{5}$ f) $\dfrac{351}{500}$ g) $\dfrac{39}{200}$ **BONUS ▶** $\dfrac{5}{16}$

A **repeating decimal** is a decimal with a digit or group of digits that repeats forever.

The digit or sequence of digits that repeats can be shown by a bar. Example: $4.121212\ldots = 4.\overline{12}$.

A **terminating decimal** is a decimal that does not go on forever. Examples: 5.68, 0.444

Some decimals do not terminate or repeat. Example: $\pi = 3.14159\ldots$

1. Write each decimal to eight decimal places.

   a) $0.\overline{3} \approx 0.\underline{\,3\,}$ __ __ __ __ __ __ __

   b) $0.0\overline{3} \approx 0.\underline{\,0\,}$ $\underline{\,3\,}$ $\underline{\,3\,}$ $\underline{\,3\,}$ __ __ __ __

   c) $0.00\overline{3} \approx 0.$__ __ __ __ __ __ __ __

   d) $0.\overline{52} \approx 0.$__ __ __ __ __ __ __ __

   e) $0.\overline{817} \approx 0.$__ __ __ __ __ __ __ __

   f) $0.8\overline{17} \approx 0.$__ __ __ __ __ __ __ __

   g) $0.9\overline{26} \approx 0.$__ __ __ __ __ __ __ __

   h) $0.25\overline{37} \approx 0.$__ __ __ __ __ __ __ __

   i) $7.2\overline{3} \approx 7.$__ __ __ __ __ __ __ __

   j) $8.2\overline{539} \approx 8.$__ __ __ __ __ __ __ __

2. Circle the repeating decimals.

   0.123412312   0.77   0.222222222…   0.512512512…   0.123238…

3. Write each repeating decimal using bar notation.

   a) 0.555555… = _____

   b) 2.343434… = _____

   c) 5.237237… = _____

   d) 57.121212… = _____

   e) 8.162626… = _____

   f) 0.910591059105 = _____

4. Find the decimal value of each fraction to 3 decimal places. Then write the fraction as a repeating decimal.

   a) $3\overline{)1.0\,0\,0}$ $\dfrac{1}{3} \approx$

   b) $3\overline{)2.0\,0\,0}$ $\dfrac{2}{3} \approx$

5. Use long division to calculate the decimal equivalent of the fraction to 6 decimal places. Then write the decimal using bar notation.

   a) $\dfrac{1}{6}$

   b) $\dfrac{4}{9}$

   c) $\dfrac{1}{11}$

   d) $\dfrac{5}{12}$

6. Match the fractions with their decimal equivalents. Use a calculator.

A $\dfrac{1}{3}$ B $\dfrac{55}{99}$ C $\dfrac{2}{3}$ D $\dfrac{2}{9}$ ___ $0.\overline{6}$ ___ $0.\overline{2}$ ___ $0.\overline{3}$ ___ $0.\overline{5}$

7. Round the repeating decimals to the nearest tenth, hundredth, and thousandth.

	nearest tenth	nearest hundredth	nearest thousandth
$\dfrac{2}{7} = 0.285714285714285714285714...$			
$\dfrac{5}{13} = 0.384615384615384615384615...$			

How to Compare Decimals   Example: $.678 \boxed{?} .\overline{67}$

Step 1: Write out the first few digits of each decimal.
(Add zeros at the end of terminating decimals.)

$.6\ 7\ \boxed{8}\ 0\ 0\ 0$

Step 2: Circle the first digits where the decimals differ.

$.6\ 7\ \boxed{6}\ 7\ 6\ 7$

Step 3: The decimal with the greater circled digit is greater.

$.678 \boxed{>} .\overline{67}$

8. Compare the decimals.

a) $.349 \boxed{} .3\overline{49}$

b) $.278 \boxed{} .\overline{27}$

c) $.\overline{613} \boxed{} .61\overline{3}$

9. Write each group of numbers in order from least to greatest.

a) $0.4 \quad 0.4\overline{2} \quad 0.\overline{42} \quad 0.42$

b) $0.16 \quad 0.\overline{1} \quad 0.1\overline{6} \quad 0.\overline{16}$

c) $0.387 \quad 0.38\overline{7} \quad 0.3\overline{87} \quad 0.\overline{387}$

d) $0.546 \quad 0.54\overline{6} \quad 0.5\overline{46} \quad 0.\overline{546}$

e) $0.383 \quad 0.38\overline{3} \quad 0.3\overline{83} \quad 0.\overline{383}$

f) $0.786 \quad 0.78\overline{6} \quad 0.7\overline{86} \quad 0.\overline{786}$

10. a) Use long division to write the fractions as repeating decimals. Copy your answers below.

$\dfrac{1}{9} =$ $\dfrac{2}{9} =$ $\dfrac{3}{9} =$ $\dfrac{4}{9} =$

b) Use the pattern you found in part a) to find...

$\dfrac{5}{9} =$ $\dfrac{6}{9} =$ $\dfrac{7}{9} =$ $\dfrac{8}{9} =$ $\dfrac{9}{9} =$

NS7-59 Using Decimals to Compare Fractions

1. Write each fraction as a decimal. Circle the decimal that is closest to the fraction.

   a) $\frac{1}{4} = $ _.25_

      $\frac{1}{4}$ is closest to: 0.2   0.4   0.6

   b) $\frac{3}{4} = $ _____

      $\frac{3}{4}$ is closest to: 0.5   0.7   0.9

   c) $\frac{1}{5} = $ _____

      $\frac{1}{5}$ is closest to: 0.14   0.25   0.36

   d) $\frac{2}{5} = $ _____

      $\frac{2}{5}$ is closest to: 0.25   0.42   0.52

2. Express each fraction as a decimal (round your answer to three decimal places).
   Circle the fraction that is closest to the decimal.

   a) $\frac{4}{5}$ [.800] $\frac{7}{10}$ [   ] $\frac{2}{3}$ [   ]   0.65 is closest to: $\frac{4}{5}$ $\frac{7}{10}$ $\frac{2}{3}$

   b) $\frac{1}{7}$ [   ] $\frac{1}{8}$ [   ] $\frac{1}{9}$ [   ]   0.125 is closest to: $\frac{1}{7}$ $\frac{1}{8}$ $\frac{1}{9}$

   c) $3\frac{1}{2}$ [   ] $\frac{10}{3}$ [   ] $\frac{8}{3}$ [   ]   3.28 is closest to: $3\frac{1}{2}$ $\frac{10}{3}$ $\frac{8}{3}$

3. Use decimal equivalents to order these fractions from greatest to least: $\frac{5}{6}, \frac{13}{17}, \frac{56}{73}, \frac{4}{5}$.

4. a) Compare each fraction and decimal by writing them as fractions with
      a common denominator.

      i)   0.57 and $\frac{3}{5}$ ii)   0.83 and $\frac{4}{5}$ iii) $\frac{2}{3}$ and 0.37

   b) Compare each fraction and decimal from part a) by writing the fraction
      as a decimal.

   c) Do you prefer the method you used in part a) or part b)? Explain.

5. a) Which of $\frac{6}{11}, \frac{23}{45}$, and $\frac{11}{21}$ is closest to $\frac{1}{2}$?   b) Which of 0.285, $0.\overline{286}$, and $0.28\overline{5}$ is closest to $\frac{2}{7}$?

6. 0.24 is close to 0.25, so a fraction close to 0.24 is $\frac{1}{4}$. Write a fraction that is close to...

   a) 0.52   b) 0.32   c) 0.298   d) 0.38   e) 0.59   f) 0.12

7. a) Use a calculator to write each fraction as a decimal: $\frac{8}{13}, \frac{9}{11}, \frac{5}{36}, \frac{3}{17}, \frac{89}{121}$.

   b) Order the fractions in part a) from least to greatest.

INVESTIGATION ▶ How can you tell from the fraction whether the equivalent decimal repeats or terminates?

A. Write three different fractions, one with each denominator: 10, 100, and 1 000. Will the decimal representations of these fractions terminate? Explain.

B. Why can a terminating decimal always be written as a decimal fraction?

Examples: $0.3 = \dfrac{3}{10}$, $0.17 = \dfrac{17}{100}$

C. Divide using a calculator. Does the decimal equivalent of the fraction terminate or repeat?

a) $\dfrac{5}{8}$ b) $\dfrac{7}{12}$ c) $\dfrac{6}{13}$ d) $\dfrac{7}{15}$ e) $\dfrac{3}{17}$ f) $\dfrac{13}{2000}$

Write the fractions with equivalent terminating decimals as decimal fractions.

D. $10 = 2 \times 5$. Write 100 and 1 000 as a product of 2s and 5s.

E. Write a fraction with a denominator that is a product of 2s, 5s, or a combination of 2s and 5s. Use a calculator to divide the numerator by the denominator. Does the equivalent decimal terminate?

F. Write $\dfrac{1}{6}, \dfrac{2}{6}, \dfrac{3}{6}, \dfrac{4}{6}$, and $\dfrac{5}{6}$ in simplest form. Why is $\dfrac{3}{6}$ the only one of the sixths that terminates?

How to Decide If a Fraction Is Equivalent to a Terminating Decimal or a Repeating Decimal

Step 1: Write the fraction in **lowest terms**.

Step 2: Look at the **denominator**.
If it can be written as a product of only 2s and/or 5s, the decimal terminates.
If it cannot be written as a product of only 2s and/or 5s, the decimal repeats.

---

1. a) Calculate the first few powers of 3 (3, 3×3, $3 \times 3 \times 3$, …).

     b) Are the decimal equivalents for $\dfrac{1}{3}, \dfrac{1}{9}$, and $\dfrac{1}{27}$ repeating decimals? How can you tell without calculating the decimal?

2. a) Write out the twelfths from $\dfrac{1}{12}$ to $\dfrac{11}{12}$. Write them all in lowest terms.

     b) Predict which of the twelfths will terminate. Explain.
     c) Use a calculator to calculate the decimal equivalents for all the twelfths.
     d) Which of the twelfths terminate? Was your prediction in part b) correct?

3. The denominators of $\dfrac{3}{6}, \dfrac{3}{12}, \dfrac{6}{12}, \dfrac{3}{15}, \dfrac{6}{15}, \dfrac{9}{15}$ and $\dfrac{12}{15}$, all have 3 as a factor. But they are all terminating decimals. Why?

NS7-61 Adding and Subtracting Repeating Decimals

1. Add or subtract the decimals by lining up the decimal places.

a) $.\overline{25} + .33 = .58\overline{25}$

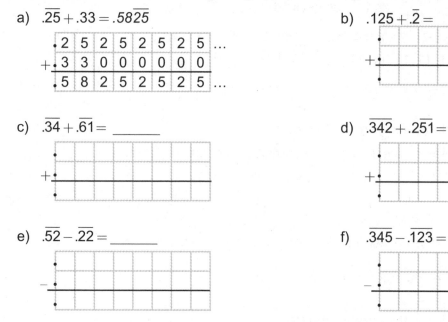

b) $.125 + .\overline{2} =$

c) $.\overline{34} + .\overline{61} =$ _____

d) $.\overline{342} + .2\overline{51} =$ _____

e) $.\overline{52} - .\overline{22} =$ _____

f) $.\overline{345} - .\overline{123} =$ _____

2. $\dfrac{1}{9} = 0.111...$, $\dfrac{2}{9} = 0.222...$, $\dfrac{3}{9} = 0.333...$, and so on.

a) Add the repeating decimals by lining up the decimal places.

   i) $0.\overline{1} + 0.\overline{2} =$ _____   ii) $0.\overline{2} + 0.\overline{5} =$ _____   iii) $0.\overline{4} + 0.\overline{4} =$ _____

b) Add the repeating decimals in part a) by changing them to fractions, adding the fractions, then writing the sum as a decimal.

c) Do you prefer the method you used in part a) or part b)? Explain.

3. a) Add by lining up the decimal places.

   i) $0.3 + 0.7$ ii) $0.33 + 0.77$ iii) $0.333 + 0.777$ iv) $0.3333 + 0.7777$

b) Use the pattern in part a) to predict $0.\overline{3} + 0.\overline{7}$.

c) Why is it not possible to add $0.\overline{3} + 0.\overline{7}$ by lining up the decimal places?

d) Change the repeating decimals in part b) to fractions. (Hint: Use the pattern in Question 2.)

   Add the fractions. Was your prediction in part b) correct?

4. Add or subtract by...

a) lining up the decimal places.

b) changing the decimals to fractions, adding or subtracting the fractions, then changing the fraction to a decimal by dividing.

   i) $0.25 + 0.\overline{3}$ ii) $0.\overline{3} - 0.25$ iii) $0.5 + 0.\overline{4}$ iv) $0.5 - 0.\overline{4}$

1. a) Use long division to write $\dfrac{1}{11}, \dfrac{2}{11}, \dfrac{3}{11}$, and $\dfrac{4}{11}$ as decimals.

   b) Extend the pattern to find $\dfrac{5}{11}, \dfrac{6}{11}, \dfrac{7}{11}, \dfrac{8}{11}, \dfrac{9}{11}, \dfrac{10}{11}$, and $\dfrac{11}{11}$.

   c) Use $\dfrac{9}{9} = \dfrac{11}{11} = 0.\overline{9}$ to show that $0.\overline{9} = 1$.

   d) Calculate the first three products, then predict the fourth.

   $\begin{array}{r} 0.09 \\ \times 5 \\ \hline \end{array}$ $\begin{array}{r} 0.0909 \\ \times 5 \\ \hline \end{array}$ $\begin{array}{r} 0.090909 \\ \times 5 \\ \hline \end{array}$ $\begin{array}{r} 0.\overline{09} \\ \times 5 \\ \hline \end{array}$

   e) Calculate $0.\overline{09} \times 5$ by changing the decimal to a fraction. Then change your answer back to a decimal. Was your prediction correct?

2. a) Use long division to show that $\dfrac{1}{99} = 0.\overline{01}$.

   b) Calculate the first three products, then predict the fourth.

   $\begin{array}{r} 0.01 \\ \times 17 \\ \hline \end{array}$ $\begin{array}{r} 0.0101 \\ \times 17 \\ \hline \end{array}$ $\begin{array}{r} 0.010101 \\ \times 17 \\ \hline \end{array}$ $\begin{array}{r} 0.\overline{01} \\ \times 17 \\ \hline \end{array}$

   c) Write $\dfrac{17}{99}$ as a repeating decimal. Explain your answer.

3. Write the fraction as a repeating decimal.

   a) $\dfrac{25}{99}$ b) $\dfrac{38}{99}$ c) $\dfrac{97}{99}$ d) $\dfrac{86}{99}$ e) $\dfrac{7}{99}$ f) $\dfrac{4}{99}$

4. Change the fraction to an equivalent fraction with denominator 9 or 99. Then write the repeating decimal.

   a) $\dfrac{13}{33}$ b) $\dfrac{2}{3}$ c) $\dfrac{4}{11}$ d) $\dfrac{34}{66}$ e) $\dfrac{10}{18}$ f) $\dfrac{30}{55}$

5. Change each repeating decimal to a fraction. Write your answer in lowest terms.

   a) $0.\overline{46}$ b) $0.\overline{07}$ c) $0.\overline{15}$ d) $0.\overline{98}$ e) $0.\overline{6}$ f) $0.\overline{48}$

6. a) We know that $\dfrac{1}{9} = 0.\overline{1}$ and $\dfrac{1}{99} = 0.\overline{01}$.   Predict: $\dfrac{1}{999} = $ _____

   Check your answer by long division.

   b) Use your answer in part a) to calculate the equivalent decimal for…

   i) $\dfrac{34}{999}$ ii) $\dfrac{8}{999}$ iii) $\dfrac{734}{999}$ iv) $\dfrac{46}{999}$ v) $\dfrac{25}{333}$ vi) $\dfrac{47}{111}$

1. Write the repeating decimal as a fraction.

   a) $0.\overline{7} = \dfrac{}{9}$ b) $0.\overline{23} = \dfrac{}{99}$ c) $0.0\overline{5} = \dfrac{}{99}$ d) $0.\overline{441} = \dfrac{}{999}$ e) $0.\overline{652} = \dfrac{}{999}$

   f) $0.\overline{98} =$ g) $0.\overline{5} =$ h) $0.\overline{461} =$ i) $0.\overline{38} =$ j) $0.\overline{061} =$

2. Multiply or divide by moving the decimal point the correct number of places, left or right.

   a) $25.44444... \times 10$ b) $2.66666... \times 100$ c) $24.919191... \div 10$

   d) $0.\overline{32} \times 100$ e) $0.\overline{32} \div 100$ f) $54.\overline{361} \times 100$

   g) $0.\overline{341} \div 10$ h) $7.\overline{432} \div 1000$ i) $36.\overline{432} \times 10$

3. a) $\dfrac{1}{9} = \underline{\quad 0.111... \quad}$ b) $\dfrac{4}{9} = \underline{\qquad}$ c) $\dfrac{2}{3} = \underline{\qquad}$

   So $\dfrac{1}{90} = \underline{\quad 0.0111... \quad}$ So $\dfrac{4}{900} = \underline{\qquad}$ So $\dfrac{2}{3000} = \underline{\qquad}$

4. $\dfrac{137}{999} = 0.\overline{137}$. What is $\dfrac{137}{9990}$? $\underline{\qquad\qquad}$

5. a) $13 \times 0.01 = \underline{\qquad}$ $13 \times 0.011 = \underline{\qquad}$ $13 \times 0.0111 = \underline{\qquad}$

   b) Predict: $13 \times 0.0111... = \underline{\qquad}$

   c) Why should $\dfrac{13}{90}$ be equal to your answer to part b)? Check using a calculator.

   d) Use $\dfrac{13}{9} = 1\dfrac{4}{9}$ to find $\dfrac{13}{90}$ in a different way.

6. Write each decimal as a fraction.

   a) $0.\overline{1} = \underline{\quad}$ $0.\overline{8} = \underline{\quad}$ $0.0\overline{8} = \underline{\quad}$ b) $0.\overline{01} = \underline{\quad}$ $0.\overline{27} = \underline{\quad}$ $0.0\overline{27} = \underline{\quad}$

   $0.5\overline{8} = 0.5 + 0.0\overline{8} = \underline{\quad} + \underline{\quad} = \underline{\quad}$ $0.4\overline{27} = 0.4 + 0.0\overline{27} = \underline{\quad} + \underline{\quad} = \underline{\quad}$

   c) $0.\overline{001} = \underline{\quad}$ $0.\overline{253} = \underline{\quad}$ $0.0\overline{253} = \underline{\quad}$ d) $0.\overline{5} = \underline{\quad}$ so $4.\overline{5} = \underline{\quad}$

   $5.6\overline{253} = \underline{\quad} + \underline{\quad} = \underline{\quad} + \underline{\quad} = \underline{\quad}$ $0.0\overline{5} = \underline{\quad}$ so $4.0\overline{5} = \underline{\quad}$

   e) $0.1\overline{5}$ f) $1.\overline{7}$ g) $2.3\overline{5}$ h) $0.24\overline{361}$ i) $2.4\overline{361}$

NS7-64 Percents

The words "per cent" mean "out of 100." A percent is a ratio that compares a number or amount to 100.

The symbol for percent is %. Example: $45\% = 45 : 100 = \dfrac{45}{100}$

1. a) 30 out of 100 squares are shaded. The ratio of shaded squares

    to all squares is ____ : 100.

    So, ____% of the grid is shaded.

    b) 47 out of 100 letters are Bs. The ratio of Bs to all letters

    in the set is ____ : 100.

    So, ____% of the letters are Bs.

    ABBBCCBBAABBCABBBCCB
    AAABBBCCBBAABAAABBBC
    CBCABBBCCBBBCCBBAAAB
    BAAABBABCBBAABCCBBAB
    BCCBAABBAAAABBCCABAA

2. Write the ratio as a percent.

    a) 20 : 100 = ____%   b) 63 : 100 = ____%   c) 5 : 100 = ____%   d) 55 : 100 = ____%

3. Write the percent as a ratio.

    a) 30% = ____ : *100*   b) 12% = ____ : ____   c) 25% = ____ : ____   d) 34% = ____ : ____

4. Write the ratio as a fraction and as a percent.

    a) 50 : 100 = $\dfrac{}{100}$ = ____%   b) 10 : 100 = $\dfrac{}{100}$ = ____%

5. Write the fraction as a percent.

    a) $\dfrac{40}{100}$ = ____%   b) $\dfrac{28}{100}$ = ____%   c) $\dfrac{43}{100}$ =   d) $\dfrac{1}{100}$ =   e) $\dfrac{10}{100}$ =

6. Write the percent as a fraction.

    a) 11% = $\dfrac{}{100}$ b) 89% = $\dfrac{}{100}$ c) 9% =   d) 75% =   e) 100% =

7. Complete the chart.

Drawing				
Fraction	$\dfrac{23}{100}$	$\dfrac{}{100}$	$\dfrac{45}{100}$	$\dfrac{}{100}$
Percent	23%	63%	____ %	____ %

NS7-65 Adding and Subtracting Percents

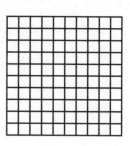

1. There are 100 squares on the grid.

   Colour 10 out of 100 squares red. The red area is ____% of the grid.

   Colour 40 out of 100 squares blue. The blue area is ____% of the grid.

   There are now 10 + 40 = ____ coloured squares on the grid.

   So, ____% of the grid is coloured.

2. Write the percents as fractions. Add or subtract. Then write the sum or difference as a percent.

   a) $30\% + 20\% = \dfrac{}{100} + \dfrac{}{100} = \dfrac{}{100} =$ ____%   b) $10\% + 50\% = \dfrac{}{100} + \dfrac{}{100} = \dfrac{}{100} =$ ____%

   c) $50\% - 25\% = \dfrac{}{100} - \dfrac{}{100} = \dfrac{}{100} =$ ____%   d) $70\% - 30\% = \dfrac{}{100} - \dfrac{}{100} = \dfrac{}{100} =$ ____%

3. Calculate.

   a) $12\% + 20\% =$ ____%   b) $33\% + 44\% =$ ____%   c) $56\% - 23\% + 8\% =$ ____%

4. Determine the missing percent in the circle graph. The whole circle represents 100%.

   a) **Gases in Earth's Atmosphere**   b) **Composition of Earth's Water**   c) **Land Cover in North America**

   oxygen ←
   ←1% other
   78% nitrogen

   oxygen: _____%

   2% frozen   unfrozen
   in ice caps fresh water
   97% ocean

   unfrozen fresh water: _____%

   27% forest
   pasture
   ←20% residential
   ←5% commercial
   ←5% open water
   ←2% orchards

   pasture: _____%

5. a) The ratio of cents in a penny to cents in a dollar is 1 : 100, so a penny is ____% of a dollar.

   The ratio of cents in a dime to cents in a dollar is ____ : 100, so a dime is ____% of a dollar.

   A quarter is ____ cents out of 100, so a quarter is ____% of a dollar.

   b) What percent of a dollar is 35 cents? _____%

   What percent of a dollar is two pennies and two quarters? ____%

   c) You have a dollar and you spend 26¢. What percent of the dollar do you

   have left? ____%

NS7-66 Tenths, Decimals, and Percents

1. Shade the percent.

   a) 50%

   b) 30%

   $\dfrac{1}{10} = 10\% = 0.1$

   1 whole = 100%

2. ____% of the 10 dots are white.

   ____% of the 10 dots are grey.

3. a) Shade 80% of the 10 dots.

   b) What percent of the dots are not shaded? _____

4. 10% of 100 marbles are blue. How many of the marbles are not blue? _____

5. Write the percent as a fraction and then as a decimal.

   a) $90\% = \dfrac{}{100} = 0.\underline{}\,\underline{}$ b) $35\% = \dfrac{}{100} = 0.\underline{}\,\underline{}$ c) $22\% = \dfrac{}{100} = 0.\underline{}\,\underline{}$ d) $6\% = \dfrac{}{100} = 0.\underline{}\,\underline{}$

   e) $52\% = \underline{} = \underline{}$ f) $2\% = \underline{} = \underline{}$ g) $60\% = \underline{} = \underline{}$ h) $100\% = \underline{} = \underline{}$

6. Write the percent as a decimal.

   a) $25\% = 0.\underline{}\,\underline{}$ b) $75\% = 0.\underline{}\,\underline{}$ c) $13\% = \underline{}$ d) $40\% = \underline{}$

   e) $7\% = \underline{}$ f) $9\% = \underline{}$ g) $70\% = \underline{}$ h) $1\% = \underline{}$

7. Write the decimal as a percent.

   a) $0.2 = \dfrac{2}{10} = \dfrac{}{100} = \underline{}\%$ b) $0.3 = \dfrac{}{10} = \dfrac{}{100} = \underline{}\%$ c) $0.7 =$

   d) $0.23 = \dfrac{}{100} = \underline{}\%$ e) $0.57 =$ f) $0.08 =$

8. Write the decimal as a percent by moving the decimal point two places to the right.

   a) $0.4 = \underline{}\%$ b) $0.6 = \underline{}\%$ c) $0.3 =$ d) $0.1 =$ e) $0.8 =$

   f) $0.72 = \underline{}\%$ g) $0.20 = \underline{}\%$ h) $0.45 =$ i) $0.06 =$ j) $0.88 =$

9. Approximately what percent does the decimal represent? Example: $0.1234 \approx 0.12 = 12\%$.
   Hint: Remember to round to two decimal places.

   a) $0.382 \approx \underline{}\%$ b) $0.925 \approx \underline{}\%$ c) $0.3779 \approx$ d) $0.1036 \approx$

10. Kay bought 6 jazz CDs and 4 rock CDs. What fraction of the CDs are jazz?
    What percent are rock?

1. Write the fraction as a percent by changing it to a fraction over 100.

   a) $\dfrac{3 \times 20}{5 \times 20} = \dfrac{60}{100} = 60\%$

   b) $\dfrac{4}{5}$

   c) $\dfrac{3}{20}$

   d) $\dfrac{8}{25}$

2. Two out of five friends, or $\dfrac{2}{5}$, ordered pizza. What percent ordered pizza? ____

3. Change the fraction to a percent. Reduce the fraction to lowest terms if necessary.

   a) $\dfrac{9}{15} = \dfrac{3}{5} = \dfrac{60}{100} = 60\%$

   b) $\dfrac{3}{15} =$

   c) $\dfrac{9}{18} =$

   d) $\dfrac{6}{24} =$

   e) $\dfrac{3}{4}$

   f) $\dfrac{1}{2}$

   g) $\dfrac{4}{10}$

   h) $\dfrac{18}{25}$

   i) $\dfrac{28}{40}$

4. Divide to change the fraction to a decimal. Then write the decimal as a percent.

   a) $\dfrac{3}{4} = 3 \div 4 = 0.$____ ____ $=$ ____%

   b) $\dfrac{4}{5}$

   c) $\dfrac{3}{15}$

   d) $\dfrac{15}{25}$

   e) $\dfrac{65}{500}$

5. Write the percent as a decimal, then as a fraction, then in lowest terms.

   a) 40%   b) 75%   c) 65%   d) 5%   e) 80%

6. Is the fraction closest to 10%, 25%, 50%, 75%, or 100%?

   a) $\dfrac{4}{5}$ b) $\dfrac{2}{10}$ c) $\dfrac{2}{5}$ d) $\dfrac{9}{10}$ e) $\dfrac{11}{20}$ f) $\dfrac{16}{20}$ g) $\dfrac{4}{25}$

7. Estimate what percent the fraction is. Say what fraction you used to make your estimate. Then divide to change the fraction to a decimal. Was your estimate close?

   a) $\dfrac{11}{40}$ b) $\dfrac{23}{49}$ c) $\dfrac{60}{84}$ d) $\dfrac{14}{24}$ e) $\dfrac{4}{42}$ f) $\dfrac{21}{31}$

8. Write the fraction as a decimal. Round to two decimal places. Write the approximate percent.

   a) $\dfrac{5}{12} = 5 \div 12 = 0.41\overline{6} \approx 0.42 =$ ____%   b) $\dfrac{1}{3}$ c) $\dfrac{2}{3}$ d) $\dfrac{2}{9}$ e) $\dfrac{5}{6}$ f) $\dfrac{1}{7}$

NS7-68 Visual Representations of Percents

1. What percent of the figure is shaded?

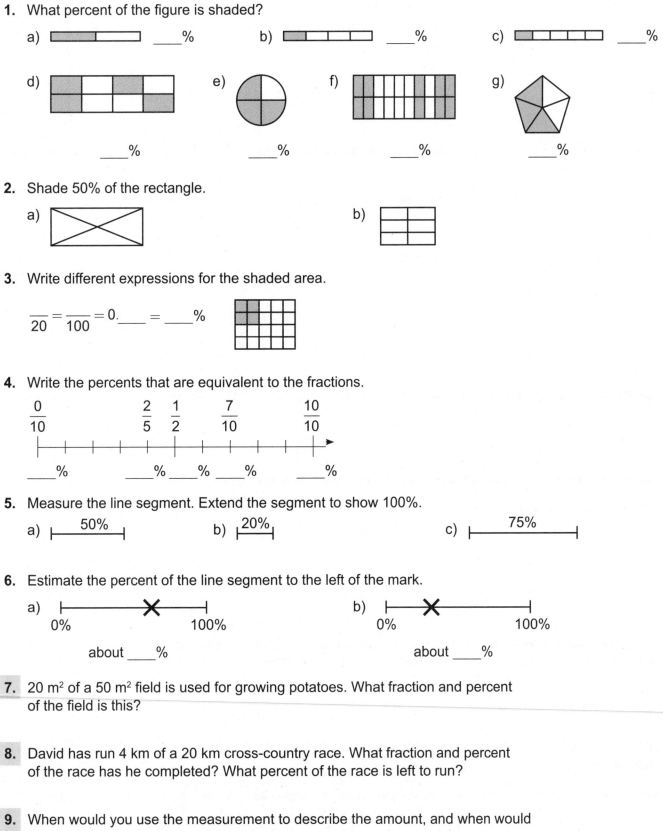

a) ____%

b) ____%

c) ____%

d) ____%

e) ____%

f) ____%

g) ____%

2. Shade 50% of the rectangle.

a)

b)

3. Write different expressions for the shaded area.

$$\frac{}{20} = \frac{}{100} = 0.\underline{} = \underline{}\%$$

4. Write the percents that are equivalent to the fractions.

$$\frac{0}{10} \qquad \frac{2}{5} \quad \frac{1}{2} \qquad \frac{7}{10} \qquad \frac{10}{10}$$

____% ____% ____% ____% ____%

5. Measure the line segment. Extend the segment to show 100%.

a) 50%

b) 20%

c) 75%

6. Estimate the percent of the line segment to the left of the mark.

a) 0%   100%

about ____%

b) 0%   100%

about ____%

7. 20 m² of a 50 m² field is used for growing potatoes. What fraction and percent of the field is this?

8. David has run 4 km of a 20 km cross-country race. What fraction and percent of the race has he completed? What percent of the race is left to run?

9. When would you use the measurement to describe the amount, and when would you use the percent (if ever)? Write a sentence using each expression.

   a) 3 h of the school day or 50% of the school day

   b) 12 kg of berries or 40% of the berries

1. Complete the chart.

Fraction	$\frac{1}{4}$		$\frac{3}{20}$			$\frac{6}{15}$	$\frac{23}{25}$		
Decimal		0.35			0.60				0.55
Percent				40%				75%	

2. Write $<$ or $>$ or $=$ between each pair of numbers. First change the numbers to a pair of decimal fractions with the same denominator.

a) $\frac{1}{2}$ 47%   b) $\frac{1}{2}$ 53%   c) $\frac{1}{4}$ 23%   d) $\frac{3}{4}$ 70%

$\frac{1 \times 50}{2 \times 50}$ $\frac{47}{100}$

$\frac{50}{100}$ $\boxed{>}$ $\frac{47}{100}$ □   □   □

e) $\frac{2}{5}$ 32%   f) 0.27   62%   g) 0.02   11%   h) $\frac{1}{10}$ 10%

□   □   □   □

i) $\frac{19}{25}$ 93%   j) $\frac{23}{50}$ 46%   k) 0.9   10%   l) $\frac{11}{20}$ 19%

□   □   □   □

3. Change the numbers in each set to decimals. Then order the decimals from least to greatest.

a) $\frac{3}{5}$, 42%, 0.73   b) $\frac{1}{2}$, 0.73, 80%   c) $\frac{1}{4}$, 0.09, 15%

4. a) In Abeed's school, $\frac{3}{5}$ of students like gym and 65% like drama. Which class is more popular?

b) In Rachel's class, 0.45 of the students like pepperoni pizza best, 35% like cheese, and $\frac{1}{5}$ like vegetarian. Which type of pizza do the most students like best?

NS7-70 Finding Percents

If you use a thousands cube to represent 1 whole, you can see that taking $\frac{1}{10}$ of a number is the same as dividing by 10 (the decimal shifts one place left):

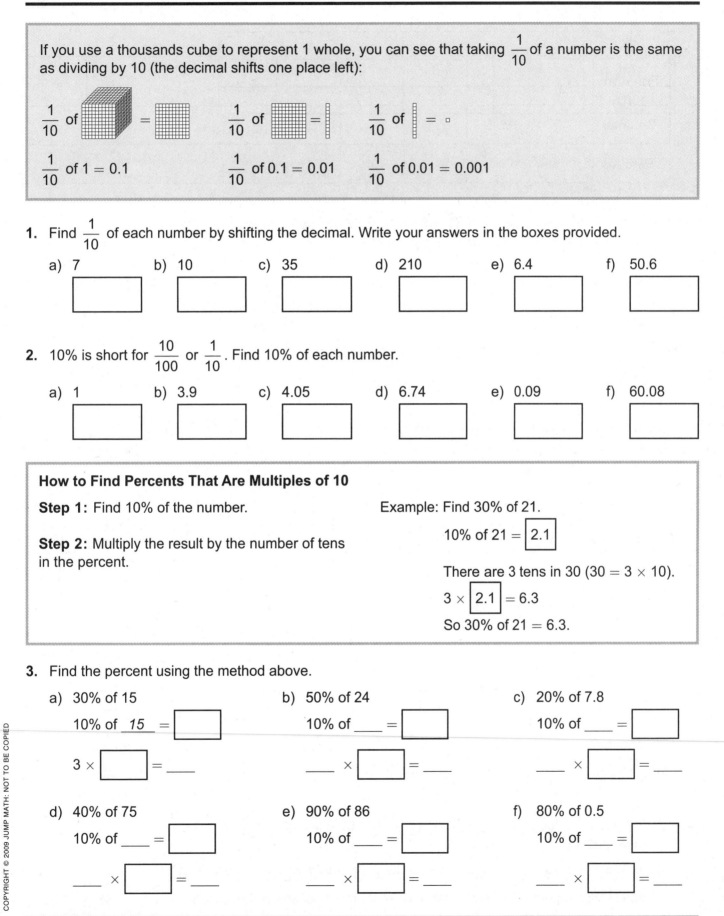

$\frac{1}{10}$ of 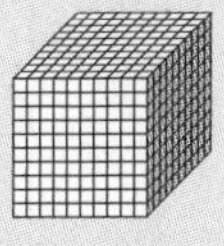 = 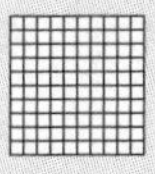 $\frac{1}{10}$ of  =  $\frac{1}{10}$ of  = 

$\frac{1}{10}$ of 1 = 0.1 $\frac{1}{10}$ of 0.1 = 0.01 $\frac{1}{10}$ of 0.01 = 0.001

1. Find $\frac{1}{10}$ of each number by shifting the decimal. Write your answers in the boxes provided.

a) 7 b) 10 c) 35 d) 210 e) 6.4 f) 50.6

2. 10% is short for $\frac{10}{100}$ or $\frac{1}{10}$. Find 10% of each number.

a) 1 b) 3.9 c) 4.05 d) 6.74 e) 0.09 f) 60.08

How to Find Percents That Are Multiples of 10

Step 1: Find 10% of the number.

Step 2: Multiply the result by the number of tens in the percent.

Example: Find 30% of 21.

10% of 21 = 2.1

There are 3 tens in 30 (30 = 3 × 10).

3 × 2.1 = 6.3

So 30% of 21 = 6.3.

3. Find the percent using the method above.

a) 30% of 15
10% of _15_ = ☐
3 × ☐ = ___

b) 50% of 24
10% of ___ = ☐
___ × ☐ = ___

c) 20% of 7.8
10% of ___ = ☐
___ × ☐ = ___

d) 40% of 75
10% of ___ = ☐
___ × ☐ = ___

e) 90% of 86
10% of ___ = ☐
___ × ☐ = ___

f) 80% of 0.5
10% of ___ = ☐
___ × ☐ = ___

4. If you know 10% of a number n, then 5% of n is 10% divided by 2. Complete the chart.

5%	3			
10%	6	20	42	1
100%	60			

> Use these steps to find 1% of a number:
>
> **Step 1:** Change the percent to a decimal and replace "of" with "×."
>
> **Step 2:** Multiply by 0.01 by shifting the decimal two places left.

5. Fill in the blanks.

   a) 1% of 300 = _0.01_ × _300_ = ____   b) 1% of 2000 = ____ × ____ = ____

   c) 1% of 15 = ____ × ____ = ____   d) 1% of 60 = ____ × ____ = ____

6. Find 1% of 200 and use your answer to calculate each percent.

   a) 2% of 200 = _____   b) 3% of 200 = _____   c) 12% of 200 = _____

7. Use the method of Question 6 to calculate…

   a) 4% of 800   b) 2% of 50   c) 11% of 60   d) 2% of 4   e) 7% of 45

8. Fill in the missing numbers. (Hint: 8% = 4% + 4%.)

2%	4%	8%	10%	20%	50%	25%	100%
	20						
	30						
					60		
			50				

9. a) If 45% is 9, what is 90%?   b) If 3% is 12, what is 1%?
   c) If 40% is 64, what is 100%?   d) If 20% is 13, what is 100%?

10. Arti wants to leave a 15% tip on a meal that cost $60. How much tip should she leave? (Hint: 15% = 10% + 5%.)

11. a) A shirt that usually costs $40 is on sale for 25% off. What is 25% of $40? What is $40 − (25% of $40)? What is the sale price of the shirt?

    b) How would you estimate the price if a shirt that usually costs $32.99 is on sale for 25% off?

NS7-71 Further Percents

35% is short for $\frac{35}{100}$. To find 35% of 27, Sadie finds $\frac{35}{100}$ of 27.

Step 1: She multiplies 27 by 35.

2	3	
	2	7
×	3	5
1	3	5
8	1	0
9	4	5

Step 2: She divides the result by 100.

$945 \div 100 = 9.45$

So 35% of 27 is 9.45.

1. Find the percent using Sadie's method.

a) 25% of 44

Step 1:

Step 2: _______ ÷ 100 = _______

So _______ of _______ is _______.

b) 18% of 92

Step 1:

Step 2: _______ ÷ 100 = _______

So _______ of _______ is _______.

2. Find the percent using Sadie's method.

a) 23% of 23
b) 15% of 26
c) 26% of 15
d) 64% of 58
e) 58% of 64
f) 50% of 81
g) 81% of 50
h) 92% of 11

3. a) Find 35% of 40 in two ways. Do you get the same answer both ways?

i) Use Sadie's method.

ii) Use 35% = 25% + 10%.

b) 35% is less than 50% = $\frac{1}{2}$. Is your answer to part a) less than half of 40?

c) Is 35% closer to 0 or $\frac{1}{2}$? _______

Was your answer to part a) closer to 0 or to half of 40? _______

Is your answer to part a) reasonable? Explain.

4. Find 30% of 50 and 50% of 30. What do you notice? Why is this the case?

NS7-72 Writing Equivalent Statements for Proportions

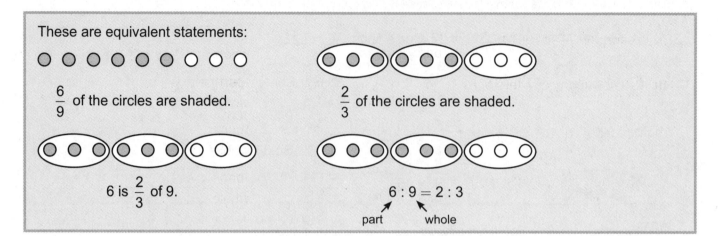

These are equivalent statements:

$\frac{6}{9}$ of the circles are shaded.

$\frac{2}{3}$ of the circles are shaded.

6 is $\frac{2}{3}$ of 9.

$6 : 9 = 2 : 3$

part   whole

1. Write four equivalent statements for each picture.

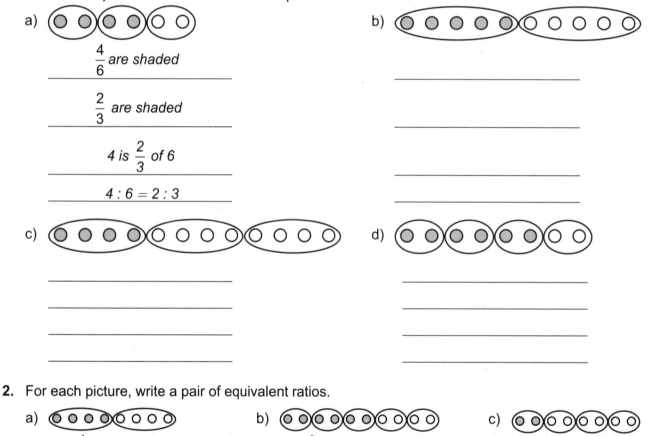

a)

$\frac{4}{6}$ are shaded

_____

$\frac{2}{3}$ are shaded

_____

4 is $\frac{2}{3}$ of 6

_____

$4 : 6 = 2 : 3$

b)

_____

_____

_____

_____

c)

_____

_____

_____

_____

d)

_____

_____

_____

_____

2. For each picture, write a pair of equivalent ratios.

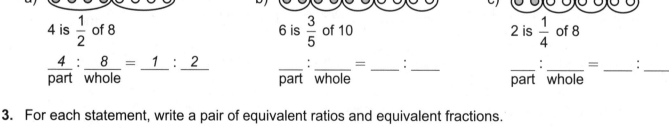

a)

4 is $\frac{1}{2}$ of 8

$\frac{4}{\text{part}} : \frac{8}{\text{whole}} = \frac{1}{\quad} : \frac{2}{\quad}$

b)

6 is $\frac{3}{5}$ of 10

$\underset{\text{part}}{\rule{2em}{0.4pt}} : \underset{\text{whole}}{\rule{2em}{0.4pt}} = \rule{2em}{0.4pt} : \rule{2em}{0.4pt}$

c)

2 is $\frac{1}{4}$ of 8

$\underset{\text{part}}{\rule{2em}{0.4pt}} : \underset{\text{whole}}{\rule{2em}{0.4pt}} = \rule{2em}{0.4pt} : \rule{2em}{0.4pt}$

3. For each statement, write a pair of equivalent ratios and equivalent fractions.

a) 15 is $\frac{3}{4}$ of 20 $\underset{\text{part}}{\rule{2em}{0.4pt}} : \underset{\text{whole}}{\rule{2em}{0.4pt}} = \rule{2em}{0.4pt} : \rule{2em}{0.4pt}$ $\dfrac{\text{part}}{\text{whole}} \rule{2em}{0.4pt} = \rule{2em}{0.4pt}$

b) 18 is $\frac{9}{10}$ of 20 $\underset{\text{part}}{\rule{2em}{0.4pt}} : \underset{\text{whole}}{\rule{2em}{0.4pt}} = \rule{2em}{0.4pt} : \rule{2em}{0.4pt}$ $\dfrac{\text{part}}{\text{whole}} \rule{2em}{0.4pt} = \rule{2em}{0.4pt}$

4. Write a question mark where you are missing a piece of information.

a) 12 is $\frac{4}{5}$ of what number? $\dfrac{12}{\text{part}} : \dfrac{?}{\text{whole}} = \underline{\ 4\ } : \underline{\ 5\ }$ $\dfrac{\text{part}}{\text{whole}}$ $\dfrac{12}{?} = \dfrac{4}{5}$

b) 6 is how many quarters of 8? $\dfrac{6}{\text{part}} : \dfrac{8}{\text{whole}} = \underline{\ ?\ } : \underline{\ 4\ }$ $\dfrac{\text{part}}{\text{whole}}$ $\underline{\ \ \ } = \underline{\ \ \ }$

c) What is $\frac{3}{4}$ of 16? $\dfrac{\ \ \ \ }{\text{part}} : \dfrac{\ \ \ \ }{\text{whole}} = \underline{\ \ \ } : \underline{\ \ \ }$ $\dfrac{\text{part}}{\text{whole}}$ $\underline{\ \ \ } = \underline{\ \ \ }$

d) 20 is how many thirds of 30? $\dfrac{\ \ \ \ }{\text{part}} : \dfrac{\ \ \ \ }{\text{whole}} = \underline{\ \ \ } : \underline{\ \ \ }$ $\dfrac{\text{part}}{\text{whole}}$ $\underline{\ \ \ } = \underline{\ \ \ }$

5. For each statement, write a pair of equivalent ratios and a pair of equivalent fractions.

a) 15 is what percent of 20? $\dfrac{15}{\text{part}} : \dfrac{20}{\text{whole}} = \underline{\ ?\ } : \underline{\ 100\ }$ $\dfrac{\text{part}}{\text{whole}}$ $\dfrac{15}{20} = \dfrac{?}{100}$

b) What is 25% of 80? $\dfrac{\ \ \ \ }{\text{part}} : \dfrac{\ \ \ \ }{\text{whole}} = \underline{\ \ \ } : \underline{\ \ \ }$ $\dfrac{\text{part}}{\text{whole}}$ $\underline{\ \ \ } = \underline{\ \ \ }$

c) 9 is what percent of 12? $\dfrac{\ \ \ \ }{\text{part}} : \dfrac{\ \ \ \ }{\text{whole}} = \underline{\ \ \ } : \underline{\ \ \ }$ $\dfrac{\text{part}}{\text{whole}}$ $\underline{\ \ \ } = \underline{\ \ \ }$

d) 18 is 3% of what number? $\dfrac{\ \ \ \ }{\text{part}} : \dfrac{\ \ \ \ }{\text{whole}} = \underline{\ \ \ } : \underline{\ \ \ }$ $\dfrac{\text{part}}{\text{whole}}$ $\underline{\ \ \ } = \underline{\ \ \ }$

6. Write the two pieces of information you are given and what you need to find (?). Then write an equation for the problem.

a) What percent of 30 is 5?   part __5__   whole __30__   percent __?__ $\dfrac{5}{30} = \dfrac{?}{100}$

b) If 7 is 20%, what is 100%?   part ____   whole __?__   percent ____ $\dfrac{\ \ \ }{?} = \dfrac{\ \ \ }{100}$

c) What is 6% of 24?   part __?__   whole ____   percent ____ $\dfrac{?}{\ \ \ } = \dfrac{\ \ \ }{100}$

d) If 3 is 12%, what is 100%?   part ____   whole ____   percent ____ $\dfrac{\ \ \ }{\ \ \ } = \dfrac{\ \ \ }{100}$

e) What percent of 90 is 4?   part ____   whole ____   percent ____ $\dfrac{\ \ \ }{\ \ \ } = \dfrac{\ \ \ }{100}$

f) What is 52% of 18?   part ____   whole ____   percent ____ $\dfrac{\ \ \ }{\ \ \ } = \dfrac{\ \ \ }{100}$

g) 7 is what percent of 25?   part ____   whole ____   percent ____ $\dfrac{\ \ \ }{\ \ \ } = \dfrac{\ \ \ }{100}$

If 5 subway tickets cost $4, how much do 20 tickets cost? Write the ratio of tickets to dollars as a fraction, then find an equivalent fraction by multiplying.

Step 1: $\dfrac{4}{5} = \dfrac{?}{20}$	Step 2: $\dfrac{4}{5} \overset{\times 4}{\underset{\times 4}{\Rightarrow}} \dfrac{}{20}$	Step 3: $\dfrac{4}{5} \overset{\times 4}{\underset{\times 4}{\Rightarrow}} \dfrac{16}{20}$

1. Solve the ratio. Draw arrows and show what you multiply by.

   a) $\dfrac{3}{4} = \dfrac{}{20}$ b) $\dfrac{1}{5} = \dfrac{}{15}$ c) $\dfrac{3}{5} = \dfrac{}{35}$ d) $\dfrac{4}{7} = \dfrac{}{49}$

   e) $\dfrac{3}{8} = \dfrac{}{24}$ f) $\dfrac{2}{3} = \dfrac{}{18}$ g) $\dfrac{13}{20} = \dfrac{}{100}$ h) $\dfrac{5}{9} = \dfrac{}{72}$

2. Solve the ratio as you did in Question 1. Note: The arrows will point from right to left.

   a) $\dfrac{15}{} = \dfrac{3}{4}$ b) $\dfrac{12}{} = \dfrac{2}{5}$ c) $\dfrac{15}{} = \dfrac{3}{7}$ d) $\dfrac{12}{18} = \dfrac{}{3}$

3. For each question, you will have to reduce the fraction given before you can find the equivalent fraction. The first one has been started for you.

   a) $\dfrac{8}{10} = \dfrac{4}{5} = \dfrac{}{15}$ b) $\dfrac{4}{6} = \dfrac{}{} = \dfrac{}{15}$ c) $\dfrac{40}{100} = \dfrac{}{} = \dfrac{}{45}$

   d) $\dfrac{15}{18} = \dfrac{}{} = \dfrac{}{30}$ e) $\dfrac{70}{100} = \dfrac{}{} = \dfrac{}{90}$ f) $\dfrac{50}{75} = \dfrac{}{} = \dfrac{}{36}$

4. Write a proportion to represent the percent problem. Solve the proportion.

   a) What percent of 20 is 4?   part ____   whole ____   percent ____ $\dfrac{}{} = \dfrac{}{100}$

   b) If 6 is 25%, what is 100%?   part ____   whole ____   percent ____ $\dfrac{}{} = \dfrac{}{100}$

   c) What is 17% of 10?   part ____   whole ____   percent ____ $\dfrac{}{} = \dfrac{}{100}$

   d) What is 17% of 50?   part ____   whole ____   percent ____ $\dfrac{}{} = \dfrac{}{100}$

   e) 4 is what percent of 5?

   f) 6 is 25% of what number?

   g) 24 is 80% of what number?

5. Explain why the proportion $\dfrac{3}{25} = \dfrac{x}{100}$ will be easy to solve.

6. Write a proportion $\dfrac{a}{b} = \dfrac{x}{100}$ to represent each problem. Solve by first writing $\dfrac{a}{b}$ in lowest terms.

a) What percent of 15 is 3?   b) What percent of 24 is 6?   c) What percent of 30 is 12?

7. Write a proportion to represent the percent problem. Find an equivalent ratio to rewrite the proportion. Solve the new proportion.

a) If 6 is 40%, what is 100%?   part __6__   whole __?__   percent __40__ $\dfrac{6}{?} = \dfrac{40}{100}$ $\dfrac{6}{?} = \dfrac{2}{5}$

Hint: Start by writing $\dfrac{40}{100}$ as an equivalent ratio with numerator 2.

b) What is 75% of 48?   part ____   whole ____   percent ____ $\dfrac{}{} = \dfrac{}{100}$ $\dfrac{}{} = \dfrac{}{}$

Hint: Start by writing 75% as an equivalent ratio with denominator 4.

c) What percent of 60 is 45?   part ____   whole ____   percent ____ $\dfrac{}{} = \dfrac{}{100}$ $\dfrac{}{} = \dfrac{}{}$

Hint: Start by writing $\dfrac{45}{60}$ as an equivalent ratio with denominator 20.

d) What is 64% of 15?   part ____   whole ____   percent ____ $\dfrac{}{} = \dfrac{}{100}$ $\dfrac{}{} = \dfrac{}{}$

Hint: Start by writing $\dfrac{64}{100}$ as an equivalent ratio with denominator 5.

8. Explain why the proportions in Question 7 were more challenging to solve than those in Question 4, parts a)–e).

9. Solve.

a) 9 is 60% of what number?   b) What is 75% of 24?

c) 16 is 80% of what number?   d) What percent of 360 is 72?

10. If 5 of 20 cars are red, what percent of the cars are red? What percent are not red?

11. If 35% of 120 students use an MP3 player, how many of the students use an MP3 player?

12. Ten students in a class (40% of the class) bike to school. How many students are in the class?

1. Calculate.

   a) 90% – 75% + 34% = _____   b) 39% + _____ = 100%   c) 86% – _____ = 14%

2. What is the sales tax where you live? _____

   Calculate the amount of tax you would pay on each price.

   a) $20 _____   b) $35 _____   c) $82.75 _____   d) $93.24 _____

3. In the school elections, $\frac{3}{5}$ of the students voted for Laura and 12% voted for Zamir.

   The rest voted for Shaw-Han. What percent voted for Shaw-Han?

4. A painter spent $500.00 on art supplies. Complete the chart.

Item	Money spent		
	Fraction	Percent	$ Amount
Brushes			$125.00
Paint	$\frac{3}{10}$		
Canvas		45%	

5. A student hopes to raise $200 for his favourite charity. He has already raised $60 by having a garage sale. What percent of the $200 does he still need to raise?

6. Complete the chart.

Item	Regular Price	Discount (percent)	Discount ($ amount)	Sale Price
Sweater	$52.00	10%	$5.20	$52.00 – $5.20 = $46.80
Boots	$38.96	25%		
Book	$9.80	30%		

7. Simone bought a bass guitar at a 20% discount. She paid $600. How many dollars did she save by buying the guitar at a discount?

8. Stephen spent $670 on furniture. He spent 25% on a chair, $234.50 on a table, and the rest on a sofa. What fraction and what percent of the $670 did he spend on each item?

9. A lake has about 1 200 fish, 12% of them sturgeon. As part of a conservation program, 200 more sturgeon are released into the lake. How many sturgeon are now in the lake? What percent and what fraction of the fish in the lake are sturgeon?

1. Write the number of boys (**b**), girls (**g**), and children (**c**) in each class.

   a) There are 8 boys and 5 girls in a class.   **b** _____   **g** _____   **c** _____

   b) There are 4 boys and 7 girls in a class.   **b** _____   **g** _____   **c** _____

   c) There are 12 boys and 15 girls in a class.   **b** _____   **g** _____   **c** _____

   d) There are 9 girls in a class of 20 children. **b** _____   **g** _____   **c** _____

2. Write the number of boys, girls, and children in each class. Then write the fraction of children who are boys and the fraction who are girls in the boxes provided.

   a) There are 5 boys and 6 girls in a class.   **b** ___☐   **g** ___☐   **c** ___

   b) There are 15 children in the class   **b** ___☐   **g** ___☐   **c** ___
      and 8 are boys.

3. Fill in the missing numbers for each classroom.

	Ratio of boys to girls	Fraction of boys	Fraction of girls	Percentage of boys	Percentage of girls
a)	3 : 2	$\dfrac{3}{5}$	$\dfrac{2}{5}$	$\dfrac{3}{5} = \dfrac{60}{100} = 60\%$	40%
b)	1 : 4				
c)		$\dfrac{3}{4}$			
d)				20%	
e)		$\dfrac{27}{50}$			
f)	9 : 16				
g)			$\dfrac{11}{20}$		
h)					35%
i)				44%	

4. Fill in the missing numbers for each classroom.

	Number of students	Fraction of boys	Fraction of girls	Number of boys	Number of girls
a)	20	$\dfrac{4}{5}$	$\dfrac{1}{5}$	$\dfrac{4}{5} \times 20 = 16$	4
b)	30	$\dfrac{1}{3}$			
c)	28		$\dfrac{3}{4}$		
d)	26	$\dfrac{7}{13}$			

5. Determine the number of girls and boys in each class.

a) There are 20 children and $\dfrac{2}{5}$ are boys.

b) There are 42 children and $\dfrac{3}{7}$ are girls.

c) There are 15 children.
The ratio of girls to boys is 3 : 2.

d) There are 24 children.
The ratio of girls to boys is 3 : 5.

e) There are 25 children and 60% are girls.

f) There are 28 children and 25% are boys.

6. For each question, say which classroom has more girls.

a) In classroom A, there are 40 children and 60% are girls.
In classroom B, there are 36 children. The ratio of boys to girls is 5 : 4.

b) In classroom A, there are 28 children. The ratio of boys to girls is 5 : 2.

In classroom B, there are 30 children and $\dfrac{3}{5}$ of the children are boys.

7. Ron and Ella shared $35 in the ratio 4 : 3. What fraction of the money did each person receive? What amount of money did each person receive?

8. Indra spent 1 hour doing homework. The chart shows the time she spent on each subject. Complete the chart. How did you find the amount of time Indra spent on math?

Subject	Time			
	Fraction of an hour	Percent	Decimal (hours)	Minutes
English	$\dfrac{1}{4}$		.25	15
Science		5%		
Math				
French			.20	

1. Fill in the blank.

a) A ▢▢▢
   B ▢▢▢▢▢

   Bar A is $\dfrac{3}{5}$ the length of B.

b) A ▢▢
   B ▢▢▢▢

   Bar A is ____ the length of B.

c) A ▢▢▢
   B ▢▢▢▢▢

   Bar A is ____ the length of B.

Problem: Seventy-five students are on a bus. There are $\dfrac{2}{3}$ as many boys as girls. How many boys are there?

Solution: The 5 units in the diagram represent the 75 students. So 1 unit represents $75 \div 5 = 15$ students. The bar representing boys is 2 units long. So there are $2 \times 15 = 30$ boys.

Boys ▢▢
Girls ▢▢▢ } 75

1 unit

---

2. Find the number of boys by drawing a linear model, as in the example above.

a) There are 40 students on a bus. There are $\dfrac{3}{5}$ as many girls as boys.

b) There are 27 students on a bus. There are $\dfrac{2}{7}$ as many boys as girls.

3. The bars below represent the number of red (r) and green (g) beads in a box. Fill in the blanks.

a) g ▢▢▢
   r ▢▢▢▢

   10 more red than green

   1 unit = _____ beads

   _____ beads altogether

b) g ▢▢▢
   r ▢▢▢▢▢

   8 more red than green

   1 unit = _____ beads

   _____ beads altogether

c) g ▢▢▢▢
   r ▢▢▢▢▢▢▢

   40 more red than green

   1 unit = _____ beads

   _____ beads altogether

4. Draw a model to find the number of red and green beads in each problem.

a) $\dfrac{2}{3}$ as many green beads as red beads

   10 more red beads than green beads

b) red beads : green beads = 3 : 5

   6 more green beads than red beads

5. Solve the following problem using the diagram as a model.

   One quarter of the fish in a tank are red. The rest are blue and green. There are 6 more green fish than red fish. There are 24 blue fish.

   How many fish are in the tank?

   red   green   blue

   ▢▢▢▢

   $\dfrac{1}{4}$ $\dfrac{1}{4}$ 6   24

6. Draw a model to solve this problem: One third of the fish in a tank are orange. The rest are yellow and blue. There are 9 more yellow fish than orange fish. There are 10 blue fish. How many fish are in the tank?

$\frac{2}{3}$ of a number is 100. What is the number?

$\frac{2}{3} = \frac{100}{?}$ part, whole $\qquad$ $\frac{2}{3} \overset{\times 50}{\underset{\times 50}{\rightrightarrows}} \frac{100}{?}$ $\qquad$ $\frac{2}{3} = \frac{100}{150}$ $\qquad$ The number is 150.

1. Find the number.

   a) $\frac{2}{5}$ of a number is 4. $\qquad$ b) $\frac{3}{7}$ of a number is 9. $\qquad$ c) $\frac{5}{11}$ of a number is 25.

2. A box holds red and blue beads. Find the total number of beads in the box.

   a) $\frac{3}{4}$ of the beads are red. Six beads are red.

   b) $\frac{3}{5}$ of the beads are blue. Twelve beads are blue.

   c) 60% of the beads are red. Fifteen beads are red.

   d) The ratio of red to blue beads is 4 : 5. There are 20 red beads.

3. Ron and Lisa share a sum of money. Ron receives $\frac{2}{5}$ of the money. Lisa receives $24.

   a) What fraction of the sum does Lisa receive? $\qquad$ b) How much money do Ron and Lisa share?

4. At Franklin Middle School, $\frac{3}{8}$ of the students take a bus to school, $\frac{3}{5}$ walk, and the rest bike. There are 20 students who bike to school. How many students are in the school?

5. In a fish tank, $\frac{2}{3}$ of the fish are red, $\frac{1}{4}$ are yellow, and the rest are green. There are 42 more red fish than green fish.

   a) What fraction of the fish are green?

   b) What fraction of the total number of fish does 42 represent? Hint: 42 is the difference between the number of red and green fish.

   c) How many fish are in the tank?

6. In Tina's stamp collection, 70% of the stamps are Canadian and the rest are international. Tina has 500 more Canadian stamps than international stamps. How many stamps does she have?

7. On a neon sign, $\frac{1}{5}$ of the lights are yellow and the rest are blue and red. There are twice as many blue lights as yellow lights, and there are 200 red lights on the sign.

   How many lights of all colours are on the sign?

> **REMINDER** ▶ Multiplication is a short form for addition.
>
> $3 \times 4 = 4 + 4 + 4$ $5 \times 7 = 7 + 7 + 7 + 7 + 7$ $2 \times 9 = 9 + 9$

1. Write each product as a sum.

a) $3 \times \dfrac{1}{4} = \dfrac{1}{4} + \dfrac{1}{4} + \dfrac{1}{4}$ b) $2 \times \dfrac{3}{7} =$ c) $4 \times \dfrac{5}{11} =$

2. Write each sum as a product.

a) $\dfrac{1}{2} + \dfrac{1}{2} + \dfrac{1}{2} =$ b) $\dfrac{5}{9} + \dfrac{5}{9} =$ c) $\dfrac{3}{4} + \dfrac{3}{4} + \dfrac{3}{4} + \dfrac{3}{4} + \dfrac{3}{4} =$

> **REMINDER** ▶ To add fractions with the same denominator, add the numerators.

3. Find each product by first writing it as a sum.

a) $4 \times \dfrac{3}{5} = \dfrac{3}{5} + \dfrac{3}{5} + \dfrac{3}{5} + \dfrac{3}{5}$ b) $2 \times \dfrac{3}{4} =$ c) $2 \times \dfrac{4}{7} =$

$= \dfrac{12}{5} = 2\dfrac{2}{5}$

d) $5 \times \dfrac{4}{11} =$ e) $6 \times \dfrac{3}{7} =$

> To multiply a fraction with a whole number, multiply the numerator by the whole number and leave the denominator the same.
>
> Example: $\dfrac{2}{9} + \dfrac{2}{9} + \dfrac{2}{9} = \dfrac{2+2+2}{9}$ so $3 \times \dfrac{2}{9} = \dfrac{3 \times 2}{9}$

4. Multiply the fraction with the whole number. Write your answer as a mixed number.

a) $4 \times \dfrac{3}{7} = \dfrac{4 \times 3}{7} = \dfrac{12}{7} = 1\dfrac{5}{7}$ b) $5 \times \dfrac{2}{3} = \dfrac{}{3} = \dfrac{}{3} = \dfrac{}{3}$

c) $3 \times \dfrac{4}{5} = \dfrac{}{5} = \dfrac{}{5} = \dfrac{}{5}$

5. Find the product. Simplify your answer. (Show your work in your notebook.)

a) $3 \times \dfrac{4}{6} = \dfrac{12}{6} = 2$ b) $8 \times \dfrac{3}{4} =$ c) $5 \times \dfrac{4}{10} =$ d) $3 \times \dfrac{6}{9} =$ e) $12 \times \dfrac{2}{8} =$

6. Find the product.

a) $4 \times \dfrac{5}{4} = \dfrac{20}{4} = 5$ b) $3 \times \dfrac{2}{3} =$ c) $7 \times \dfrac{9}{7} =$ d) $8 \times \dfrac{5}{8} =$ e) $a \times \dfrac{b}{a} =$

In mathematics, the word "of" can mean multiply.

Examples: "2 groups of 3" means 2×3

"6 groups of $\frac{1}{2}$" means $6 \times \frac{1}{2} = \frac{1}{2} + \frac{1}{2} + \frac{1}{2} + \frac{1}{2} + \frac{1}{2} + \frac{1}{2}$

"$\frac{1}{2}$ of 6" means $\frac{1}{2} \times 6$ Reminder: $\frac{a}{b}$ of c is $a \times c \div b$

7. Calculate each product by finding the fraction of the whole number.

a) $\frac{1}{3}$ of $6 = $ _____ so $\frac{1}{3} \times 6 = $ _____   b) $\frac{3}{5}$ of $10 = $ _____ so $\frac{3}{5} \times 10 = $ _____

c) $\frac{2}{3}$ of $6 = $ _____ so $\frac{2}{3} \times 6 = $ _____   d) $\frac{3}{4}$ of $20 = $ _____ so $\frac{3}{4} \times 20 = $ _____

When multiplying whole numbers, the order we multiply in does not affect the answer.

Examples: $2 \times 3 = 3 \times 2 = 6$ $4 \times 5 = 5 \times 4 = 20$

INVESTIGATION 1 ▶ When multiplying a fraction and a whole number, does the order we multiply in affect the answer?

A. Calculate the product in both orders.

i) $8 \times \frac{1}{4} = \frac{1}{4} + \frac{1}{4} + \frac{1}{4} + \frac{1}{4} + \frac{1}{4} + \frac{1}{4} + \frac{1}{4} + \frac{1}{4} = $ _____   ii) $6 \times \frac{2}{3} = \frac{2}{3} + \frac{2}{3} + \frac{2}{3} + \frac{2}{3} + \frac{2}{3} + \frac{2}{3} = $ _____

$\frac{1}{4} \times 8 = \frac{1}{4}$ of $8 = $ _____ $\frac{2}{3} \times 6 = \frac{2}{3}$ of $6 = $ _____

iii) $10 \times \frac{3}{5}$ and $\frac{3}{5} \times 10$ iv) $12 \times \frac{5}{6}$ and $\frac{5}{6} \times 12$

B. Does changing the order we multiply in affect the answer? _____

INVESTIGATION 2 ▶ The fractions $\frac{1}{3}$ and $\frac{2}{6}$ are equivalent. Does multiplying by $\frac{2}{6}$ result in the same answer as multiplying by $\frac{1}{3}$?

A. Multiply these numbers by both $\frac{1}{3}$ and $\frac{2}{6}$. Reduce your answer to lowest terms.

i) $4 \times \frac{1}{3} = $ _____ $4 \times \frac{2}{6} = $ _____ $ = $ _____   ii) $11 \times \frac{1}{3} = $ _____ $11 \times \frac{2}{6} = $ _____ $ = $ _____

B. Does multiplying by $\frac{2}{6}$ result in the same answer as multiplying by $\frac{1}{3}$? _____

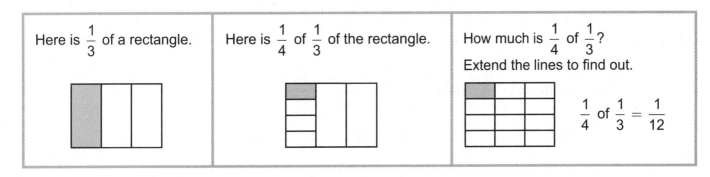

Here is $\frac{1}{3}$ of a rectangle.

Here is $\frac{1}{4}$ of $\frac{1}{3}$ of the rectangle.

How much is $\frac{1}{4}$ of $\frac{1}{3}$?

Extend the lines to find out.

$\frac{1}{4}$ of $\frac{1}{3} = \frac{1}{12}$

1. Extend the horizontal lines in each picture, then write a fraction statement for each figure using the word "of."

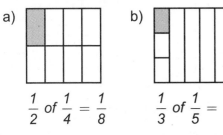 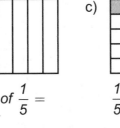 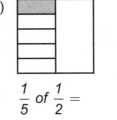 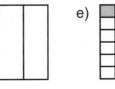

a) $\frac{1}{2}$ of $\frac{1}{4} = \frac{1}{8}$ b) $\frac{1}{3}$ of $\frac{1}{5} =$ c) $\frac{1}{5}$ of $\frac{1}{2} =$ d)   e)

2. Rewrite the fraction statements from Question 1 using the multiplication sign instead of the word "of."

a) $\frac{1}{2} \times \frac{1}{4} = \frac{1}{8}$ b)   c)   d)   e)

3. Write a multiplication statement for each figure.

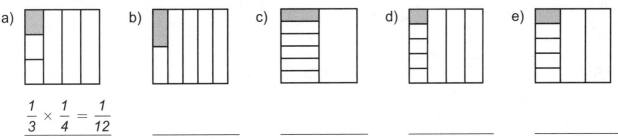

a) $\frac{1}{3} \times \frac{1}{4} = \frac{1}{12}$ b) _____   c) _____   d) _____   e) _____

4. Write a formula for multiplying fractions that both have numerator 1.

$\frac{1}{a} \times \frac{1}{b} =$ _____

5. Multiply.

a) $\frac{1}{2} \times \frac{1}{5} =$ b) $\frac{1}{2} \times \frac{1}{7} =$ c) $\frac{1}{3} \times \frac{1}{6} =$ d) $\frac{1}{5} \times \frac{1}{7} =$

e) $\frac{1}{5} \times \frac{1}{2} =$ f) $\frac{1}{7} \times \frac{1}{2} =$ g) $\frac{1}{6} \times \frac{1}{3} =$ h) $\frac{1}{7} \times \frac{1}{5} =$

6. Look at your answers to Question 5. Does the order you multiply in affect the answer? _____

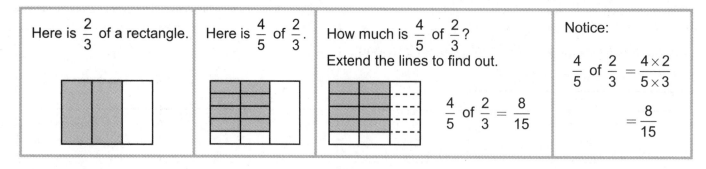

Here is $\frac{2}{3}$ of a rectangle.	Here is $\frac{4}{5}$ of $\frac{2}{3}$.	How much is $\frac{4}{5}$ of $\frac{2}{3}$? Extend the lines to find out. $\frac{4}{5}$ of $\frac{2}{3} = \frac{8}{15}$	Notice: $\frac{4}{5}$ of $\frac{2}{3} = \frac{4 \times 2}{5 \times 3}$ $= \frac{8}{15}$

7. Write a fraction statement for each figure. Use multiplication instead of the word "of."

   a)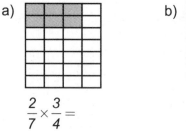
   $$\frac{2}{7} \times \frac{3}{4} =$$

   b)
   $$\frac{5}{7} \times \frac{2}{3} =$$

   c)

   d)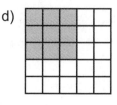

8. Find each amount by multiplying the numerators and denominators of the fractions.

   a) $\frac{2}{3} \times \frac{4}{7} = \frac{8}{21}$
   b) $\frac{1}{2} \times \frac{3}{5} =$
   c) $\frac{3}{4} \times \frac{5}{7} =$
   d) $\frac{2}{5} \times \frac{3}{8} =$

9. Write a formula for multiplying fractions by fractions.

   $$\frac{a}{b} \times \frac{c}{d} = \underline{\hspace{4cm}}$$

10. Multiply the fractions. (Reduce your answer to lowest terms.)

   a) $\frac{2}{3} \times \frac{3}{5} =$
   b) $\frac{3}{4} \times \frac{5}{7} =$
   c) $\frac{1}{3} \times \frac{4}{5} =$
   d) $\frac{4}{6} \times \frac{8}{7} =$
   e) $\frac{3}{7} \times \frac{8}{9} =$

11. Multiply the fractions. (Reduce your answer to lowest terms.) What do you notice?

   a) $\frac{3}{5} \times \frac{5}{3}$
   b) $\frac{2}{7} \times \frac{7}{2}$
   c) $\frac{3}{2} \times \frac{2}{3}$
   d) $\frac{4}{5} \times \frac{5}{4}$
   e) $\frac{7}{9} \times \frac{9}{7}$

12. a) Circle the fractions that are more than $\frac{2}{3}$.

   $\frac{5}{7}$ $\qquad$ $\frac{5}{8}$ $\qquad$ $\frac{3}{5}$ $\qquad$ $\frac{7}{10}$

   b) Without calculating the products, circle the products that are greater than 1 $(= \frac{2}{3} \times \frac{3}{2})$.

   $\frac{5}{7} \times \frac{3}{2}$ $\qquad$ $\frac{5}{8} \times \frac{3}{2}$ $\qquad$ $\frac{3}{5} \times \frac{3}{2}$ $\qquad$ $\frac{7}{10} \times \frac{3}{2}$

   c) Verify your answers to part b) by calculating the products.

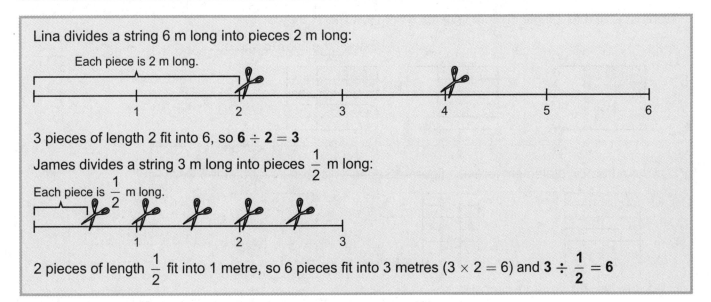

Lina divides a string 6 m long into pieces 2 m long:

Each piece is 2 m long.

3 pieces of length 2 fit into 6, so $6 \div 2 = 3$

James divides a string 3 m long into pieces $\frac{1}{2}$ m long:

Each piece is $\frac{1}{2}$ m long.

2 pieces of length $\frac{1}{2}$ fit into 1 metre, so 6 pieces fit into 3 metres ($3 \times 2 = 6$) and $3 \div \frac{1}{2} = 6$

1. Answer the questions and complete the division statements.

   a) How many pieces of length $\frac{1}{3}$ fit into 1? _____3_____ $1 \div \frac{1}{3} =$ _____3_____

      How many pieces of length $\frac{1}{3}$ fit into 2? __$2 \times 3 = 6$__ $2 \div \frac{1}{3} =$ _____6_____

      How many pieces of length $\frac{1}{3}$ fit into 5? _____ $5 \div \frac{1}{3} =$ _____

   b) How many pieces of length $\frac{1}{4}$ fit into 1? _____ $1 \div \frac{1}{4} =$ _____

      How many pieces of length $\frac{1}{4}$ fit into 3? _____ $3 \div \frac{1}{4} =$ _____

      How many pieces of length $\frac{1}{4}$ fit into 7? _____ $7 \div \frac{1}{4} =$ _____

   c) How many pieces of length $\frac{1}{a}$ fit into 1? _____ $1 \div \frac{1}{a} =$ _____

      How many pieces of length $\frac{1}{a}$ fit into 3? _____ $3 \div \frac{1}{a} =$ _____

      How many pieces of length $\frac{1}{a}$ fit into b? _____ $b \div \frac{1}{a} =$ _____

2. Find each quotient.

   a) $9 \div \frac{1}{5} =$ ___ × ___ = ___   b) $8 \div \frac{1}{4} =$ ___ × ___ = ___   c) $7 \div \frac{1}{6} =$ ___ × ___ = ___

   d) $8 \div \frac{1}{3} =$ ___   e) $6 \div \frac{1}{6} =$ ___   f) $5 \div \frac{1}{7} =$ ___

   g) $7 \div \frac{1}{7} =$ ___   h) $8 \div \frac{1}{9} =$ ___

How many strings of length $\frac{2}{5}$ m fit along a string of length 4 m?

Step 1: Calculate how many strings of length $\frac{1}{5}$ m fit along a string of length 4 m.

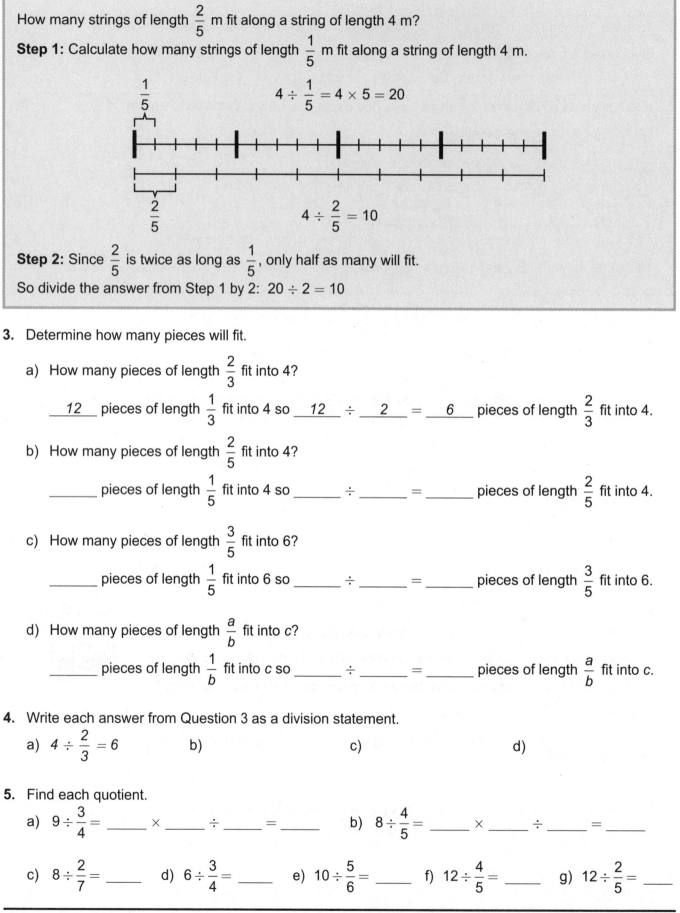

$$4 \div \frac{1}{5} = 4 \times 5 = 20$$

$$4 \div \frac{2}{5} = 10$$

Step 2: Since $\frac{2}{5}$ is twice as long as $\frac{1}{5}$, only half as many will fit.

So divide the answer from Step 1 by 2: $20 \div 2 = 10$

3. Determine how many pieces will fit.

   a) How many pieces of length $\frac{2}{3}$ fit into 4?

      ___12___ pieces of length $\frac{1}{3}$ fit into 4 so ___12___ ÷ ___2___ = ___6___ pieces of length $\frac{2}{3}$ fit into 4.

   b) How many pieces of length $\frac{2}{5}$ fit into 4?

      _____ pieces of length $\frac{1}{5}$ fit into 4 so _____ ÷ _____ = _____ pieces of length $\frac{2}{5}$ fit into 4.

   c) How many pieces of length $\frac{3}{5}$ fit into 6?

      _____ pieces of length $\frac{1}{5}$ fit into 6 so _____ ÷ _____ = _____ pieces of length $\frac{3}{5}$ fit into 6.

   d) How many pieces of length $\frac{a}{b}$ fit into c?

      _____ pieces of length $\frac{1}{b}$ fit into c so _____ ÷ _____ = _____ pieces of length $\frac{a}{b}$ fit into c.

4. Write each answer from Question 3 as a division statement.

   a) $4 \div \frac{2}{3} = 6$ b)   c)   d)

5. Find each quotient.

   a) $9 \div \frac{3}{4} =$ _____ × _____ ÷ _____ = _____   b) $8 \div \frac{4}{5} =$ _____ × _____ ÷ _____ = _____

   c) $8 \div \frac{2}{7} =$ _____   d) $6 \div \frac{3}{4} =$ _____   e) $10 \div \frac{5}{6} =$ _____   f) $12 \div \frac{4}{5} =$ _____   g) $12 \div \frac{2}{5} =$ _____

NS7-81 Word Problems

1. To make 1 pie, a recipe calls for $\frac{3}{4}$ of a cup of blueberries. How many cups of blueberries are needed for 3 pies?

2. Kira's exercise routine takes $\frac{2}{3}$ of an hour. She exercises 4 days a week. How many hours a week does she exercise?

3. How many people will 9 pizzas feed if each person eats $\frac{3}{4}$ of a pizza?

4. Paul cuts a rope into pieces. Each piece is $\frac{3}{5}$ of a metre long. The rope was 60 m long. How many pieces has Paul made?

5. It takes $\frac{3}{4}$ of an hour to pick the peaches on one tree. How long will it take to pick the peaches on 12 trees?

6. Anne took $\frac{1}{5}$ of a pie. She gave $\frac{2}{3}$ of her piece to Ron. What fraction of a pie did Ron get?

7. a) What fraction of a year is a month?
   b) What fraction of a decade is a year?
   c) What fraction of a decade is a month?

8. Philip gave away 35% of his hockey cards.
   a) What fraction of his cards did Philip keep?
   b) Philip put his remaining cards in a scrapbook. Each page holds 18 cards and he filled $46\frac{2}{9}$ pages. How many cards did he put in the scrapbook?
   c) How many cards did Philip have before he gave part of his collection away?

9. Two-thirds of Helen's age is half of Dale's age. Dale is 10 years older than Helen. How old is Helen?

10. Ron's age is two-thirds of Mark's age. Mark's age is three-fifths of Sara's age. Sara is 9 years older than Ron. How old is Mark?

NS7-82 Multiplying Decimals by 0.1, 0.01, and 0.001

1. To multiply a number by 10, move the decimal point ___1___ place to the _____*right*_____.

   To multiply a number by 100, move the decimal point _____ places to the _____.

   To multiply a number by 1 000, move the decimal point _____ places to the _____.

2. a) Multiply by 10, 100, or 1 000. Use the rules in Question 1.

   $10 \times 0.1 =$ __*1.0*__ $100 \times 0.1 =$ _____ $1\ 000 \times 0.1 =$ _____

   b) Rule: To multiply a number by 0.1, move the decimal point _____ place to the _____.

   c) Use your rule from part b) to find these products.

   i) $0.1 \times 0.1 =$ _____   ii) $0.01 \times 0.1 =$ _____   iii) $0.001 \times 0.1 =$ _____

   iv) $5 \times 0.1 =$ _____   v) $0.2 \times 0.1 =$ _____   vi) $0.07 \times 0.1 =$ _____

3. a) Multiply by moving the decimal point. Use the rules in Question 1.

   $10 \times 0.01 =$ _____ $100 \times 0.01 =$ _____ $1\ 000 \times 0.01 =$ _____

   b) Rule: To multiply a number by 0.01, move the decimal point _____ places to the _____.

   c) Predict: To multiply a number by 0.001, move the decimal point _____ places to the _____.

   d) Use your rule from part b) and your prediction from part c) to determine these products. Use a calculator to check your answers.

   i) $0.1 \times 0.01 =$ _____   ii) $0.01 \times 0.01 =$ _____   iii) $0.3 \times 0.001 =$ _____

   iv) $2.5 \times 0.01 =$ _____   v) $13.9 \times 0.001 =$ _____   vi) $810.6 \times 0.001 =$ _____

4. Multiply.

   a) 0.05×0.01 b) 0.32×0.001 c) 50×0.01 d) 57.2×0.0001

5. When you multiply a number *n* by a number less than 1, the product is _____ than *n*.

6. Convert the measurement. Use 1 mm = 0.1 cm, 1 cm = 0.01 m, 1 m = 0.001 km.

   a) 36 mm = (36 × __*0.1*__) cm   b) 470 cm = (470 × _____) m   c) 85 m = (85 × _____) km

   = _____ cm   = _____ m   = _____ km

7. a) Rewrite each decimal as a product with one factor that is 0.1, 0.01, or 0.001.

   i) $0.2 = 2 \times$ __*0.1*__   ii) $0.7 = 7 \times$ _____   iii) $0.03 =$ _____ $\times 0.01$ iv) $0.005 = 5 \times$ _____

   b) Rewrite the decimal as you did in part a). Then multiply.

   i) $16 \times 0.2 = 16 \times 2 \times 0.1$ ii) $75 \times 0.04 = 75 \times$ _____ $\times 0.01$ iii) $18 \times 0.005 = 18 \times$ _____ $\times 0.001$

   = _____ $\times 0.1$ = _____ $\times 0.01$ = _____ $\times 0.001$

   = _____   = _____   = _____

A place value after the decimal point is called a **decimal place**.

1. How many decimal places does each number have?

   a) 201.4 has _____   b) 72.03 has _____   c) 214.126 has _____   d) 80.023 007 has _____

2. a) Change each decimal to a fraction with denominator 10, 100, or 1 000.

   i) $0.2 =$ _____   ii) $0.02 =$ _____   iii) $0.12 =$ _____   iv) $5.1 =$ _____   v) $8.247 =$ _____

   b) Compare the number of zeros in the denominator of the fraction to the number
      of decimal places in the decimal. What do you notice?

3. Shade squares to show each amount. Find the product.

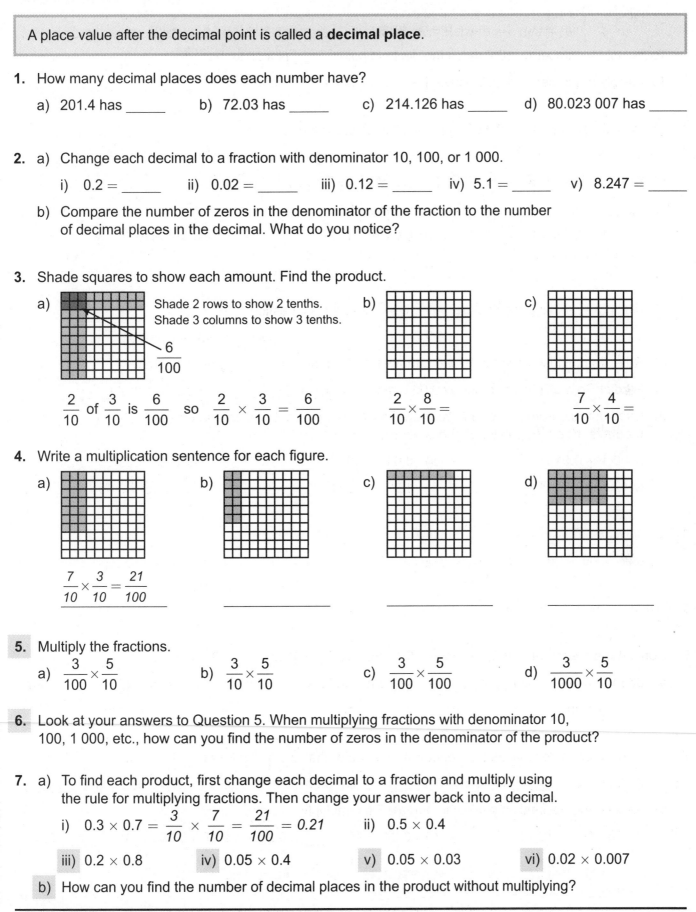

   a) Shade 2 rows to show 2 tenths.
      Shade 3 columns to show 3 tenths.

      $\frac{6}{100}$

      $\frac{2}{10}$ of $\frac{3}{10}$ is $\frac{6}{100}$ so $\frac{2}{10} \times \frac{3}{10} = \frac{6}{100}$

   b) $\frac{2}{10} \times \frac{8}{10} =$

   c) $\frac{7}{10} \times \frac{4}{10} =$

4. Write a multiplication sentence for each figure.

   a) $\frac{7}{10} \times \frac{3}{10} = \frac{21}{100}$

   b) _____

   c) _____

   d) _____

5. Multiply the fractions.

   a) $\frac{3}{100} \times \frac{5}{10}$ b) $\frac{3}{10} \times \frac{5}{10}$ c) $\frac{3}{100} \times \frac{5}{100}$ d) $\frac{3}{1000} \times \frac{5}{10}$

6. Look at your answers to Question 5. When multiplying fractions with denominator 10,
   100, 1 000, etc., how can you find the number of zeros in the denominator of the product?

7. a) To find each product, first change each decimal to a fraction and multiply using
      the rule for multiplying fractions. Then change your answer back into a decimal.

      i) $0.3 \times 0.7 = \frac{3}{10} \times \frac{7}{10} = \frac{21}{100} = 0.21$ ii) 0.5×0.4

      iii) 0.2×0.8 iv) 0.05×0.4 v) 0.05×0.03 vi) 0.02×0.007

   b) How can you find the number of decimal places in the product without multiplying?

Example: 0.28×0.4	**Step 1:** Multiply the decimals as if they were whole numbers. $28 \times 4 = 112$	**Step 2:** 0.28 has 2 decimal places and 0.4 has 1 decimal place. So the product should have **2 + 1 = 3** decimal places. $0.28 \times 0.4 = 0.112$

8. Using the rule given above, multiply the decimals in your notebook.

   a) 0.5×0.8 b) 0.7×0.9 c) 0.2×0.6 d) 0.15×0.8 e) 0.26×0.3

   f) 0.4×0.67 g) 0.32×0.9 h) 0.04×0.7 i) 0.2×0.7 j) 0.8×0.46

9. Round each decimal number to the first digit from the left that is not 0 — this is called the **leading digit**.

   a) $0.023\,7 \approx \underline{\ \ 0.02\ \ }$ b) $0.003\,89 \approx \underline{\quad}$ c) $92.156 \approx \underline{\quad}$ d) $0.007\,777\,77 \approx \underline{\quad}$

10. Estimate the product.

   a) $2.1 \times 6.8 \approx \underline{\quad} \times \underline{\quad} = \underline{\quad}$ b) $6.54 \times 3.417 \approx \underline{\quad} \times \underline{\quad} = \underline{\quad}$

   c) 3.25×5.498 d) 15.125×2.064 e) 9.678×44.7 f) 35.78×46.72

11. Estimate the product, then place the decimal point correctly in each answer.

   a) $7.8 \times 4 = 3\ 1\ 2$ b) $35.60 \times 4.8 = 1\ 7\ 0\ 8\ 8$

   c) $5.25 \times 1.78 = 9\ 3\ 4\ 5$ d) $47.35 \times 3.187 = 1\ 5\ 0\ 9\ 0\ 4\ 4\ 5$

12. Estimate each product, then correct the answers that are wrong.

   a) $3.4 \times 2.01 = 6\,.\,8\ 3\ 4$ b) $3.4 \times 2.05 = 0\,.\,6\ 9\ 7$

   c) $3.4 \times 2.056 = 6\,.\,9\ 9\ 0\ 4$ d) $76.35 \times 11.23 = 8\ 5\ 7\,.\,4\ 1\ 0\ 5$

13. Multiply as if the numbers were whole numbers. Then estimate to place the decimal point.

   a) 2.7×3.6 b) 6.8×0.73 c) 4.5×3.9

14. $a \times b = 0.6$. Write as many possible values for a and b as you can find.

15. A yard has dimensions 8.5 m by 5.3 m. What is the area of the yard?

16. A bottle holds 0.7 litres of liquid. How many litres will 2 1/2 bottles hold?
    Hint: Change the fraction to a decimal.

There are 10 mm in 1 cm.   10 cm = 1 dm

There are 10 cm in 1 dm.   There are 100 cm in 1 m.   There are 10 dm in 1 m.

There are 1000 m in 1 km.

1. Fill in the blank.

a) There are _____ mm in 1 dm. b) There are _____ cm in 1 km. c) There are _____ dm in a 1 km.

2. Complete each statement.

a) There are ___10___ cm in 1 dm, so 1 cm = $\dfrac{1}{10}$ dm = ___0.1___ dm.

b) There are ___100___ cm in 1 m, so 1 cm = $\dfrac{1}{100}$ m = ___0.01___ m.

c) There are _____ mm in 1 cm, so 1 mm = ☐ cm = _____ cm.

d) There are _____ mm in 1 dm, so 1 mm = ☐ dm = _____ dm.

e) There are _____ dm in 1 m, so 1 dm = ☐ m = _____ m.

3. Complete the statements.

a) 1 cm = $\dfrac{1}{10}$ of a ___dm___

   1 cm = 0.1 ___dm___

b) 1 mm = $\dfrac{1}{10}$ of a _____

   1 mm = 0.1 _____

c) 1 dm = $\dfrac{1}{10}$ of a _____

   1 dm = 0.1 _____

d) 1 cm = $\dfrac{1}{100}$ of a _____

   1 cm = 0.01 _____

e) 1 mm = $\dfrac{1}{100}$ of a _____

   1 mm = 0.01 _____

f) 1 mm = $\dfrac{1}{1000}$ of a _____

   1 mm = 0.001 _____

To answer parts g) to i), first picture the amount in your mind. Then ask yourself, What larger unit is the amount a **tenth** of? or What unit would the amount fit into ten times?

g) 10 cm = $\dfrac{1}{10}$ of a _____

   10 cm = 0.1 _____

h) 10 mm = $\dfrac{1}{10}$ of a _____

   10 mm = 0.1 _____

i) 100 m = $\dfrac{1}{10}$ of a _____

   100 m = 0.1 _____

4. a) How many pennies make 4 dollars and 23 cents? Write 4 dollars 23 cents in decimal notation for dollars.

b) How many centimetres are in 4 m 23 cm? Write 4 m 23 cm in decimal notation for metres.

c) How are the questions above the same?

5. Is 5 m 28 cm equal to 5.28 m or 5.28 cm? Explain.

1. Change each measurement to the smaller unit.

   a) 8 m = _____ cm   b) 9 m = _____ dm   c) 5 cm = _____ mm

   d) 9 dm = _____ cm   e) 3 m = _____ cm   f) 14 m = _____ dm

   g) 45 dm = _____ mm   h) 20 cm = _____ mm   i) 300 m = _____ dm

   j) 25 cm = _____ mm   k) 850 dm = _____ mm   l) 99 m = _____ cm

2. Change each measurement to the smaller unit.

   a) 7 m 2 cm = _700_ cm + _2_ cm = _702_ cm   b) 9 m 52 cm = ___ cm + ___ cm = ___ cm

   c) 4 m 3 dm = ___ dm + ___ dm = ___ dm   d) 8 m 5 dm = ___ dm + ___ dm = ___ dm

   e) 5 cm 2 mm = ___ mm + ___ mm = ___ mm   f) 6 dm 75 mm = ___ mm + ___ mm = ___ mm

   g) 2 km 352 m = ___ m + ___ m = ___ m   h) 4 m 13 mm = ___ mm + ___ mm = ___ mm

3. Fill in the missing numbers to make the equivalent fractions.

   a) $.5 \text{ m} = \dfrac{\quad}{10} \text{ m} = \dfrac{\quad}{100} \text{ m} = \dfrac{\quad}{1000} \text{ m}$ b) $.72 \text{ m} = \dfrac{\quad}{100} \text{ m} = \dfrac{\quad}{1000} \text{ m}$

   c) $.7 \text{ dm} = \dfrac{\quad}{100} \text{ dm}$ d) $.85 \text{ m} = \dfrac{\quad}{1000} \text{ m}$

   e) $.9 \text{ m} = \dfrac{\quad}{100} \text{ m}$

4. What unit will fit into…

   a) a metre 100 times? _____*a centimetre*_____   b) a centimetre 10 times? _____

   c) a decimetre 100 times? _____   d) a metre 10 times? _____

5. Express each measurement in a whole number of units. Hint: To express $\dfrac{57}{100}$ m

   in a whole number of units, think: "What unit will fit into a metre 100 times? Since

   there are 100 cm in a metre, $\dfrac{57}{100}$ m = 57 cm."

   a) $\dfrac{7}{10}$ m = _____*7 dm*_____   b) $\dfrac{4}{10}$ m = _____   c) $\dfrac{93}{100}$ m = _____

   d) $\dfrac{2}{10}$ dm = _____   e) $\dfrac{37}{100}$ dm = _____   f) $\dfrac{56}{1000}$ m = _____

   g) $\dfrac{72}{100}$ dm = _____   h) $\dfrac{8}{10}$ cm = _____   i) $\dfrac{75}{1000}$ km = _____

6. Change each measurement to the unit given in the box. Hint: To change .7 dm to millimetres, think: "There are 100 mm in a decimetre, so I should change .7 to a fraction with denominator 100: .7 dm = $\frac{70}{100}$ dm = 70 mm."

a) $\boxed{\text{mm}}$ .3 cm = $\frac{3}{10}$ cm = 3 mm

b) $\boxed{\text{cm}}$ .52 m =

c) $\boxed{\text{mm}}$ .6 dm =

d) $\boxed{\text{mm}}$ .52 m =

7. Change each measurement to the unit given in the box.

a) $\boxed{\text{cm}}$ 3.5 m = 3 m + $\frac{5}{10}$ m = 3 m + $\frac{50}{100}$ m = 300 cm + 50 cm = 350 cm

b) $\boxed{\text{cm}}$ 4.2 m =

c) $\boxed{\text{dm}}$ 4.7 m

d) $\boxed{\text{cm}}$ 6.8 dm

e) $\boxed{\text{mm}}$ 8.73 dm

f) $\boxed{\text{mm}}$ 2.3 cm

8. Write each measurement in mixed units.

a) 2.357 m = ____ m ____ dm ____ cm ____ mm

b) 3.52 dm = ____ dm ____ cm ____ mm

c) 5.006 m = ____ m ____ dm ____ cm ____ mm

d) 8.04 dm = ____ dm ____ cm ____ mm

e) 3.5 cm = ____ cm ____ mm

f) 20.54 dm = ____ dm ____ cm ____ mm

9. Underline the digit that stands for the unit given in the box.

a) $\boxed{\text{cm}}$ 3.7 2 3 m

b) $\boxed{\text{mm}}$ 1 7 . 5 2 dm

c) $\boxed{\text{dm}}$ 1 0 . 7 9 cm

d) $\boxed{\text{dm}}$ 2 3 . 4 5 9 m

e) $\boxed{\text{m}}$ 5 8 . 4 1 dm

f) $\boxed{\text{dm}}$ 1 2 1 mm

10. In the measurement 2 . 3 7 5 km, underline the digit that represents metres.

11. $1.72 stands for 1 dollar 7 dimes 2 pennies. In the measurement 1.72 m, are the centimetres like dimes or like pennies? Explain.

12. Carl has a set of sticks: some are 5 cm long and some are 3 cm long. Show how each of the following measurements could be made by lining the sticks up end to end.

a) 18 cm

b) 19 cm

c) 100 mm

d) 280 mm

13. Most provinces in Canada have an official tree. Change each measurement to the smallest unit used in the chart, and then order the provincial trees from tallest to shortest.

Tree	Height
White Birch (Saskatchewan)	20 m
Lodgepole Pine (Alberta)	3 050 cm
Western Red Cedar (British Columbia)	59 m
Red Oak (Prince Edward Island)	24 m

ME7-22 Volume of Rectangular Prisms

> **Volume** is the amount of space taken up by a three-dimensional object.
>
> To measure volume, we can use 1 cm³ blocks. These blocks are uniform cubes with length, width, and height all 1 cm. They are also called centimetre cubes.
>
> **1 cm³ block**
>
>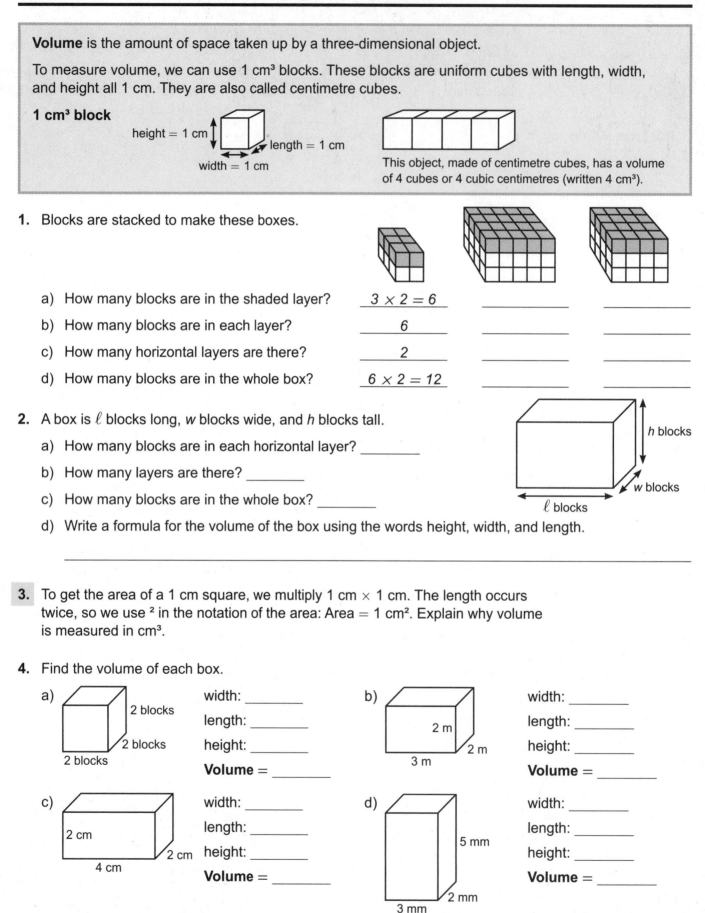
>
> height = 1 cm
> length = 1 cm
> width = 1 cm
>
> This object, made of centimetre cubes, has a volume of 4 cubes or 4 cubic centimetres (written 4 cm³).

1. Blocks are stacked to make these boxes.

   a) How many blocks are in the shaded layer? $3 \times 2 = 6$ _____ _____

   b) How many blocks are in each layer? 6 _____ _____

   c) How many horizontal layers are there? 2 _____ _____

   d) How many blocks are in the whole box? $6 \times 2 = 12$ _____ _____

2. A box is ℓ blocks long, w blocks wide, and h blocks tall.

   a) How many blocks are in each horizontal layer? _____

   b) How many layers are there? _____

   c) How many blocks are in the whole box? _____

   d) Write a formula for the volume of the box using the words height, width, and length.

   _____

   h blocks
   w blocks
   ℓ blocks

3. To get the area of a 1 cm square, we multiply 1 cm × 1 cm. The length occurs twice, so we use ² in the notation of the area: Area = 1 cm². Explain why volume is measured in cm³.

4. Find the volume of each box.

   a)
   2 blocks
   2 blocks
   2 blocks

   width: _____
   length: _____
   height: _____
   Volume = _____

   b)
   2 m
   2 m
   3 m

   width: _____
   length: _____
   height: _____
   Volume = _____

   c)
   2 cm
   2 cm
   4 cm

   width: _____
   length: _____
   height: _____
   Volume = _____

   d)
   5 mm
   2 mm
   3 mm

   width: _____
   length: _____
   height: _____
   Volume = _____

ME7-23 Right and Skew Prisms

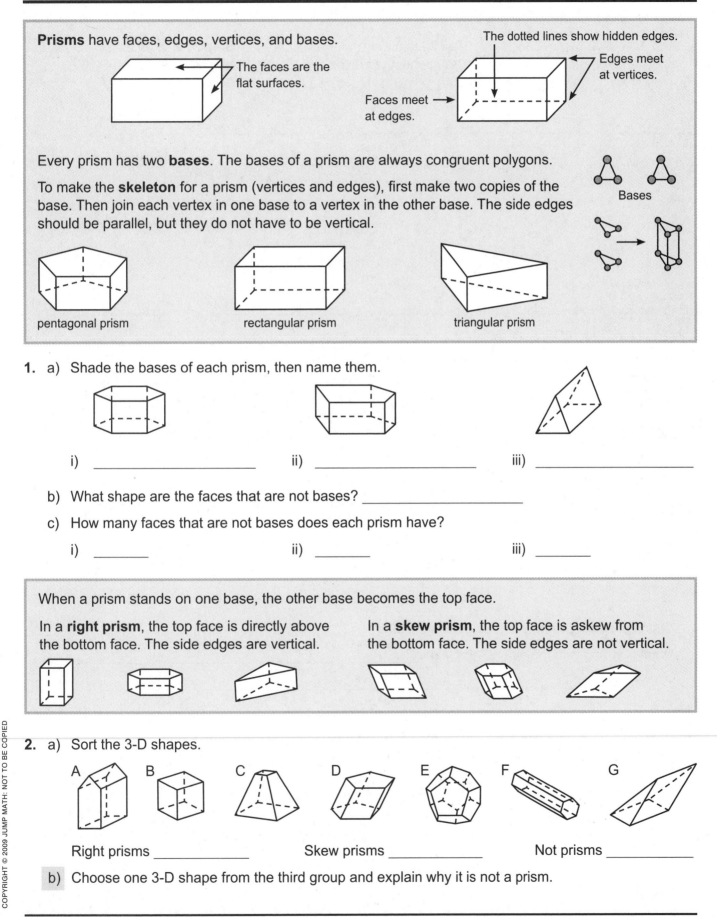

Prisms have faces, edges, vertices, and bases.

The faces are the flat surfaces.

The dotted lines show hidden edges.

Edges meet at vertices.

Faces meet at edges.

Every prism has two **bases**. The bases of a prism are always congruent polygons.

To make the **skeleton** for a prism (vertices and edges), first make two copies of the base. Then join each vertex in one base to a vertex in the other base. The side edges should be parallel, but they do not have to be vertical.

Bases

pentagonal prism   rectangular prism   triangular prism

1. a) Shade the bases of each prism, then name them.

   i) _____   ii) _____   iii) _____

   b) What shape are the faces that are not bases? _____

   c) How many faces that are not bases does each prism have?

   i) _____   ii) _____   iii) _____

When a prism stands on one base, the other base becomes the top face.

In a **right prism**, the top face is directly above the bottom face. The side edges are vertical.

In a **skew prism**, the top face is askew from the bottom face. The side edges are not vertical.

2. a) Sort the 3-D shapes.

   A   B   C   D   E   F   G

   Right prisms _____   Skew prisms _____   Not prisms _____

   b) Choose one 3-D shape from the third group and explain why it is not a prism.

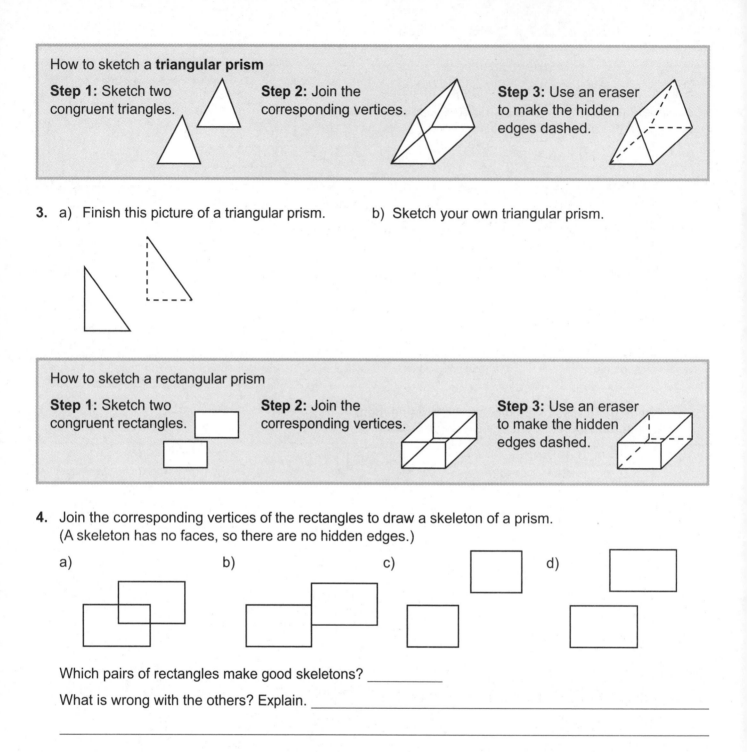

How to sketch a **triangular prism**

Step 1: Sketch two congruent triangles.

Step 2: Join the corresponding vertices.

Step 3: Use an eraser to make the hidden edges dashed.

3. a) Finish this picture of a triangular prism.

b) Sketch your own triangular prism.

How to sketch a rectangular prism

Step 1: Sketch two congruent rectangles.

Step 2: Join the corresponding vertices.

Step 3: Use an eraser to make the hidden edges dashed.

4. Join the corresponding vertices of the rectangles to draw a skeleton of a prism.
(A skeleton has no faces, so there are no hidden edges.)

a)   b)   c)   d)

Which pairs of rectangles make good skeletons? _____

What is wrong with the others? Explain. _____

_____

5. Now sketch two different rectangular prisms. Make the hidden edges dashed, and make sure none of your edges overlap!

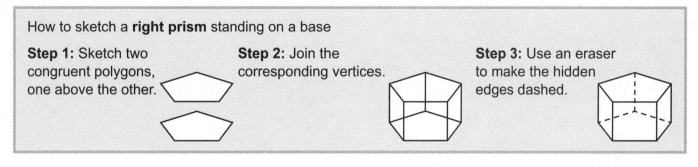

How to sketch a **right prism** standing on a base

Step 1: Sketch two congruent polygons, one above the other.

Step 2: Join the corresponding vertices.

Step 3: Use an eraser to make the hidden edges dashed.

6. Sketch three prisms with bases of different shapes.

7. a) Match each set of dimensions to the sketch that fits best. Then mark the length, height, and width of each prism on the sketch.

_____ 5 m, 3 m, 7 m   _____ 3 cm, 3 cm, 4 cm   _____ 2 km, 4 km, 4 km

A   B   C

b) Find the volume of each right rectangular prism.

Volume A: _____   Volume B: _____   Volume C: _____

8. a) Write 200 as a multiple of three numbers in three different ways.

200 = ____ × ____ × ____   200 = ____ × ____ × ____   200 = ____ × ____ × ____

b) Use the numbers from part a) to sketch three rectangular prisms with volume 200 cm³.

1. a) What fraction of the rectangle is shaded? _____

    b) What is the area of the rectangle in square units? _____

    c) What is the area of the shaded part? _____

2. a) What fraction of the volume of each rectangular prism (r.p.) below is the volume of the triangular prism (t.p.)? _____

    b) What would you divide the volume of each rectangular prism by to find the volume of the triangular prism? _____

    c) Calculate the volumes to fill in the blanks.

    i)   ii)   iii)

    Volume of r.p. = _____   Volume of r.p. = _____   Volume of r.p. = _____

    Volume of t.p. = _____   Volume of t.p. = _____   Volume of t.p. = _____

> Remember: The area of a triangle is $\frac{1}{2}$ of (base × height) or (base × height) ÷ 2.

3. a) These are bases of the triangular prisms in Question 2. Calculate the area of each triangular base.

    i)   ii)   iii)

    Area of base = _____   Area of base = _____   Area of base = _____

    b) Mark an edge perpendicular to a base of each prism in Question 2. Then multiply the area of the triangular base by the length of that edge perpendicular (⊥) to the base.

    i)   ii)   iii)

    $\underline{\quad 1 \quad}$ × $\underline{\quad 4 \quad}$ = _____   _____ × _____ = _____   _____ × _____ = _____
    area   ⊥ edge   area   ⊥ edge   area   ⊥ edge
    of base   of base   of base

    c) Compare the numbers you calculated in Question 3 b) with the volumes of the triangular prisms you calculated in Question 2 c). What do you notice?

4. You can divide any triangle into 2 right triangles. Divide this rectangle into 2 smaller rectangles that contain the right triangles.

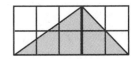

What fraction of the area of each smaller rectangle is the right triangle? _____

What fraction of the area of the whole rectangle is the whole triangle? _____

5. You can divide a rectangular prism into two smaller rectangular prisms.

What fraction of each rectangular prism is the triangular prism? _____

6. Find the volume of each rectangular prism, then the volume of each triangular prism.

a)

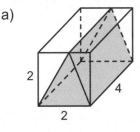

fraction shaded _____

volume of rectangular prism _____

volume of triangular prism _____

b)

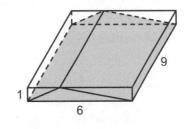

fraction shaded _____

volume of rectangular prism _____

volume of triangular prism _____

c)

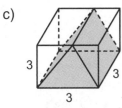

fraction shaded _____

volume of rectangular prism _____

volume of triangular prism _____

d)

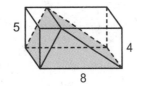

fraction shaded _____

volume of rectangular prism _____

volume of triangular prism _____

e)

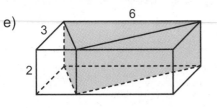

fraction shaded _____

volume of rectangular prism _____

volume of triangular prism _____

f)

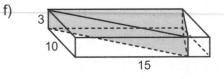

fraction shaded _____

volume of rectangular prism _____

volume of triangular prism _____

ME7-25 Volume of Polygonal Prisms

INVESTIGATION 1 ▶ How is the area of the base related to the volume of a rectangular prism made of blocks?

A. Each of these prisms is made from 1 cm³ blocks.

i) ii) 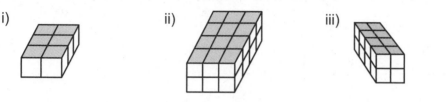 iii) iv)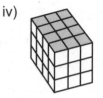

The base of each prism is shaded. What is the area of the base?

B. What is the volume of one horizontal layer of blocks in each prism?

C. What do you notice about the answers in parts A and B?

D. What is the height of each prism?

E. Find the volume of each prism.

F. For each prism, what can you multiply the volume of one layer of blocks by to get the volume of the prism?

G. Will the method from part F work for all rectangular prisms? Build 3 rectangular prisms from blocks and check. Use your models to write a formula for the area of a rectangular prism using the area of the base and the height.

Volume of a rectangular prism = _____

INVESTIGATION 2 ▶ Does the formula from Investigation 1 work for any prism made of blocks?

A. What is the area of the base of each structure?

i) 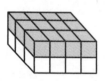 ii) 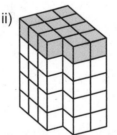 iii)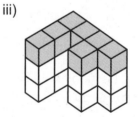

B. What is the volume of one horizontal layer of each structure?

C. What is the volume of each structure?

D. Are these structures prisms? Explain.

_____

_____

E. Does the formula from Investigation 1 work here? _____

1. Make a conjecture about the volume of any right prism, the area of the base, and the height.

   Conjecture: Volume of a right prism = _____

   Check your conjecture for the triangular prism inside each rectangular prism.

   The picture below the prisms shows the base of the triangular prism.

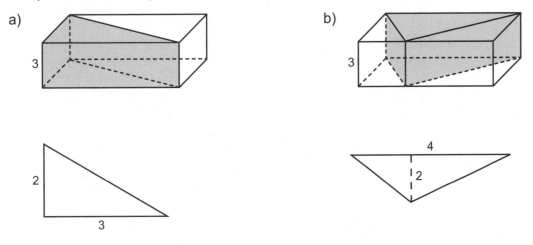

2. Find the volume of each prism. The picture below the prism shows the base of the prism. Remember: Any polygon can be divided into triangles and/or rectangles.

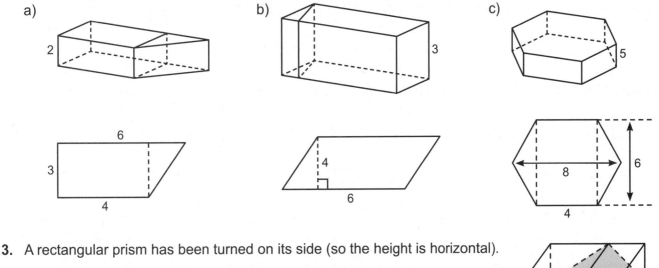

3. A rectangular prism has been turned on its side (so the height is horizontal).

   The volume of the rectangular prism is: width × length × height

   The volume of the triangular prism is: width × length × height ÷ 2

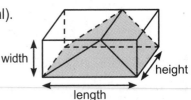

   a) One of the faces of the triangular prism has an area that can be calculated by multiplying width × length ÷ 2.

   What is the shape of the face? _____

   b) Explain why the volume of the triangular prism can be calculated by multiplying Area of triangular base × height.

4. A prism has the base shown and height h cm.

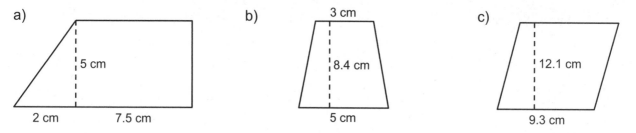

  a) Explain why the volume of the prism is $15 \times h + 20 \times h$ cm³.

  b) Is the expression $15 \times h + 20 \times h$ equal to the expression $(15 + 20) \times h$?

  c) How does your answer to part b) show that the volume of the prism is equal to **Area of base** $\times$ **h**?

5. Estimate, then calculate the volume of a prism with height 10 cm and the base shown.

  a)

  5 cm

  2 cm   7.5 cm

  b)

  3 cm

  8.4 cm

  5 cm

  c)

  12.1 cm

  9.3 cm

6. Sketch two prisms with different bases that have volume 300 cm³.

A centimetre cube has **volume** 1 cm³. It can hold 1 mL of water, so its **capacity** is 1 mL.

---

7. a) $1\,L = $ _____ mL

  b) A 1 L jar has volume _____ cm³.

8. Find the volume and the capacity of each box.

  a)

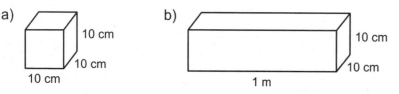

  10 cm

  10 cm

  10 cm

  b)

  10 cm

  10 cm

  1 m

  c)

  1 m

  1 m

  1 m

9. Find the capacity of each prism in Question 5.

10. A juice carton has a capacity of 1.89 L. What is its volume?

11. The volume of a right triangular prism is 300 cm³. Its height is 15 cm. What is the area of the base of this prism? Explain how you found your answer.

12. A rectangular juice carton can hold 2 L of juice. It is 25 cm tall. What is the area of the base of the carton?

BONUS ▶ A small milk carton holds 250 mL of milk. Use the measurements given on the sketch to find the total height of the carton.

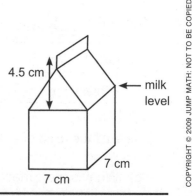

4.5 cm

← milk level

7 cm

7 cm

Note: Pictures are not drawn to scale.

1. In each prism, shade **all** the edges that have the same length as the edge marked.

Example: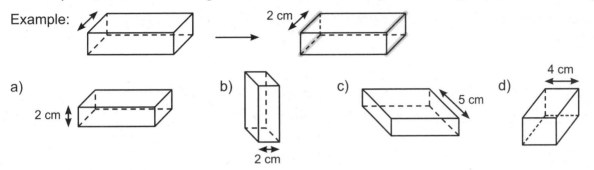

a)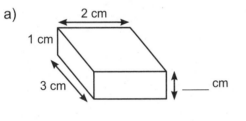

b) c) d)

2. Find the missing edge length.

a)

2 cm
1 cm
3 cm
_____ cm

b)

3 cm
4 cm
2 cm
_____ cm

c)

_____ cm
5 cm
2 cm
4 cm

3. a) Draw each face of this prism on the 1 cm grid paper.

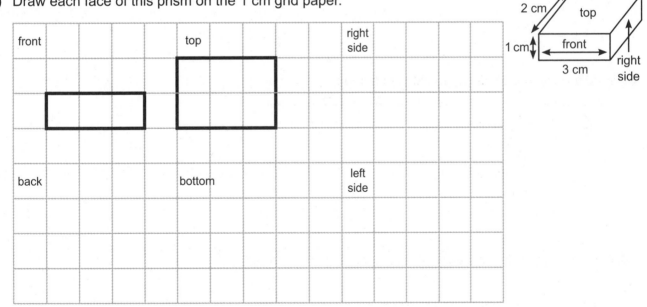

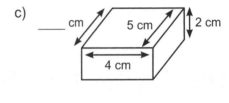

2 cm
1 cm
top
front
3 cm
right side

b) What is the area of each face of the prism?

front _3 cm²_	top _____	right side _____
back _____	bottom _____	left side _____

The **surface area** of a 3-D shape is the total area of all the faces of the shape.

c) What is the surface area of the prism? _____

4. Shade the face that has the same area as the already shaded face.

a)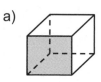

b)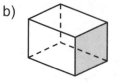

c)

5. The area of each visible face is given. What is the area of each hidden face?

a)
```
      top
      12 cm²      right
  front           8 cm²
  6 cm²
```

back _____

bottom _____

left _____

b)
```
           top
  left      6 cm²
  10 cm²  front
          15 cm²
```

back _____

bottom _____

right _____

c)
```
        top
        18 m²       right
  front 12 m²       6 m²
```

left _____

bottom _____

back _____

d) Frank says that the surface area of the prism in part a) is 26 cm². Is he correct? Explain why or why not.

_____

_____

6. a) Write the area of each visible face directly on the face. Then double each area to find the total area of each pair of congruent faces.

i)
```
  5 cm      top
            right
  2 cm  front
        6 cm²
        3 cm
```

ii)
```
  4 cm      top
            right
  3 cm   front
         3 cm
```

front + back = __6 × 2__ = __12 cm²__

top + bottom = _____ = _____

_____ + _____ = _____ = _____

_____

_____

_____

b) What is the surface area of each prism?

i) _____

ii) _____

7. a) Alexandra says that she only needs to find the area of two faces of this prism to calculate the surface area. Is she correct? Explain.

b) What is the surface area of the prism?

```
  8 cm
  5 cm
         8 cm
```

1. These polygons are the faces of a prism. Name the prism you could make if you assembled the faces.

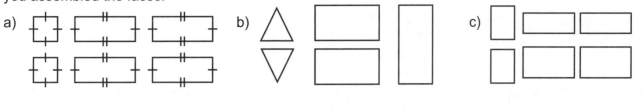

   a)

   b)

   c)

   _____   _____   _____

   Mark the equal sides on all the faces above. Part a) is done for you.

2. Shade the bases of each shape and then complete the chart.

Number of sides on each base				
Number of (non-base) rectangular faces				

   What relationship do you see between the number of sides on each base and the number of (non-base) rectangular faces on a prism?

   _____

3. How many of each type of face would you need to make the prism?

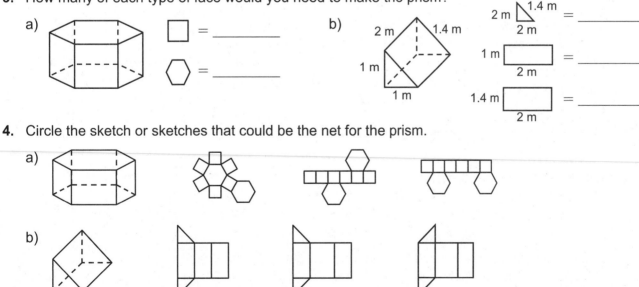

   a)   □ = _____

         ⬡ = _____

   b)   2 m   1.4 m   1 m   1 m

         2 m ◺ 1.4 m / 2 m = _____

         1 m ▭ 2 m = _____

         1.4 m ▭ 2 m = _____

4. Circle the sketch or sketches that could be the net for the prism.

   a)

   b)

   c) Explain what is wrong with the sketches you did not circle.

5. Circle the shape that could be the missing face for the net. Then add this face to the net.

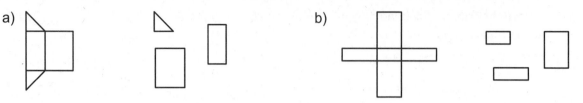

a)   b)

6. Mark the edges that will be glued together on the net. Part a) is started for you.

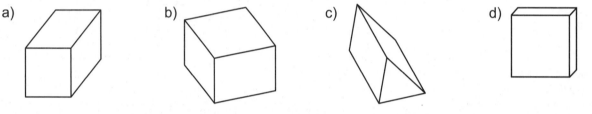

a)   b)   c)

7. Sketch a net for the prism. Name the prism.

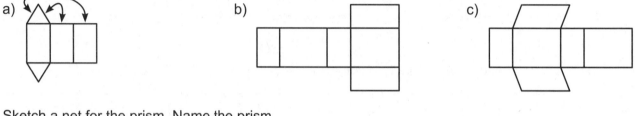

a)   b)   c)   d)

8. Draw a net for the box on the grid paper and label each face. Part a) is done for you.

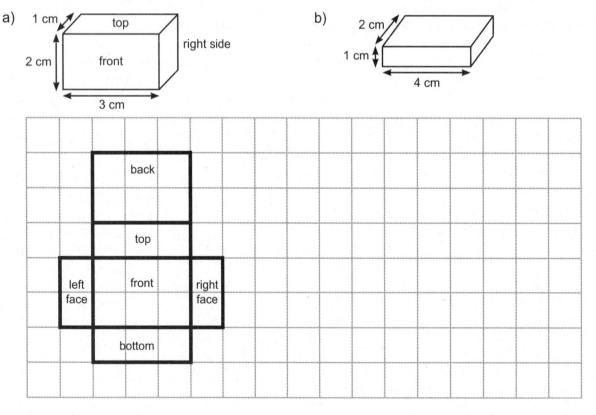

a) 1 cm top right side 2 cm front 3 cm

b) 2 cm 1 cm 4 cm

	back	
	top	
left face	front	right face
	bottom	

9. Write a multiplication statement giving the area of each face for each prism in
Question 8. Then calculate the surface area of the prism.

a) front __2 × 3 = 6 cm²__ back _____

    right face _____ left face _____

    top _____ bottom _____

    surface area of prism _____

b) front _____ back _____

    right face _____ left face _____

    top _____ bottom _____

    surface area of prism _____

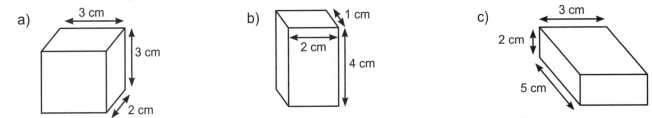

REMINDER ▶ Volume of a right prism = area of base × height

10. Draw a net for the prism on 1 cm grid paper. Then find the surface area and
the volume of the prism.

a)
   3 cm
   3 cm
   2 cm

b)
   1 cm
   2 cm
   4 cm

c)
   3 cm
   2 cm
   5 cm

11. a) Write the name of each face of the prism on the net. Then write the length of
each edge on the net. (The right face is done for you.)

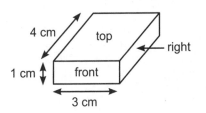

4 cm top right

1 cm front

3 cm

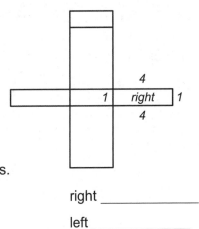

4

1 right 1

4

b) Find the area of each face. Do not forget to include the units.

    top _____ cm² _____ front _____ right _____

    bottom _____ back _____ left _____

c) Add the areas to find the surface area. Surface area: _____

12.

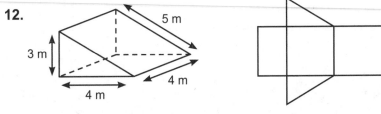

5 m

3 m

4 m

4 m

a) Write the length of each edge on the net.

b) Find the surface area of the prism. Surface area: _____

c) Find the volume of the prism. Volume: _____

ME7-28 Volume and Surface Area

1. Find the surface area of the prism by any method.

a)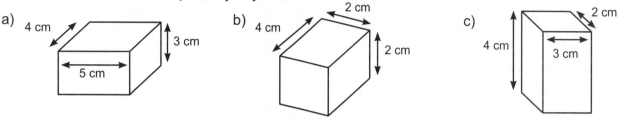
4 cm 3 cm 5 cm

b) 2 cm 4 cm 2 cm

c) 2 cm 4 cm 3 cm

2. Crystal knows that the surface areas of the front, top, and right faces of a prism add to 20 cm². How can she find the **total** surface area of the prism? Explain.

_____

_____

3. Sally's teacher tells her that she can find the surface area of a prism by adding the areas of three faces and then multiplying by two. Which of the following will give Sally the correct answer? Circle all the correct answers.

(area of top + area of bottom + area of right side) × 2   (area of top + area of left side + area of back) × 2

(area of top + area of right side + area of front) × 2   (area of bottom + area of right side + area of left side) × 2

(area of bottom + area of left side + area of front) × 2   (area of bottom + area of front + area of top) × 2

4. Find the missing length.

a)
3 m | Area = 12 m²
_____ m

b)
5 m
_____ m | Area = 15 m²

c)
2 m | Area = 14 m²
_____ m

5. Find the missing edge length.

a)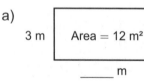
m
4 m 6 m 20 m²

b)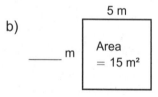
3 m 7 m 15 m² _____ m

c)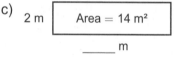
12 m² _____ m 3 m 2 m

6. Edges a, b, and c have lengths that are whole numbers. The surface area of each face is written directly on the face. What are some possible lengths for edges a, b, and c? (Hint: Why can edge a not be 4 m long?)

18 m² b
a
12 m² c 6 m²

7. Describe two different ways of finding the surface area of a rectangular prism. Which do you prefer?

8. Write a formula for the surface area of the prism using the length (ℓ), width (w), and height (h).

h w ℓ

9. A rectangular box is 30 cm long, 25 cm wide, and 20 cm tall.

    a) Sketch the box.

    b) Write the dimensions of the box on your sketch.

    c) Find the area of each face of the box.

    d) The box has a lid. Mark it on your sketch. What are the dimensions of the face that is the lid?

    e) Find the surface area of the box without the lid.

A **regular** polygon has all sides equal and all angles equal.

---

10. A box has the shape of a right prism with a regular hexagon for its base. The sides in the base are 10 cm long. The box is 20 cm high and the area of the base is 520 cm².

    a) How many faces of each type does the box without the lid have?

    _____ hexagons and _____ rectangles

    b) Sketch the faces of the box. Write the dimensions on the faces.

    c) Find the surface area of the box without the lid.

11. a) Write the formula for the volume of a right prism using the area of the base and the height.

    Volume of a right prism = _____

    b) Find the volume of each box in Questions 9 and 10.

12. Find the missing edge of the prism.

    a) Volume = 36 m³

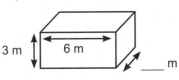

    b) Volume = 105 m³

    c) Volume = 24 m³

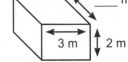

13. a) Bilal says that the volume of this box is 40 m³. Is he correct? Explain why or why not.

    b) Change the measurements of the box into centimetres and find the volume and the surface area.

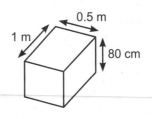

14. A rectangular prism has volume 60 cm³. It is 5 cm long and 3 cm high.

    a) Sketch the prism.

    b) Find the missing dimension of the prism.

    c) Find the surface area of the prism.

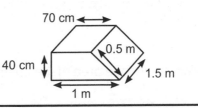

15. Find the volume and the surface area of this prism.

PDM7-6 Bar Graphs

A **bar graph** has four parts: vertical and horizontal **axes**, a **scale**, **labels** (including a title), and **data** (given by the bars).

▶ The bars in a bar graph can be vertical or horizontal.
▶ The scale tells how much each interval on the axis represents.
▶ The labels indicate what the data in the bars is.

1. A teacher made a bar graph (Figure 1) to show the distribution of marks on a test.

   a) Draw a horizontal bar graph (in Figure 2) to show the same data as on the vertical bar graph.

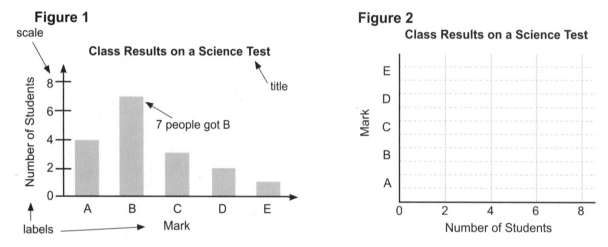

Figure 1

scale

Class Results on a Science Test

title

7 people got B

Number of Students

labels → Mark

Figure 2

Class Results on a Science Test

Mark

Number of Students

   b) What scale was used in the bar graphs? Do you think it was a good choice? Why or why not?

2. Draw a bar graph for each frequency table (use the grids at the bottom of the page). For each graph, you will first need to decide the scale. Example: In part b), you might use the scale 5, 10, 15, 20, 25. In this scale, 5 students are represented by each division.

   a)
Mark	A	B	C	D	E
Frequency	2	9	6	1	0

   ___2___ students should be represented by each division in the scale.

   b)
Mark	A	B	C	D	E
Frequency	16	23	17	5	2

   _____ students should be represented by each division in the scale.

   c)
Mark	A	B	C	D	E
Frequency	19	24	13	3	2

   _____ students should be represented by each division in the scale.

   d)
Mark	A	B	C	D	E
Frequency	10	46	30	8	3

   _____ students should be represented by each division in the scale.

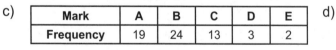

a)
Number of Students
A B C D E
Mark

b)
Number of Students
A B C D E
Mark

c)
Number of Students
A B C D E
Mark

d)
Number of Students
A B C D E
Mark

Probability and Data Management 7-6

3. A company asked 100 females and 100 males whether they agree or disagree with a statement. This was the data they collected: 62 males and 54 females agree. Look at the two graphs below.

a) Do both graphs show the same data? _____

b) Which graph makes it look as though more than half of both males and females agree? _____

c) Which graph makes it look as though very few females agree? _____

d) Which graph suggests a greater difference in opinion between males and females? _____

e) Which graph better represents the data? _____ Why? _____

4.

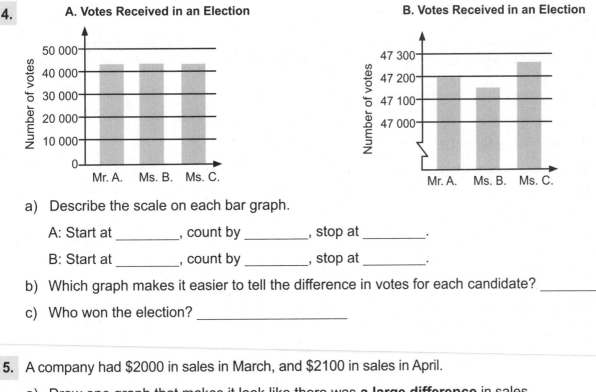

a) Describe the scale on each bar graph.

A: Start at _____, count by _____, stop at _____.

B: Start at _____, count by _____, stop at _____.

b) Which graph makes it easier to tell the difference in votes for each candidate? _____

c) Who won the election? _____

5. A company had $2000 in sales in March, and $2100 in sales in April.

a) Draw one graph that makes it look like there was **a large difference** in sales.
Draw another graph that makes it look like there was **very little difference** in sales.

b) Which do you think is the more accurate graph? Why?

6. Why is it sometimes necessary to start the numbers in a scale at a number greater than 0? Why can doing so be misleading?

PDM7-7 Double Bar Graphs

1. Two sporting goods companies graphed their sales for January through June:

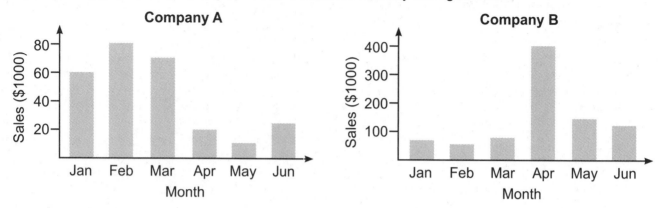

a) When you glance quickly at the two graphs, which company appears to
   have higher monthly sales? _____ Why? _____

b) When you look closely at the scales, which company actually has higher sales? _____

c) Why are most of the bars on the graph for Company B so short? _____

   _____

To compare the sales of both companies, it is convenient to put their graphs on the **same axes**.
The **key** shows you which company is represented by which kind of bar. This kind of graph is called
a **double bar graph**.

---

d) Circle the key on the double bar graph at right.

e) Complete the double bar graph by estimating
   numbers when you need to.

f) In which month(s) did Company A sell
   more than Company B?

   _____

g) During one month in this period, Company B
   had several items in their store autographed
   by a famous athlete. Which month do you
   think that was?

   _____

h) One of the companies sells mostly winter
   sporting goods (for skiing, skating, hockey,
   etc.) and the other sells mostly summer
   sporting goods (for swimming, baseball,
   tennis, etc.). Which company do you think
   is which? Why?

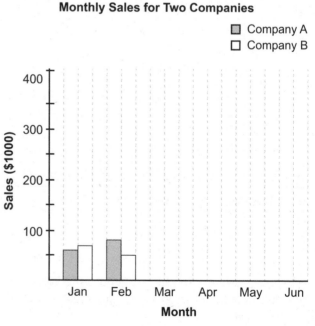

Probability and Data Management 7-7

2. A real estate agent sells both houses and condominiums. The double bar graph shows her sales over the past year.

a) The agent forgot to draw a key, but you know that May and June are the best months for selling houses. Complete the key:

▢ _____

▮ _____

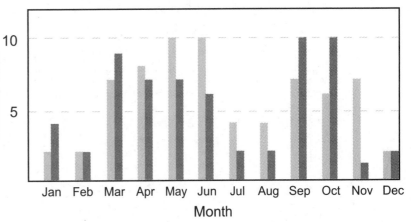

House and Condominium Sales in 2009

b) Next year, the agent wants to go on vacation for a month. In which month would you suggest she take her holiday?

_____

Why?

3. The **bar graph** and the **stem and leaf plot** at right both represent the same data.

Use the graphs to answer the questions below. Put a check mark under the name of the graph that you used to find the answer. Put a check mark under **both** if you could have used either graph to find the answer.

Stem	Leaf
4	8
5	6 9
6	2 4 6 7
7	0 1 5 5 7 8 9
8	2 3 7 7 7
9	2 5

	Bar Graph	Stem and Leaf Plot
a) How many students took the test? _____		
b) In what range were most of the marks? _____		
c) How many students had marks in the 90s? _____		
d) How many students had marks below 60? _____		
e) What was the highest mark? _____		
f) What was the most common mark? _____		

4. For some parts of Question 3, you put a checkmark in both boxes because you could find the information from either graph. Was one of the graphs easier to use? Circle its checkmark if it was.

PDM7-8 Line Graphs

1. The data shows minimum wage increases in Ontario (data from the Ontario Ministry of Labour).

   a) Graph the data on the grids below. Use line graphs.

Year	1995	2004	2005	2006	2007
Minimum Wage ($/hour)	6.85	7.15	7.45	7.75	8.0

   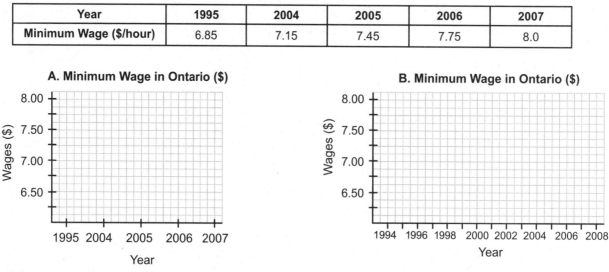

   b) Which graph makes it look as if the minimum wage increased at the same rate from 1995 to 2007? _____

   c) Which graph shows that the minimum wage started increasing more quickly in 2004? _____

   d) Which graph better represents the data? What is wrong with the other graph?

2. Sally and Daphne draw line graphs to show the colour of cars in the same parking lot.

   Sally's graph:

   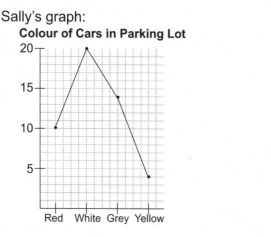

   Daphne's graph:

   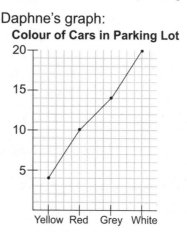

   a) Do both graphs show the same data? Other than the shape of the line, what is the only difference between the two graphs?

   b) Sally says the number of cars increases and then decreases; Daphne says the number of cars always increases. Do these descriptions of what the graphs show fit the data? Explain why line graphs are the wrong choice for this data.

   c) What type of graph would have been a better choice for this data? Why?

   d) Show the same data with your choice of graph.

Probability and Data Management 7-8

PDM7-9 Tallies and Frequency Tables

1. Renia surveyed 35 students about their favourite subject. Unfortunately, she spilled water on her paper and smeared the French tally. Can you complete her data chart?

Subject	Math	Science	History	French	Gym
Tally	~~HHT~~ ~~HHT~~ //	//	~~HHT~~ //		~~HHT~~ ~~HHT~~

a) List the subjects from **most** favourite to **least** favourite.

_____

b) There are 100 students in Renia's grade. Using the results of her survey, predict the number of students in her grade who have history as their favourite subject. _____

How did you know? _____

2. Ms. Smith records the class results from a science test. When she tallies a mark, she crosses it off her list so that she knows she has counted it.

~~A~~ ~~B~~ D C ~~B~~ ~~B~~ ~~A~~ ~~B~~ B ~~A~~ B B C C B A B D B B ~~A~~ C C

After she has finished tallying all the As and some of the Bs, her tally chart looks like this.

Mark	Tally	Frequency	Fraction of students
A	////	4	
B	////		
C			
D			

a) Did she miss any As? _____ Fill in any As she missed and correct her frequency total. Complete the tally and the frequency columns.

b) How many students wrote the test altogether? _____

c) How many students got Ds? _____

d) What fraction of the students received Ds? _____

e) What fraction of students got other marks? Complete the last column of the chart.

f) How will Ms. Smith find the average — will she use the mean, the median, or the mode?

g) Did more than half of Ms. Smith's students get at least a B?

3. A **frequency table** shows how many times a data value occurs in a set. A **relative frequency** table shows the fraction of time each data value occurs. Complete the frequency table and the relative frequency table for this tally chart in your notebook.

Favorite Types of Movies	
Comedy	~~HHT~~ ~~HHT~~ ~~HHT~~
Drama	~~HHT~~ /
Action	~~HHT~~ ~~HHT~~ ~~HHT~~

PDM7-10 Circle Graphs

Many people use **percents** to show data.

Miki surveyed 100 Grade 7 students in his city about their favourite type of movie.

Favourite Type of Movie	
Comedy	32%
Action	41%
Horror	16%
Other	11%

He uses a circle divided into **100 equal parts** to show his results.

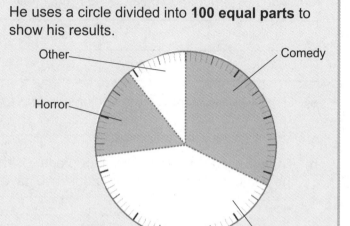

1. a) What percent of Grade 7 students like each type of movie in each school? Complete the chart.

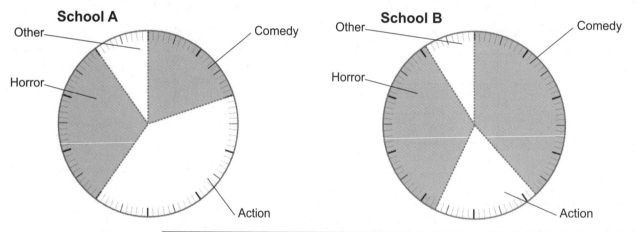

School A

School B

	Comedy	Action	Horror	Other	Total
School A					
School B					

b) What is the total percent for each school? Why does this make sense?

2. Gisela copied down the following percents from a circle graph she saw on the Internet.

Favourite Type of Movies			
Comedy	**Action**	**Horror**	**Other**
48%	21%	26%	9%

How can you tell that she made a mistake?

3. Calli and Bilal go to different schools.

They surveyed the Grade 7 students at their schools about their favourite types of music.

Calli's School	
Type of music	**Number of students**
Classical	10
Rock	20
Pop	140
Other	30

Bilal's School	
Type of music	**Number of students**
Classical	20
Rock	15
Pop	5
Other	10

a) How many Grade 7 students did Calli survey? _____ How many did Bilal survey? _____

b) Find the fraction of Grade 7 students at each school who like each type of music.
Turn the fraction into an equivalent fraction over 100, and then change it to a percent.

Example: $\dfrac{\text{number of Grade 7 students who like classical music at Calli's school}}{\text{number of Grade 7 students in total at Calli's school}} = \dfrac{10}{200} = \dfrac{5}{100} = 5\%$

c) Complete the circle graphs to show the percents you calculated in part b).

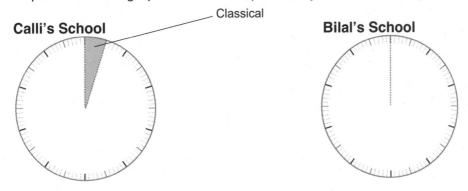

Calli's School — Classical

Bilal's School

d) More people at Calli's school than at Bilal's school like rock music. Why does your circle graph not show this?

e) Whose school do you think is more like yours—Calli's, Bilal's, or neither? Why?

4. Complete the relative frequency table, then draw a circle graph.

Favourite Type of Book	Frequency	Fraction	Percent
Mystery	16	$\dfrac{16}{40} = \dfrac{2}{5}$	$\dfrac{2 \times 20}{5 \times 20} = \dfrac{40}{100} = 40\%$
Fantasy	4		
Romance	12		
Other	8		

PDM7-11 Drawing Circle Graphs

1. a) Find the percent of students who use each mode of transportation to get to school.
   Then use a protractor to find the angle of each section in the circle.

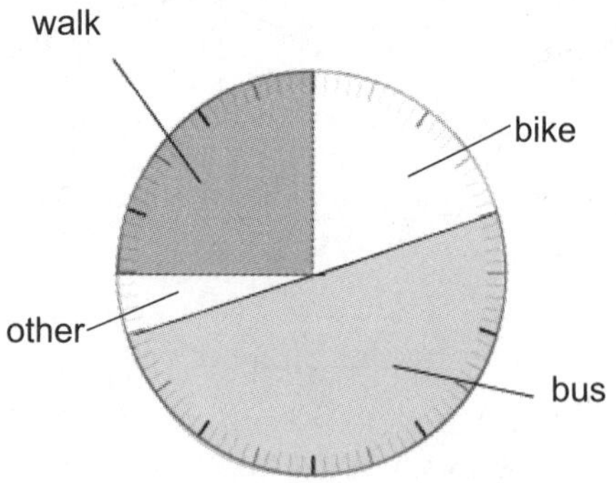

	Percent	**Angle in circle**
walk	*25%*	*90°*
bike		
bus		
other		

   b) Add the percents in your chart. _____ + _____ + _____ + _____ = _____

   Do you get a total of 100%? If not, find your mistake.

   c) Add the angles in your chart. _____ + _____ + _____ + _____ = _____

   Do you get a total of 360°? If not, find your mistake.

REMINDER ▶ To calculate 15% of 60, change 15% to a fraction ($15\% = \dfrac{15}{100}$), replace "of" with a multiplication sign ($\times$), and multiply:

$$15\% \text{ of } 60 = \frac{15}{100} \times 60$$
$$= \frac{3}{20} \times 60$$
$$= \frac{180}{20} = 9$$

---

   d) According to the "walk" section in the circle graph above, 90° is 25% of 360°.
   Check this by calculating 25% of 360°.

   e) According to the "bike" section, _____° is _____% of 360°.

   According to the "bus" section, _____° is _____% of 360°.

   According to the "other" section, _____° is _____% of 360°.

   f) Check each statement in part e) by calculating the percent.

   bike: bus: other:

Probability and Data Management 7-11

2. Complete each chart and then use your protractor to draw a circle graph. Use labels to make it clear what each part of the circle represents. Make sure all your percents total 100% and all your angles total 360°.

a) Survey results: Daily newspaper habit

Title: _____

	Percent	Angle in circle
delivered to home	40%	
buy occasionally	50%	
never look at	10%	

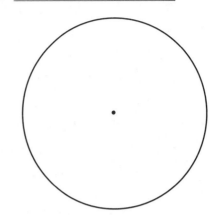

b) Survey results: How students spend money

Title: _____

	Percent	Angle in circle
entertainment (movies, CDs, etc.)	45%	
clothes and personal care	30%	
snacks	10%	
savings	15%	

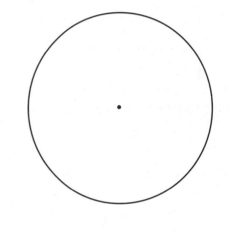

c) Survey results: Favourite kind of pie

Title: _____

	Percent	Angle in circle
apple	20%	
blueberry	15%	
cherry	10%	
other	55%	

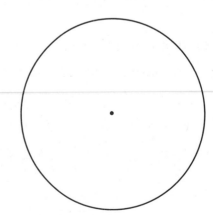

3. Write each fraction as an equivalent fraction over 100 and then as a percent.

a) $\dfrac{3}{10} = \dfrac{}{100} = $ ____ %

b) $\dfrac{7}{25} = \dfrac{}{100} = $ ____ %

c) $\dfrac{9}{20} = \dfrac{}{100} = $ ____ %

d) $\dfrac{33}{75} = \dfrac{}{25} = \dfrac{}{100} = $ ____ %

e) $\dfrac{12}{30} = \dfrac{}{10} = \dfrac{}{100} = $ ____ %

f) $\dfrac{52}{80} = \dfrac{}{20} = \dfrac{}{100} = $ ____ %

4. Write each fraction as an equivalent fraction over 360 to determine the degree measure (the angle) in a circle graph.

a) $\dfrac{9}{20} = \dfrac{}{360}$

b) $\dfrac{13}{40} = \dfrac{}{360}$

c) $\dfrac{70}{400} = \dfrac{}{40} = \dfrac{}{360}$

d) $\dfrac{21}{108} = \dfrac{}{36} = \dfrac{}{360}$

5. Complete the relative frequency chart. Then draw a circle graph.

a)

Favourite Sport	Frequency	Fraction of total	Angle in circle
Hockey	8	$\dfrac{8}{20}$	144°
Swimming	5		
Running	4		
Other	3		

Title: _____

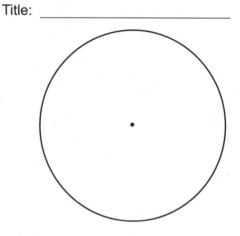

b)

Favourite Indoor Games	Frequency	Fraction of total	Angle in circle
Board games	11		
Card games	1		
Video games	21		
Other	3		

Title: _____

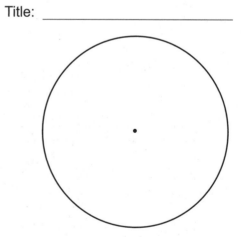

PDM7-12 Reading Circle Graphs

To find the percent of 360° that 72° represents, follow the steps below.

Write 72 as a fraction of 360. $\dfrac{72}{360}$	Reduce $\dfrac{72}{360}$ to lowest terms. $\dfrac{72}{360} = \dfrac{1}{5}$	Compare this fraction to a fraction with a denominator of 100. $\dfrac{1}{5} = \dfrac{\ }{100}$	Solve. $1 \xrightarrow{\times 20} 20$ $\dfrac{1}{5} = \dfrac{20}{100}$ $5 \xrightarrow{\times 20} 100$ So, 72 is 20% of 360.

1. Calculate the percent.

   a) 90° is _____% of 360°

   b) 36° is _____% of 360°

   c) 18° is _____% of 360°

   d) 288° is _____% of 360°

2. a) Use a protractor to determine the angle of the part-time section in each circle graph. Then find the percent of people in each company who work part-time.

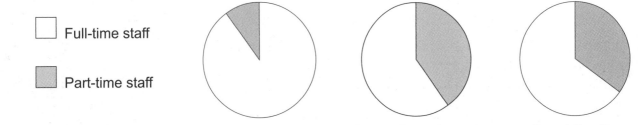

   Full-time staff

   Part-time staff

   b) Each company has 60 employees. How many employees in each company work part-time?

3. The circle graph below shows the percent of playing time a hockey coach gives each forward line. The first line receives more ice time than the second, the second line receives more ice time than the third, and the third receives more ice time than the fourth.

   a) Give the circle graph a title.   Title: _____

   b) Finish the key by labelling which line (first, second, third, or fourth) each pattern on the circle graph represents.

   ☐ _____

   ▨ _____

   ▨ _____

   ▨ _____

   c) Use a protractor to determine the angle of each section in the circle graph.

   d) Use your answer in c) to determine the percent of ice time each line receives.

   e) If the team plays a regular 60-minute game, how much time will the second line get?

   f) The team wins 3-2 after 4 minutes of overtime. Ron plays on the third line. How much time did Ron play for?

Sometimes, the angle in a circle does not correspond to a whole number percent of 360°.

Example: If the angle in a circle is 30°, $\frac{30}{360} = \frac{1}{12} = 0.08\overline{3} = 8.\overline{3}\%$, so 30° is $8.\overline{3}\%$ of 360°.

Usually, rounding the percent to 1 decimal place is enough accuracy.

Example: 30° is about 8.3% of 360°.

To change a fraction to a decimal, use long division or a calculator.

4. Change each fraction to a decimal (rounded to 3 decimal places) and then to a percent (rounded to 1 decimal place).

a) $\frac{5}{12} \approx 0.$ ___ ___ ___ $\approx$ _____ %

b) $\frac{5}{36} \approx 0.$ ___ ___ ___ $\approx$ _____ %

c) $\frac{7}{18} \approx 0.$ ___ ___ ___ $\approx$ _____ %

d) $\frac{8}{15} \approx 0.$ ___ ___ ___ $\approx$ _____ %

5. Write each angle as a fraction of 360°. Then find the percent of 360° (rounded to 1 decimal place) that each angle represents.

a) 60°   b) 200°   c) 40°   d) 210°   e) 132°

6. Lina keeps track of how many servings of each type of food she eats for a month. She draws a circle graph to show her results.

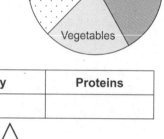

a) Use a protractor to find the angle in the circle for each type of food.

b) Find the percent of 360° (to 1 decimal place) that each angle represents. Complete the relative frequency table.

	Breads/Grains	Vegetables	Fruits	Dairy	Proteins
Percent					

c) Add the percents from part b). Do you get a total of 100%?

d) Round your answers from part b) to the nearest whole number and add the percents. Do you get a total of 100%? What happened?

e) If Lina eats 24 servings of food each day, how many servings of each type of food does she have each day?

f) Lina finds the pyramid at right on the Internet. The pyramid shows the recommended number of servings per day of each type of food. Compare what Lina eats to these recommendations. Are Lina's eating habits healthy?

INVESTIGATION ▶ Does repeating each data value the same number of times change the mean?

A. Find the mean.

a) 3 3 4 6 6   (___+___+___+___+___) ÷ 5   = ___

b) 3 3 4 6 6 3 3 4 6 6   (___+___+___+___+___) × 2 ÷ 10   = ___

c) 3 3 4 6 6 3 3 4 6 6 3 3 4 6 6   (___+___+___+___+___) × 3 ÷ 15   = ___

d) 2 5 4 1   (___+___+___+___) ÷ ___   = ___

e) 2 5 4 1 2 5 4 1 2 5 4 1   (___+___+___+___) × ___ ÷ ___   = ___

B. Does repeating each data value the same number of times change the mean? Explain.

C. Investigate what happens to the mode and the median when data values are repeated. Do the mode and the median change? Make up your own data to check.

---

1. Sally surveyed 20 families on her street to find the number of cars they have. She displays her results in both a frequency table and a circle graph.

# of cars	frequency
0	4
1	8
2	8

0 car $\frac{1}{5}$ 2 cars $\frac{2}{5}$ $\frac{2}{5}$ 1 car

To find the mean (the average number of cars on the street per family), Sally uses the frequency table:

$(0 + 0 + 0 + 0 + 1 + 1 + 1 + 1 + 1 + 1 + 1 + 1 + 2 + 2 + 2 + 2 + 2 + 2 + 2 + 2) ÷ 20$

Tina finds the mean another way. She uses the circle graph and pretends there are only 5 families:

$(0 + 1 + 1 + 2 + 2) ÷ 5$

a) What answers do Sally and Tina get?

b) Whose method do you like better? Why?

c) If Sally accidentally divides 24 by 10 instead of by 20, she gets a mean of 2.4. How can she tell immediately that she has made a mistake?

2. The circle graph shows the percent of people earning each annual income in a developing country.

a) Use the circle graph to find the mean, median, and mode. Hint: Pretend the country has only 360 people.

b) Explain why you do not need to know the population of the country to determine the mean salary.

c) Would you move to this country? Why or why not?

d) If you wanted to move to a country with a "good" average income, which average would you look at: the median, the mode, or the mean? Explain your answer.

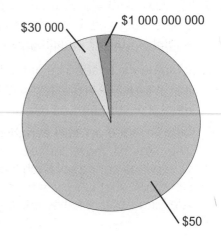

$30 000 $1 000 000 000 $50

PDM7-14 Comparing Graphs

1. Match each type of graph with its purpose.

Line Graph — Compares two sets of data

Shows a trend in data or makes a prediction (usually used when graphing change over time)

Circle Graph

Stem and Leaf Plot — Visually displays the frequency of results

Double Bar Graph — Makes it easy to see the largest, smallest, and most common data values

Bar Graph — Visually displays the relative frequency of results

2. Sally wants to donate money to a charity that sends medical supplies to developing countries. The double bar graph below shows how two charities spend their money.

a) How much does each charity spend on fundraising, shipping, administration, and medical supplies?

b) In your notebook, draw two circle graphs showing the fraction of each charity's money spent on each area.

   i) Which charity spends more on medical supplies?

   ii) Which charity spends more money altogether?

   iii) What fraction of Charity A's money is spent on medical supplies?

   iv) What fraction of Charity B's money is spent on medical supplies?

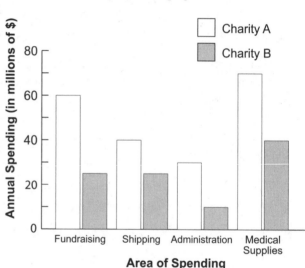

c) If Sally donates $100 to Charity A, how much of her money would go toward medical supplies?

d) If Sally donates $100 to Charity B, how much of her money would go toward medical supplies?

e) If you were Sally, which charity would you give your $100 to? Why?

f) Which type of graph gave you the most relevant information to help you decide which charity to donate money to? Explain your answer.

3. Using each type of graph (line, bar, double bar, circle, stem and leaf) only **once**,
    select the type of graph you would use to…

    a) show how many movies a month people in your
        class watch.   _____

    b) compare the number of tickets sold at a
        hockey arena and a movie theatre each month.   _____

    c) know how much of your $100-donation a charity
        will spend on building a shelter for homeless people.   _____

    d) see if there are any trends in life expectancy for
        people born in Canada from 1867 to 1997.   _____

    e) know how many people in your class are
        shorter than 143 cm or taller than 168 cm.   _____

4. In your notebook or on a computer, choose and draw an appropriate type of graph
    to represent each set of data, and then explain your choice. Use each type of graph
    (line, circle, bar, double bar, stem and leaf) only once. Be sure to include a title,
    labels, and scales on each graph.

    a) Percent of votes given to each candidate in a school election:

Candidate	Katie	John	Rita	Melanie	Paul
Fraction of Votes	40%	25%	20%	10%	5%

    b) Jessica's marks on her first five science and math tests of the year (each out of 100):

Test #	1	2	3	4	5
Science marks	70	84	85	80	82
Math marks	68	78	81	72	76

    c) A class survey showing how many pets the students have:

Number of pets	0	1	2	3	4	5 +
Frequency	8	7	6	1	2	3

    d) Thickness of rulers produced by a company (in tenths of a mm):

    28   29   31   30   28   27   24   31   31   30
    31   30   29   29   28   26   32   33   30   28

    e) Distance from home at various times:

Distance from home (m)	0	50	150	250	300	300
Time (minutes)	0	1	2	3	4	5

PDM7-15 Bias in a Sample or a Census

> If you collect information by surveying an entire population, you are using a **census**. If you survey only a part of the population, you are using a **sample**.

1. Would you use a sample or a census to find out…

   a) which movie your 5 friends want to watch? _____

   b) who your school thinks should be school president? _____

   c) how smoking affects people's lungs? _____

   d) whether people in your home city would support an NHL hockey team? _____

2. The principal of a school wants to find out if students think that school should start and finish half an hour earlier, but she does not have time to ask everyone. She surveys two groups:

   A: The first 50 students who arrive in the morning   YES 40   NO 10

   B: Five students from each of the ten classrooms   YES 20   NO 30

   a) Why did the two surveys not get the same results?

   b) Which group's opinion will be more similar to the whole school's opinion?

   c) If there are 500 people in the school, how many do you think will want school to start and finish half an hour earlier?

> A **representative sample** is similar to the whole population. A **biased sample** is not similar to the whole population because some parts are not represented.

3. Which sample in Question 2 is biased, A or B? _____

4. Decide whether the samples are biased or representative. Explain the cause of any bias.

   a) A school (grades 1–8) is planning a party and wants to have board games at the party. To find the most popular board games in the school, they ask:

   • 40 grade 7 and 8 students
   • 5 students from each grade

   b) Scientists are comparing the heart rate of 15-year-olds before and after half an hour of exercise. They test the heart rate of:

   • 25 members of a school track and field team
   • 25 students from one class

   c) A class is testing two brands of seeds to find out what percent will germinate. They plant:

   • 10 seeds from each package
   • The 10 largest seeds from each package

5. A city wants to build a new hockey arena, a new swimming pool, or a new library. Which of the following places is the best site for a survey? Why? What is wrong with the other three?

- beach
- bookstore
- professional hockey game
- shopping mall

6. Two students, Miki and Melanie, are running in student elections. They want to know how many of the school's 250 students will vote for them.

- Miki asks the 25 students in his class and finds that 15 will vote for him and 10 will not.

- Melanie gets a student list from the principal and asks every tenth student on the list. She finds that 15 will vote for her and 10 will not.

a) Whose sample is more biased? Why?
b) Who do you think will win the election? Why?

7. Marco wants to know how many hours per day his classmates spend on homework. This is the question he asked the students in his class:

How many hours per day do you spend on homework?

☐ 0–8 hours per day

☐ 8–16 hours per day

☐ 16–24 hours per day

Will Marco's survey results be useful? Explain.

8. To ask whether school uniforms should be required, two questions are proposed.

A: Do you think that students should be allowed to express themselves by what they wear?

B: Do you think that equality among students is important enough to require consistent student uniforms?

a) Which question do you think was proposed by someone in favour of

school uniforms? _____

Which was proposed by someone against school uniforms? _____

b) Write down a question they could ask instead that does not already suggest an answer.

_____

_____

PDM7-16 Designing, Displaying, and Analyzing a Survey

1. Follow these steps to conduct your own survey.

   a) A survey usually asks a particular question. Examples: How do you get to school? What is your favourite colour? How big is your family?

      What question will you ask in your survey?

   b) What responses do you expect? Do you need to include an "other" category?

   c) Is your question biased? If yes, think of a new question.

   d) Who should you survey? How many people should you survey to get an accurate response to your question? Is the sample you have chosen representative or biased?

   e) Before conducting your survey, try to predict the results. What answer do you think will be the most common? The least common?

   f) Create a table to keep track of the responses you will get. Example:

How do you get to school?	Tally
Walk	
Take the bus	
Ride my bike	

   g) Choose and draw an appropriate type of graph to display your data.

   h) Summarize your conclusions. Did your results correspond to your predictions?

2. Design an experiment.

   a) Decide on your question. Examples:

      • How does adding salt to ice affect how fast it melts?
      • Do tomato seeds grow more quickly in direct sun or shade?

   b) What do you need to measure?

   c) How will you measure your results? What materials and equipment will you need?

   d) How will you make sure your experiment gives reliable results? You will need to keep everything constant except what you want to measure.

   e) Draw the table you will use to record your results.

   f) Choose and draw an appropriate type of graph to display your data.

   g) Summarize your conclusions. Did your results correspond to your predictions?

PA7-16 Formulas

André makes a garden path using square and triangular tiles. His pattern uses 6 triangular tiles for every 1 square tile.

He writes a **formula** — an equation that shows how to calculate the number of triangles (*t*) from the number of squares (*s*).

6 × squares = triangles

or (for short) **6 × *s* = *t***

Squares (*s*)	6 × *s* = *t*	Triangles (*t*)
1	6 × 1 = 6	6
2	6 × 2 = 12	12
3	6 × 3 = 18	18

1. Each chart represents a design for a path. Complete the chart.

a)

Squares (*s*)	4 × *s* = *t*	Triangles (*t*)
1	4 × *1* = *4*	4
2	4 × *2* = __	
3	4 × *3* = __	

b)

Squares (*s*)	7 × *s* = *t*	Triangles (*t*)
1	7 × *1* = *7*	7
2	7 × *2* = __	
3	7 × *3* = __	

c)

Squares (*s*)	5 × *s* = *t*	Triangles (*t*)
2	5 × *2* = *10*	
3	5 × __ = __	
4	5 × __ = __	

d)

Squares (*s*)	4 × *s* = *t*	Triangles (*t*)
5	4 × __ = __	
6	4 × __ = __	
7	4 × __ = __	

e)

Squares (*s*)	6 × *s* = *t*	Triangles (*t*)
1		
3		
5		

f)

Squares (*s*)	6 × *s* = *t*	Triangles (*t*)
9		
12		
15		

2. Write a formula to show how to calculate the number of triangles (*t*) from the number of squares (*s*).

a)

Squares	Triangles
1	4
2	8
3	12

b)

Squares	Triangles
1	5
2	10
3	15

c)

Squares	Triangles
1	2
2	4
3	6

d)

Squares	Triangles
1	6
2	12
3	18

3. Wendy makes geometric patterns using squares (s), rectangles (r), and triangles (t) that look like this.

Complete the chart and then write a formula for the design. Example: $4 \times s = t$

a)
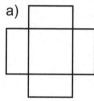

Squares (s)	Rectangles (r)
1	
2	
3	

b)
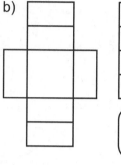

Squares (s)	Rectangles (r)
1	
2	
3	

c)
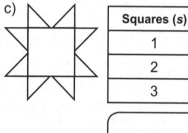

Squares (s)	Triangles (t)
1	
2	
3	

d)
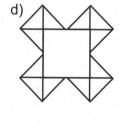

Squares (s)	Triangles (t)
1	
2	
3	

BONUS ▶ Complete the chart and write 3 formulas.

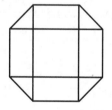

Squares (s)	Triangles (t)	Rectangles (r)
1		
2		
3		

$t =$ _____ $\times s$ $r =$ _____ $\times s$ $t =$ _____ $\times r$

4. In Question 3 a), how many rectangles will Wendy need to make a design with 7 squares?

5. Wendy has 39 triangles. Does she have enough triangles to make 7 copies of the geometric design at right? How can you tell without making a chart?

6. Create a design using squares (s) and triangles (t) to go with the formula.

   a) $6 \times s = t$ b) $5 \times s = t$ c) $7 \times s = t$

7. Create a design with squares and triangles and then write a formula for your design.

Patterns and Algebra 7-16

In the auditorium of her school, Sandra notices that the number of chairs in each row is always four greater than the number of the row. She writes a formula that shows how to calculate the number of chairs from the row number.

row number + 4 = number of chairs or $r + 4 = c$

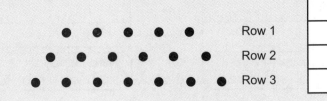

Row 1
Row 2
Row 3

Row (r)	$r + 4 = c$	Chairs (c)
1	$1 + 4 = 5$	5
2	$2 + 4 = 6$	6
3	$3 + 4 = 7$	7

8. Each chart represents an arrangement of chairs. Complete the chart.

a)

Row (r)	$r + 6 = c$	Chairs (c)
1	$\underline{1} + 6 = \underline{7}$	$\underline{7}$
2	$\underline{} + 6 = \underline{}$	
3	$\underline{} + 6 = \underline{}$	

b)

Row (r)	$r + 9 = c$	Chairs (c)
1	$\underline{} + 9 = \underline{}$	
2	$\underline{} + 9 = \underline{}$	
3	$\underline{} + 9 = \underline{}$	

9. Find the number you must add to the row number to get the number of chairs. Write a formula using r for the row number and c for the number of chairs.

a)

Row	Chairs
1	5
2	6
3	7

$r + 4 = c$

b)

Row	Chairs
1	8
2	9
3	10

c)

Row	Chairs
1	9
2	10
3	11

d)

Row	Chairs
7	12
8	13
9	14

10. Complete the chart. Then write a formula for the arrangement of chairs.

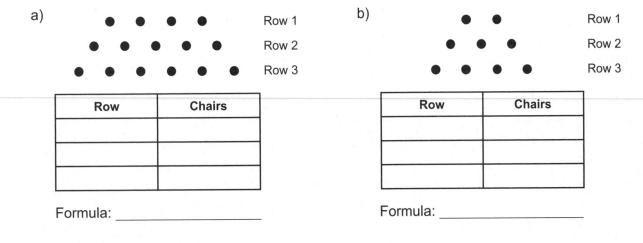

a)

Row 1
Row 2
Row 3

Row	Chairs

Formula: _____

b)

Row 1
Row 2
Row 3

Row	Chairs

Formula: _____

11. How many chairs would be in the 10th row in Question 10 a)? _____

12. Apply the given rule or formula to the numbers in the first column. Write your answers in the second column.

a)

Input	Output
0	4
1	5
2	6

Rule: Add 4 to each input number

b)

Input	Output
4	
5	
6	

Rule: Subtract 4 from each input number

c)

Input	Output
4	
7	
8	

Rule: Multiply each input number by 6

d)

Input	Output
28	
16	
40	

Rule: Divide each input number by 4

e)

Input	Output
18	
19	
20	

Rule: Add 9 to each input number

f)

Input	Output
4	
6	
9	

Rule: Multiply each input number by 8

g)

Input	Output
26	
11	
46	

Formula:
Input + 3 = Output

h)

Input	Output
15	
19	
23	

Formula:
Input − 5 = Output

i)

Input	Output
4	
7	
12	

Formula:
Input × 4 = Output

13. Give a rule or a formula that tells you how to make the output numbers from the input numbers. See Question 12 for sample rules.

a)

Input	Output
3	18
2	12
1	6

Rule:

b)

Input	Output
16	2
32	4
48	6

Rule:

c)

Input	Output
19	16
15	12
21	18

Rule:

d)

Input	Output
3	6
4	7
5	8

Formula:

e)

Input	Output
3	8
5	10
7	12

Formula:

f)

Input	Output
1	7
2	14
3	21

Formula:

1. Write the rule.

a)

Input	Output
1	3
2	6
3	9
4	12

Rule: _____*Multiply by 3*_____

Input	Output
3	1
6	2
9	3
12	4

Rule: _____

b)

Input	Output
2	7
3	8
4	9
5	10

Rule: _____

Input	Output
7	2
8	3
9	4
10	5

Rule: _____

c)

Input	Output
3	6
5	10
7	14
9	18

Rule: _____

Input	Output
6	3
10	5
14	7
18	9

Rule: _____

2. Look at your answers in Question 1. How does your rule change when you switch the input and output numbers?

An **ordered pair** consists of two numbers where the order they are written matters. We can treat input and output numbers as ordered pairs. Example:

Input	Output
1	2

⟶ (1, 2) but

Input	Output
2	1

⟶ (2, 1)

The ordered pairs (1, 2) and (2, 1) are different.

3. Write the input and output numbers as ordered pairs.

a)

Input	Output	
3	5	(3, 5)
4	6	(,)
5	7	(,)
6	8	(,)

b)

Input	Output	
10	5	(,)
8	4	(,)
6	3	(,)
4	2	(,)

c)

Input	Output	
5	10	(,)
4	8	(,)
3	6	(,)
2	4	(,)

PA7-18 Graphs

A point on a graph can represent an ordered pair.

Example: The ordered pair (2, 5) is shown as a point on the graph.

The numbers 2 and 5 are called **coordinates**.
The first coordinate is 2; the second coordinate is 5.

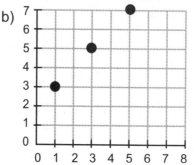

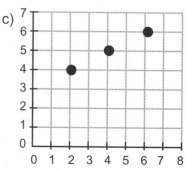

(2, 5)

The second number is on the vertical axis.

The first number is on the horizontal axis.

1. For each set of points, write a list of ordered pairs and complete the T-table.

   a)

Ordered Pairs	First Number	Second Number
(2, 1)	2	1
(,)		
(,)		

   b)

Ordered Pairs	First Number	Second Number
(,)		
(,)		
(,)		

   c)

Ordered Pairs	First Number	Second Number
(,)		
(,)		
(,)		

2. Mark 3 grid points on the line segment. Then write a list of ordered pairs and complete the T-table.

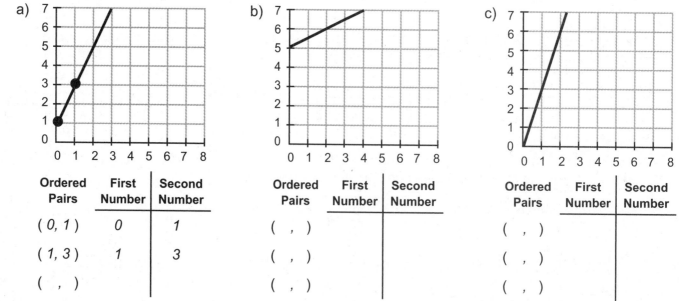

   a)

Ordered Pairs	First Number	Second Number
(0, 1)	0	1
(1, 3)	1	3
(,)		

   b)

Ordered Pairs	First Number	Second Number
(,)		
(,)		
(,)		

   c)

Ordered Pairs	First Number	Second Number
(,)		
(,)		
(,)		

3. Write a list of ordered pairs based on the T-table. Plot the ordered pairs and connect the points to form a line.

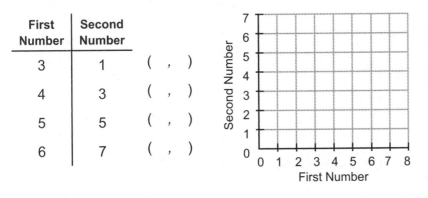

First Number	Second Number
3	1
4	3
5	5
6	7

(,)
(,)
(,)
(,)

4. Draw a graph for the T-table (as in Question 3).

a)

Input	Output
2	5
4	6
6	7
8	8

b)

Input	Output
1	7
2	6
3	5
4	4

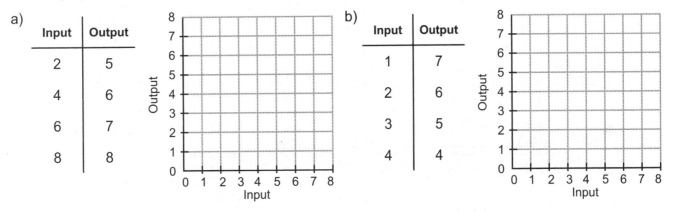

BONUS ▶ Look carefully at the scales!

c)

Input	Output
2	4
4	8
6	12
8	16

d)

Input	Output
1	6
3	8
5	10
7	12

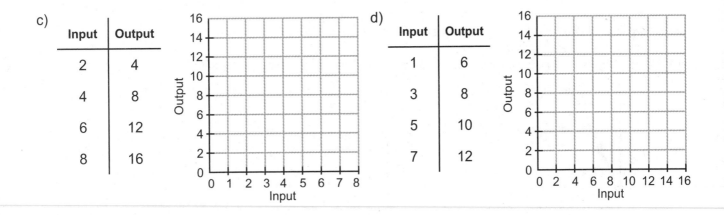

5. Draw a coordinate grid on grid paper and plot the ordered pairs.

a) (1, 2), (3, 5), (5, 8), (7, 11)

b) (0, 0), (2, 3), (4, 6), (6, 9)

c) (0, 10), (2, 7), (4, 4), (6, 1)

PA7-19 Sequences as Ordered Pairs

Look at the sequence: 1 3 5 7 9 11 13 15 17 19

The first term is 1, the second term is 3, the third term is 5, and so on.

1. Find the given term in the sequence above.

   a) The 4th term is _____   b) The 9th term is _____   c) The 6th term is _____

The position of a term in a sequence is called the **term number**. Example: In the sequence
1 3 5 7 9 11 13 15 17 19 …, 11 has term number 6, because 11 is the 6th term.

2. Put the terms in the sequence into a T-table with their term numbers.

a) 1 3 5 7

Term Number	Term
1	
2	
3	
4	

b) 2 4 6 8

Term Number	Term
1	
2	
3	
4	

c) 4 7 10 13

Term Number	Term
1	
2	
3	
4	

You can think of a sequence as a set of ordered pairs: (term number, term).
Example: **2, 5, 8, 11, 14** ⟶ (1, **2**), (2, **5**), (3, **8**), (4, **11**), (5, **14**)

3. Change the sequence to a set of ordered pairs.

   a) 1   3   5   7   9
   (1 , 1), (2 , 3), (3 , 5), (4 , 7), (5 , 9)

   b) 2   4   6   8   10
   (1 ,), (2 ,), (3 ,   ), (4 ,), (5 ,)

   c) 4 7 10 13 16

   d) 3 7 11 15 19

4. a) Change each set of ordered pairs to a sequence of numbers.

   A (1, 0), (2, 4), (3, 8), (4, 12), (5, 16)   B (1, 17), (2, 11), (3, 9), (4, 4), (5, 1)

   C (1, 2), (2, 3), (3, 4), (4, 3), (5, 2)   D (1, 4), (2, 7), (3, 4), (4, 7), (5, 4), (6, 7)

   b) Which sequence from part a) matches each description?

   i)   increases then decreases _____   ii)   increases by the same amount _____

   iii) repeats _____   iv) decreases by different amounts _____

5. a) Re-order the ordered pairs so that their first numbers are in increasing order.
      Then change each set of ordered pairs to a sequence of numbers.

   A (4, 4), (6, 3), (2, 9), (3, 6), (1, 10), (5, 4)   B (4, 7), (2, 9), (5, 6), (1, 10), (6, 5), (3, 8)

   C (3, 6), (6, 3), (1, 2), (2, 1), (4, 5), (5, 4)   D (3, 7), (5, 9), (1, 5), (6, 10), (4, 8), (2, 6)

   b) Which sequence from part a) decreases by the same amount? _____

PA7-20 Graphing Sequences

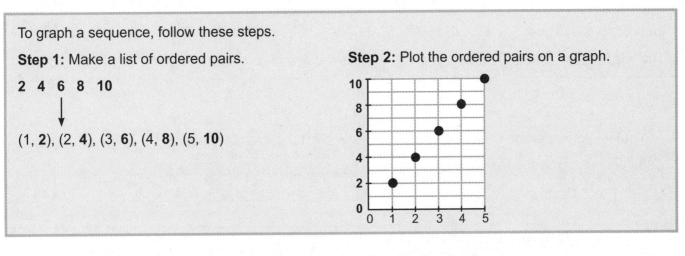

To graph a sequence, follow these steps.

Step 1: Make a list of ordered pairs.

2 4 6 8 10

↓

(1, **2**), (2, **4**), (3, **6**), (4, **8**), (5, **10**)

Step 2: Plot the ordered pairs on a graph.

1. a) Graph the sequence of numbers by first making a list of ordered pairs.

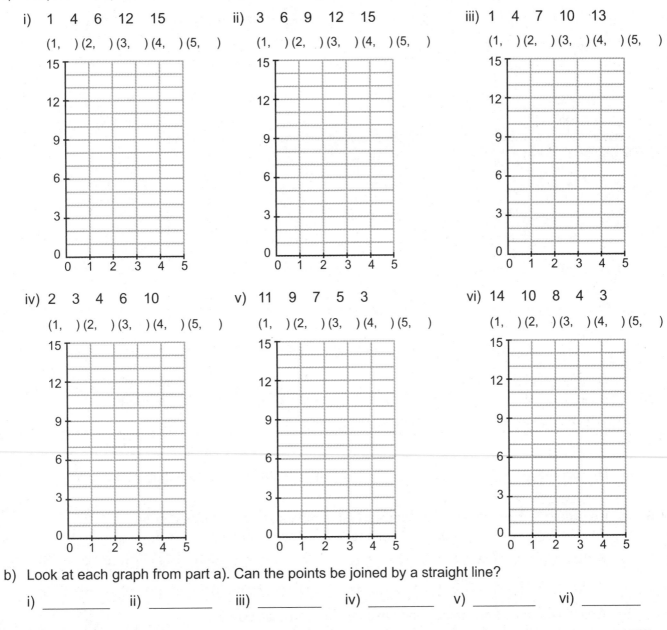

i) 1   4   6   12   15

   (1,) (2,) (3,) (4,) (5,)

ii) 3   6   9   12   15

   (1,) (2,) (3,) (4,) (5,)

iii) 1   4   7   10   13

   (1,) (2,) (3,) (4,) (5,)

iv) 2   3   4   6   10

   (1,) (2,) (3,) (4,) (5,)

v) 11   9   7   5   3

   (1,) (2,) (3,) (4,) (5,)

vi) 14   10   8   4   3

   (1,) (2,) (3,) (4,) (5,)

b) Look at each graph from part a). Can the points be joined by a straight line?

   i) _____ ii) _____ iii) _____ iv) _____ v) _____ vi) _____

2. On grid paper, graph each increasing sequence.

   a) 5   7   9   11   b) 2   6   10   14   c) 3   4   5   6

3. On grid paper, graph each decreasing sequence.

   a) 12   8   4   0   b) 11   8   5   2   c) 21   15   9   3

4. Compare your answers to Questions 2 and 3. How are the graphs of increasing

and decreasing sequences different? _____

_____

> A sequence is called **linear** if the points on its graph can be joined by a **straight line**.

INVESTIGATION 1 ▶ How can you tell from the gaps whether or not a sequence is linear?

A. Which sequences from Question 1 are linear? Find their gaps.

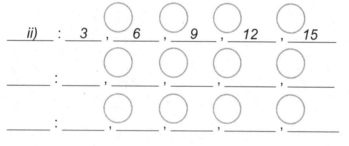

   _ii)_ : _3_ , _6_ , _9_ _12_   _15_

   _____ : _____ , _____ , _____ , _____

   _____ : _____ , _____ , _____ , _____

B. Which sequences from Question 1 are not linear? Find their gaps.

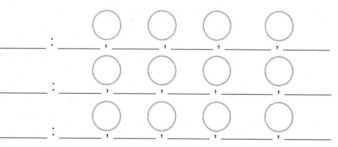

   _____ : _____ , _____ , _____ , _____

   _____ : _____ , _____ , _____ , _____

   _____ : _____ , _____ , _____ , _____

C. How can you tell by looking at the gaps of a sequence whether or not the sequence

is linear? _____

---

5. a) Decide which of these decreasing sequences is linear by finding the gaps
      between the terms.

   A _11_   _9_   _6_   _4_   _1_   **B** _13_   _10_   _7_   _4_   _1_

   _____ is linear because _____

   b) Check your answer by graphing both sequences on grid paper.

Patterns and Algebra 7-20

6. a) Find the gaps between the terms in the T-table.

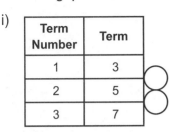

i)

Term Number	Term
1	3
2	5
3	7

ii)

Term Number	Term
1	8
2	5
3	2

iii)

Term Number	Term
1	1
2	3
3	8

b) Which sequences from part a) are increasing? _____

c) Which sequences from part a) are linear? _____

d) Match each T-table from part a) to its graph.

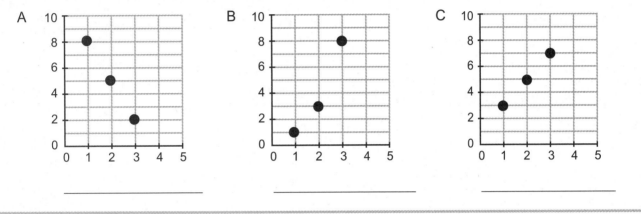

A

B

C

_____   _____   _____

~~~~~~

INVESTIGATION 2 ▶ How can you tell from its rule whether or not a sequence is linear?

A. Using the rule, write the first 4 terms of the sequence. Then find the gaps.

i)   Start at 1. Add 2 each time.

_____ _____ _____ _____

ii)   Start at 4. Add 1 each time.

_____ _____ _____ _____

iii)   Start at 1. Multiply by 2 each time.

_____ _____ _____ _____

iv)   Start at 2. Add 5. Subtract 3. Repeat.

_____ _____ _____ _____

v)   2, 7, 5, then repeat.

_____ _____ _____ _____

vi)   Start at 12. Subtract 2 each time.

_____ _____ _____ _____

vii)   Start at 2. Multiply by 3 each time.

_____ _____ _____ _____

viii) Start at 96. Divide by 2 each time.

_____ _____ _____ _____

B. Looking at the gaps, predict which sequences are linear. _____

C. Choose one sequence that you think is linear and one that you think is not linear.
Check your predictions by graphing the sequences on grid paper.

D. How can you tell from its rule whether or not a sequence is linear?

PA7-21 Interpreting Linear Graphs

1. a) Make a T-table for each set of points on the coordinate grid.

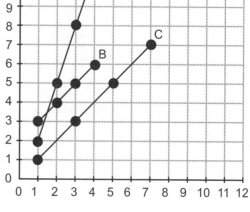

Graph A	
Input	Output

Graph B	
Input	Output

Graph C	
Input	Output

b) Write a rule for each T-table.

2. Mark a third grid point on the line and write the ordered pair for your point.

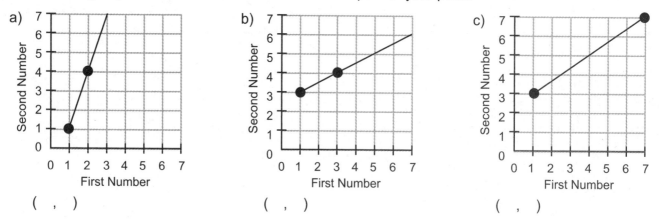

a) (,)

b) (,)

c) (,)

3. Mark four grid points that lie on a straight line in the coordinate grid. Then make a T-table for your set of points.

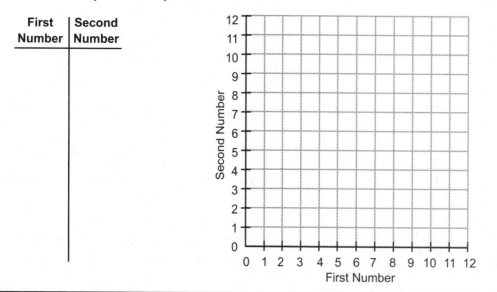

First Number	Second Number

4. The graph shows the cost of making a telephone call to New York.

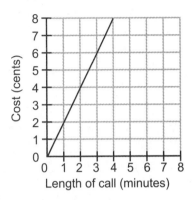

Cost (cents) vs Length of call (minutes)

a) If you talked for 2 minutes, how much would you have to pay?

b) How much does the cost rise every minute?

c) How much would you have to pay to talk for 10 minutes?

d) If you paid 6 cents, how long would you be able to talk for?

e) How much would you have to pay to talk for 30 seconds?

5. The graph shows the distance Kathy travelled on a cycling trip.

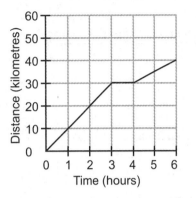

Distance (kilometres) vs Time (hours)

a) How far had Kathy cycled after 2 hours?

b) How far had Kathy travelled after 6 hours?

c) Did Kathy rest at all on her trip? How do you know?

d) When she was cycling, did Kathy always travel at the same speed?

6. The graph shows Ben and Tom's progress in a 120 m race.

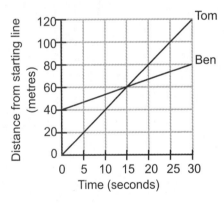

Distance from starting line (metres) vs Time (seconds)

a) How far from the start was Tom after 10 seconds?

b) How far from the start was Ben after 15 seconds?

c) Who won the race? By how much?

d) How much of a head start did Ben have?

e) How many seconds from the start did Tom overtake Ben?

7. The graph shows the cost of renting a bike from Mike's store.

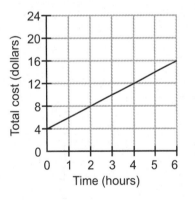

Total cost (dollars) vs Time (hours)

a) How much would you have to pay to rent the bike for…

   i) 2 hours?   ii) 4 hours?   iii) 3 hours?

b) How much do you have to pay for the bike before you have even ridden it?

c) Vi's store charges $3.50 an hour for a bike. Whose store would you rent from if you wanted the bike for 3 hours?

PA7-22 Graphing Formulas

1. Evaluate the expression $3n - 1$ for each value of n.

$n = 1$	$n = 2$	$n = 3$	$n = 4$
$3n - 1 = 3(1) - 1$	$3n - 1 = 3(2) - 1$	$3n - 1 =$	$3n - 1 =$
$\quad = 3 - 1$	$\quad =$		
$\quad = 2$	$\quad =$		

2. Evaluate the expression for $n = 1, 2, 3, 4,$ and 5. Write your answers in the T-table.

a) $2n + 3$

n	$2n + 3$
1	
2	
3	
4	
5	

b) $3n - 2$

n	$3n - 2$
1	
2	
3	
4	
5	

c) $2n - 1$

n	$2n - 1$
1	
2	
3	
4	
5	

3. Finish the T-tables, write the ordered pairs, and plot the ordered pairs on the graphs.

a)

n	$2n + 2$
1	
2	
3	
4	
5	

(1,) (2,) (3,) (4,) (5,)

b)

n	$3n - 1$
1	
2	
3	
4	
5	

(1,) (2,) (3,) (4,) (5,)

c)

n	$4n - 3$
1	
2	
3	
4	
5	

(1,) (2,) (3,) (4,) (5,)

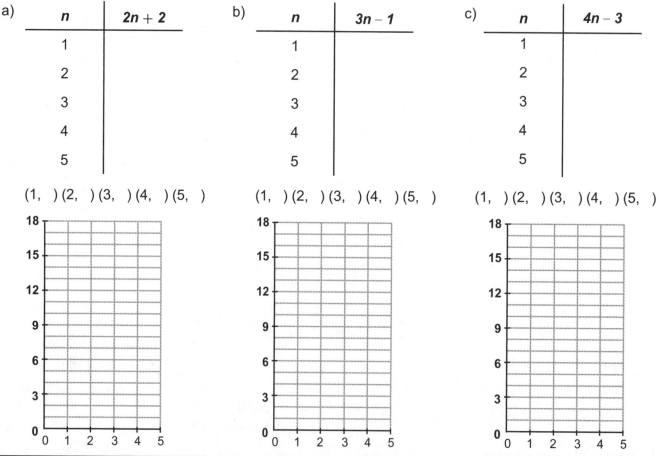

1. Write the sequence for the formula. Then find the gaps and write the rule.

   a) Term = 2 × Term Number + 1

Term Number	1	2	3	4	5
Term					

   Sequence: ___3___ (+2) ___5___ (+2) ___7___ (+2) ___9___ (+2) ___11___

   Rule: _____*Start at 3, then add 2 each time.*_____

   b) Term = 3 × Term Number – 2

Term Number	1	2	3	4	5
Term					

   Sequence: ____ ◯ ____ ◯ ____ ◯ ____ ◯ ____

   Rule: _____

   c) Term = 25 – (4 × Term Number)

Term Number	1	2	3	4	5
Term					

   Sequence: ____ ◯ ____ ◯ ____ ◯ ____ ◯ ____

   Rule: _____

   d) Term = 5 × Term Number – 3

Term Number	1	2	3	4	5
Term					

   Sequence: ____ ◯ ____ ◯ ____ ◯ ____ ◯ ____

   Rule: _____

   e) Term = 19 – (3 × Term Number)

Term Number	1	2	3	4	5
Term					

   Sequence: ____ ◯ ____ ◯ ____ ◯ ____ ◯ ____

   Rule: _____

2. Which of these can you find just by looking at the formula, without doing any calculations? Explain.

   i) the gap in a sequence   ii) the first term in a sequence   iii) the 10th term in a sequence

3. How could you use the rule to find…

   a) the gap in a sequence?   b) the first term in a sequence?   c) the 10th term in a sequence?

4. How could you use the formula to find…

   a) the gap in a sequence?   b) the first term in a sequence?   c) the 10th term in a sequence?

5. Would you use the rule or the formula to find the 50th term in a sequence? Explain.

Direct Variation

1. Fill in the chart and write a rule for the number of blocks in each figure.

a) Figure 1   Figure 2   Figure 3

Figure Number	Number of Blocks
1	4
2	8
3	12

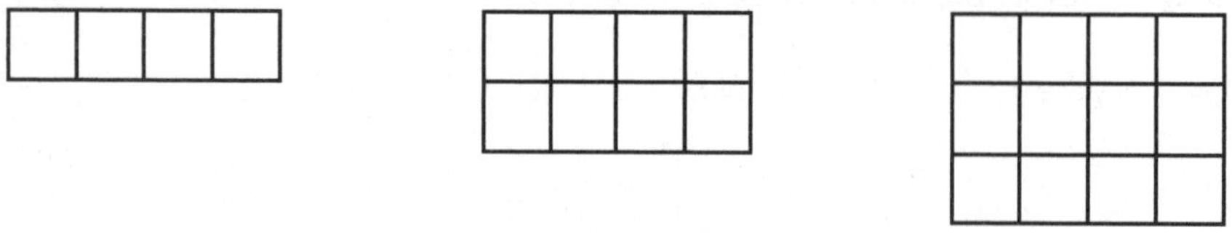

Rule: _____Multiply the Figure Number by 4._____

b) Figure 1   Figure 2   Figure 3

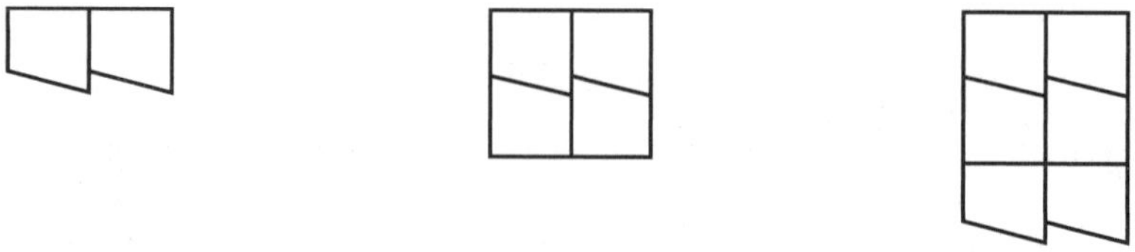

Figure Number	Number of Blocks

Rule: _____

c) Figure 1   Figure 2   Figure 3

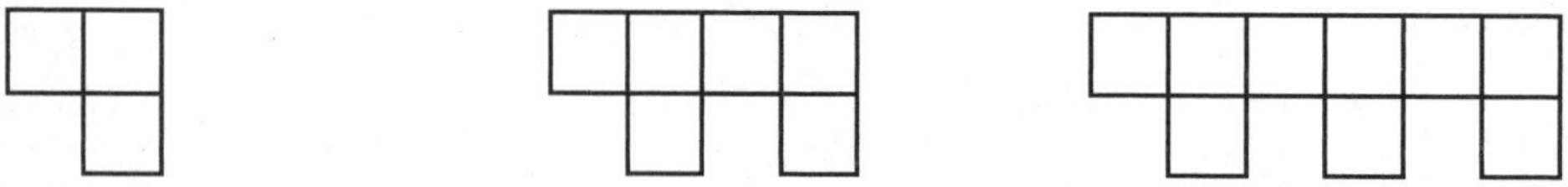

Figure Number	Number of Blocks

Rule: _____

d) Figure 1   Figure 2   Figure 3

Figure Number	Number of Blocks

Rule: _____

In each exercise above, you can find the number of blocks in any figure by multiplying the Figure Number by the number of blocks in the first figure: **Figure Number × # of blocks in Figure 1**. In such cases, we say that the number of blocks **varies directly** with the Figure Number.

2. Circle the charts where the number of blocks **varies directly** with the Figure Number.

Figure Number	Number of Blocks
1	4
2	8
3	12

Figure Number	Number of Blocks
1	5
2	8
3	11

Figure Number	Number of Blocks
1	7
2	14
3	21

Figure Number	Number of Blocks
1	3
2	6
3	10

3. In each pattern below, the number of **shaded** blocks **varies directly** with the Figure Number. The **total number of blocks**, however, **does not vary directly**.

i) Write a formula for the number of shaded blocks in each sequence.
ii) Write a formula for the total number of blocks in each sequence.

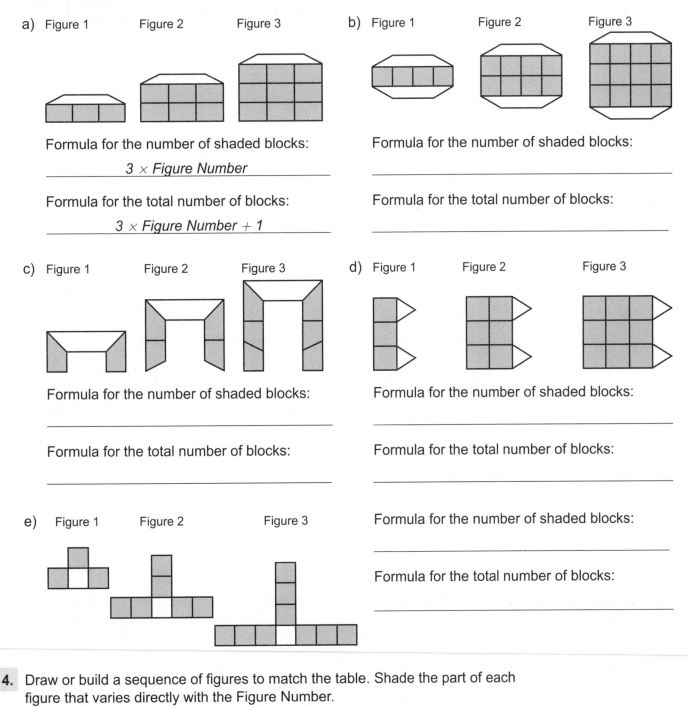

a) Figure 1   Figure 2   Figure 3

Formula for the number of shaded blocks:

_____ 3 × Figure Number _____

Formula for the total number of blocks:

_____ 3 × Figure Number + 1 _____

b) Figure 1   Figure 2   Figure 3

Formula for the number of shaded blocks:

_____

Formula for the total number of blocks:

_____

c) Figure 1   Figure 2   Figure 3

Formula for the number of shaded blocks:

_____

Formula for the total number of blocks:

_____

d) Figure 1   Figure 2   Figure 3

Formula for the number of shaded blocks:

_____

Formula for the total number of blocks:

_____

e) Figure 1   Figure 2   Figure 3

Formula for the number of shaded blocks:

_____

Formula for the total number of blocks:

_____

4. Draw or build a sequence of figures to match the table. Shade the part of each figure that varies directly with the Figure Number.

a)

Figure Number	Number of Blocks
1	7
2	9
3	11

b)

Figure Number	Number of Blocks
1	6
2	10
3	14

c)

Figure Number	Number of Blocks
1	5
2	8
3	11

Patterns and Algebra 7-24

Predicting the Gap Between Terms in a Pattern

1. Fill in the chart using the rule.

   a) Rule: Multiply by 4 and add 3

Input	Output
1	
2	
3	

   Gap: _____

   b) Rule: Multiply by 3 and subtract 2

Input	Output
1	
2	
3	

   Gap: _____

   c) Rule: Multiply by 5 and add 1

Input	Output
1	
2	
3	

   Gap: _____

   d) Rule: Multiply by 10 and subtract 4

Input	Output
1	
2	
3	

   Gap: _____

   e) Compare the gap in each pattern above to the rule for the pattern. What do you notice?

   _____

2. For each pattern below, make a T-table as shown. Fill in the total numbers of blocks (shaded and unshaded) and the gaps. Can you predict what the gap will be for each pattern before you fill in the chart?

Figure Number	Number of Blocks
1	
2	
3	

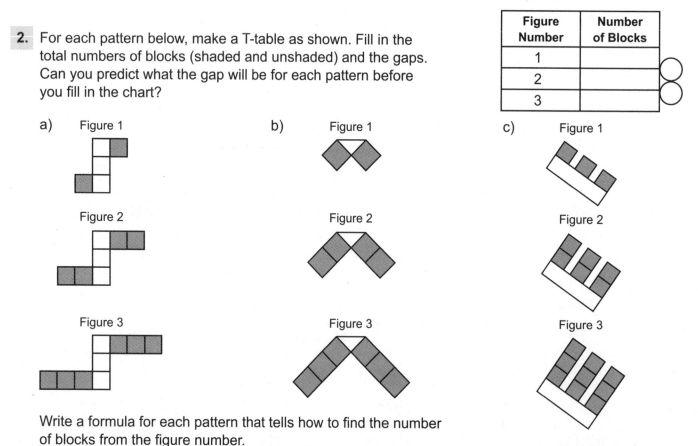

   a) Figure 1

   Figure 2

   Figure 3

   b) Figure 1

   Figure 2

   Figure 3

   c) Figure 1

   Figure 2

   Figure 3

   Write a formula for each pattern that tells how to find the number of blocks from the figure number.

In the T-table shown here, the term is calculated from the term number by two operations.

Term Number	Term
1	5
2	8
3	11

To find the operations and write the rule:

Step 1: Find the gap between the numbers in the **Term** column.

Term Number (n)	$n \times$ Gap	Term
1		5
2		8
3		11

3
3

Step 2: Multiply each **Term Number** by the gap.

Term Number (n)	$n \times$ Gap	Term
1	3	5
2	6	8
3	9	11

3
3

Step 3: What must you add (or subtract) to each number in the second column to get the term?

Term Number (n)	$n \times$ Gap	Term
1	3	5
2	6	8
3	9	11

3
3

Add 2

Step 4: Write a rule for the T-table. Rule: _____ *Multiply the term number by 3, then add 2* _____

3. Use the steps above to find the rule that tells you how to calculate the output from the input.

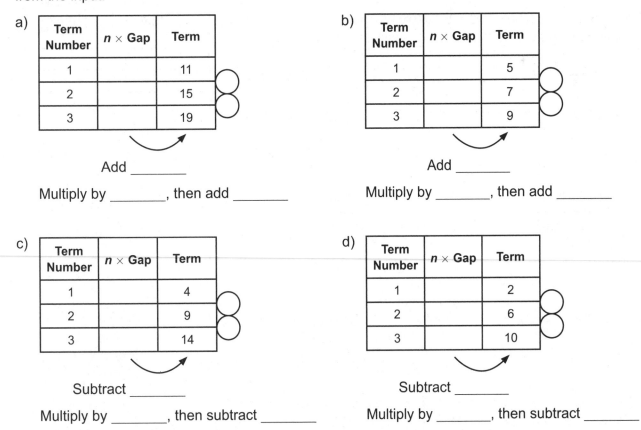

a)

Term Number	$n \times$ Gap	Term
1		11
2		15
3		19

Add _____

Multiply by _____, then add _____

b)

Term Number	$n \times$ Gap	Term
1		5
2		7
3		9

Add _____

Multiply by _____, then add _____

c)

Term Number	$n \times$ Gap	Term
1		4
2		9
3		14

Subtract _____

Multiply by _____, then subtract _____

d)

Term Number	$n \times$ Gap	Term
1		2
2		6
3		10

Subtract _____

Multiply by _____, then subtract _____

4. Use the gap in the sequence to start writing the formula. Then complete the chart to finish writing the formula.

a)

Term Number (n)	n × Gap	Term
1	5	2
2	10	7
3	15	12
4	20	17

Formula: _____ 5n – 3 _____

b)

Term Number (n)	n × Gap	Term
1		1
2		4
3		7
4		10

Formula: _____

c)

Term Number (n)	n × Gap	Term
1		3
2		7
3		11
4		15

Formula: _____

d)

Term Number (n)	n × Gap	Term
1		4
2		14
3		24
4		34

Formula: _____

e)

Term Number (n)	n × Gap	Term
1		4
2		6
3		8
4		10

Formula: _____

f)

Term Number (n)	n × Gap	Term
1		9
2		15
3		21
4		27

Formula: _____

g) 3, 5, 7, 9

h) 9, 20, 31, 42

i) 17, 27, 37, 47

j) 12, 15, 18, 21

k) 2, 14, 26, 38

l) 53, 55, 57, 59

5. Write a formula for the number of toothpicks in each figure. Use your formula to determine the number of toothpicks in the 30th figure.

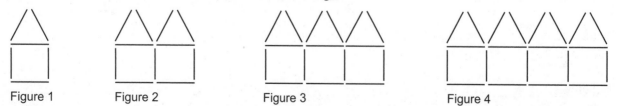

Figure 1   Figure 2   Figure 3   Figure 4

PA7-26 Matching Graphs and Formulas

1. Without writing the sequence for the pattern rule, find the gaps in the sequence.

   a) Start at 15. Subtract 4 each time. ____−4____

   b) Start at 3. Add 2 each time. _____

   c) Start at 15. Add 3 each time. _____

   d) Start at 23. Subtract 2 each time. _____

2. Without writing the sequence for the formula, find the gaps in the sequence.

   a) $3n + 2$ b) $5 - 4n$ c) $6 + 2n$ d) $5 - 3n$ e) $5n + 4$

   _____   _____   _____   _____   _____

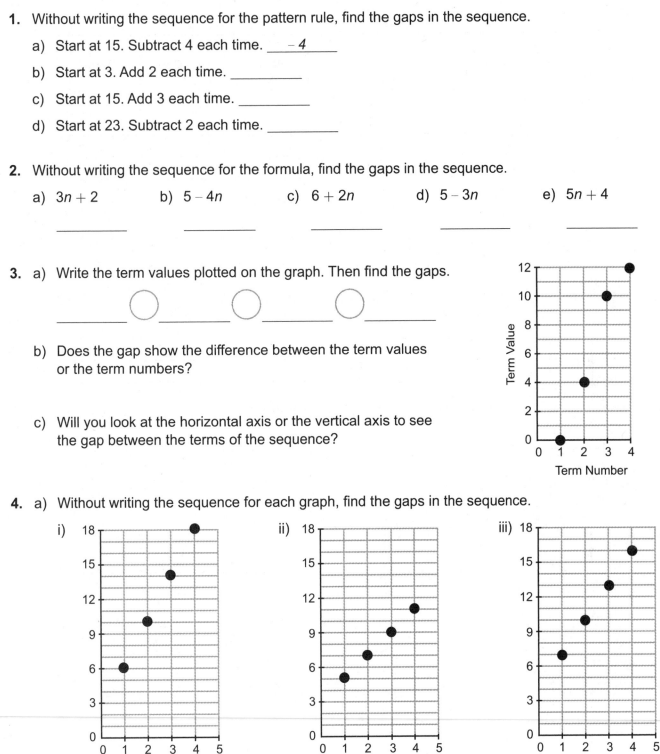

3. a) Write the term values plotted on the graph. Then find the gaps.

   _____ ◯ _____ ◯ _____ ◯ _____

   b) Does the gap show the difference between the term values
      or the term numbers?

   c) Will you look at the horizontal axis or the vertical axis to see
      the gap between the terms of the sequence?

4. a) Without writing the sequence for each graph, find the gaps in the sequence.

   i)   ii)   iii)

   _____   _____   _____

   b) Sara wrote the formulas for the graphs above: $3n + 4$, $4n + 2$, $2n + 3$.
      Which formula belongs to which graph?

      i) _____   ii) _____   iii) _____

5. a) Each formula represents a sequence.

Evaluate the formula at $n = 1$ to find the first term of the sequence.

   i) $3n + 4$ _____   ii) $3n + 2$ _____   iii) $3n - 1$ _____

b) Each graph represents a sequence. Find the first term of the sequence by finding the second coordinate when the first coordinate is 1.

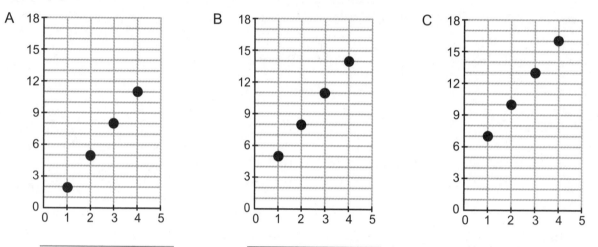

_____   _____   _____

c) Each formula from part a) represents the same sequence as a graph from part b). Which graph matches each formula?

   i) $3n + 4$ _____   ii) $3n + 2$ _____   iii) $3n - 1$ _____

6. Match each formula to a graph.

$3n - 2$ _____ $4n - 3$ _____ $3n + 1$ _____

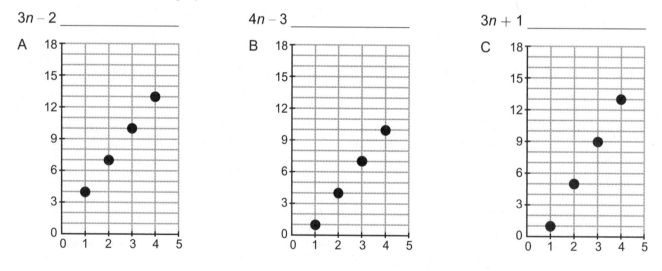

7. a) Finish writing 5 different formulas with numbers of your choice.

   $3n +$ _____ $2n +$ _____ $4n +$ _____ $3n +$ _____ $2n +$ _____

b) Draw the graphs for the formulas on grid paper, out of order.

c) Have a partner match the formulas to the graphs.

PA7-27 Using Graphs to Make Predictions

1. Use the graph to find the missing values in the table.

a)

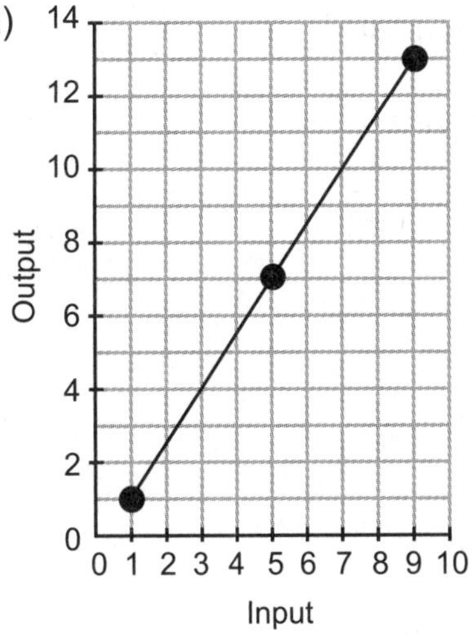

Input	Output
1	1
3	
5	7
	10
9	13

b)

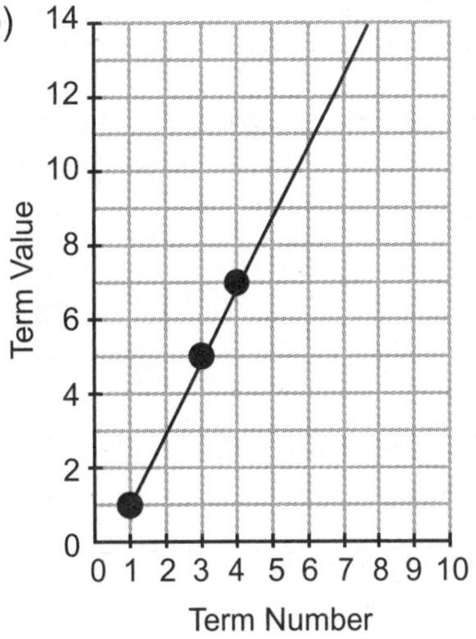

Input	Output
1	1
	3
3	5
4	7
5	

2. Extend the line to find the value of the 11th term.

a)

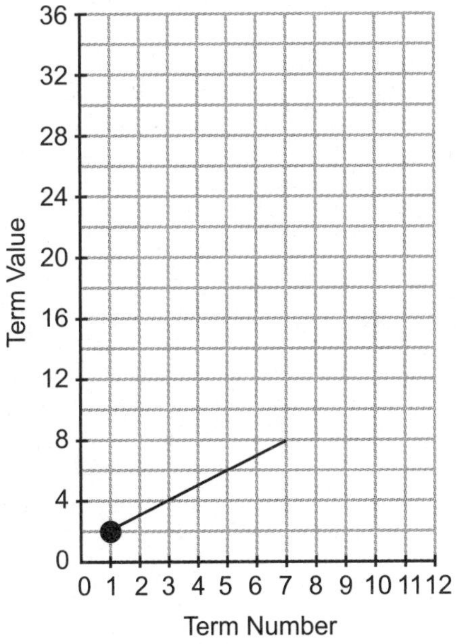

Value of the 11th term _____

b)

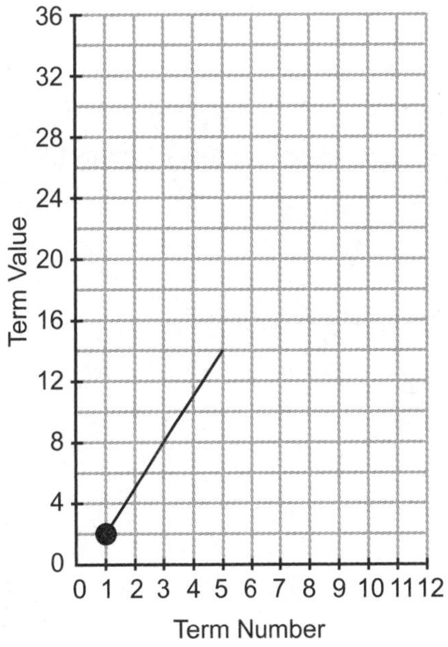

Value of the 11th term _____

3. For each sequence, make a table of values for the term numbers and the term values. Draw a graph for your table and extend the graph to find the value of the 7th term.

a) 2, 5, 8, 11

b) 1, 3, 5, 7

4. Draw a graph to show how many toothpicks would be needed for the 8th figure in the sequence.

a)

b)

5. A car is travelling at a constant speed of 40 km/h.

a) Write an expression for the distance the car has travelled after n hours.

_____

b) Create a table of values for the distance the car has travelled after n hours.

Time (n hours)	Distance Travelled (km)

c) Write the ordered pairs from the table of values. Then plot the points on the graph.

d) Join the points on the graph with a straight line. If the car travelled for 3.5 hours, how far would it go?

e) How many hours would it take the car to travel 320 km? Extend the line to find out.

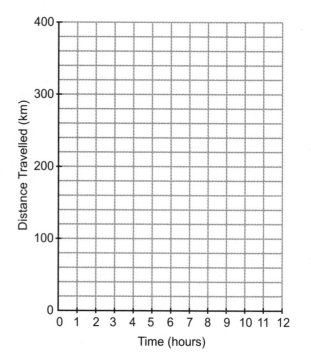

6. a) Plot the relationship between n and the given expression, for n equal to 1, 2, 3, 4, and 5. Note: Leave extra space on the horizontal axis to extend the graph.

i) $4n + 1$ ii) $5n - 2$ iii) $3n + 9$

b) Extend the line in each graph to evaluate each expression for $n = 6$. Then substitute $n = 6$ into each expression to check your answer.

c) Use the graphs to find the value of n that makes each expression equal to 33.

d) Write an equation and solve it to check your work for part c). Example: Solve $4n + 1 = 33$ to check your answer to part i).

Patterns and Algebra 7-27

PA7-28 Problems and Puzzles

Tom wants to find the 10th term in the sequence 3, 7, 11, 15, ... He makes a chart and writes a formula for the sequence.

Term Number	$n \times$ Gap	Term
1	$1 \times 4 = 4$	3
2	$2 \times 4 = 8$	7
3	$3 \times 4 = 12$	11

Formula: $4n - 1$

Using his formula, Tom can calculate the value of the 10th term: $4 \times (10) - 1 = 40 - 1 = 39$.

1. Find a formula for the sequence (let n represent the term number). Then find the value of the 10th term in the sequence.

   a) 4, 9, 14, 19   b) 4, 10, 16, 22   c) 3, 9, 15, 21   d) 5, 16, 27, 38

   e) 11, 21, 31, 41   f) 13, 15, 17, 19   g) 3, 10, 17, 24   h) 44, 47, 50, 53

2. If the pattern continues, how many letters will appear in row "K"? Hint: Write a sequence for the number of letters in each row, then write a rule for the sequence.

```
    A A
   B B B
  C C C C
 D D D D D
E E E E E E
```

3. For the pattern, write...

   i) a **sequence** giving the number of blocks in each figure.
   ii) a **rule** for the pattern.
   iii) an **algebraic expression** for the number of blocks in the nth figure.
   iv) the number of blocks in the **15th figure**.

   a)

   Figure 1   Figure 2   Figure 3

   i) _____ 4, 6, 8, _____

   ii) _____ $2 \times$ Figure Number $+ 2$ _____

   iii) _____ $2n + 2$ _____

   iv) $2 (15) + 2 = 30 + 2$

   $= 32$

   The 15th figure would have 32 blocks.

   b)

   Figure 1   Figure 2   Figure 3

   i) _____

   ii) _____

   iii) _____

   iv)

   _____

   c)

   Figure 1   Figure 2   Figure 3

   d)

   Figure 1   Figure 2   Figure 3

4. The pattern rule is: Start at 4 and add 3 each time.

a) Finish writing the formula: Term = Term Number × _____ + _____

b) Find the 23rd term in the sequence in two ways.

    i) Substitute 23 as the term number.

    ii) Substitute 20 as the term number to find the 20th term. Then extend the sequence using the pattern rule to find the 23rd term. Did you get the same answer both ways?

5. a) Complete the T-table.

1	$2^2 - 1^2 =$
2	$3^2 - 2^2 =$
3	$4^2 - 3^2 =$
4	$5^2 - 4^2 =$
5	$6^2 - 5^2 =$
6	$7^2 - 6^2 =$

b) Use your answers to part a) to write a formula for the number in the nth row of the T-table.

c) Will $23^2 - 22^2$ be in the 22nd row or the 23rd row? How do you know?

d) Use your formula to find $23^2 - 22^2$.

e) Check your answer using a calculator or long multiplication.

6. i) Write the number of blocks in each figure as a sequence.
  ii) Write an algebraic expression for the number of blocks in each figure.
  iii) Find the number of blocks in the 10th figure.

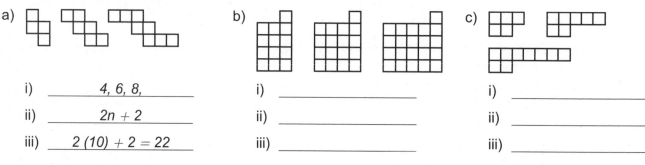

a)
  i) _____ 4, 6, 8, _____
  ii) _____ $2n + 2$ _____
  iii) _____ $2(10) + 2 = 22$

b)
  i) _____
  ii) _____
  iii) _____

c)
  i) _____
  ii) _____
  iii) _____

7. Find the number of toothpicks in the 20th figure of the sequence.

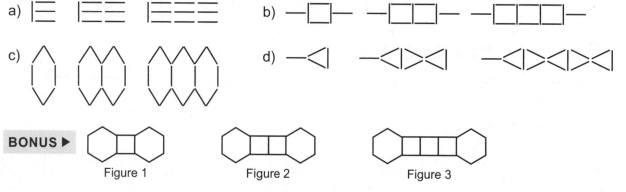

a)   b)

c)   d)

BONUS ▶

Figure 1   Figure 2   Figure 3

  i) Write an expression for the perimeter of each figure.

  ii) Which figure will have perimeter 26? Hint: Write an equation in which you make the expression you found in part i) equal to 26.

Patterns and Algebra 7-28

8. How many dots would be in Figure 8?

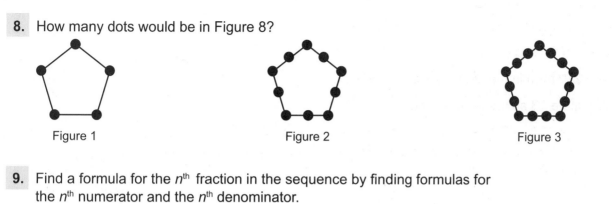

Figure 1   Figure 2   Figure 3

9. Find a formula for the nth fraction in the sequence by finding formulas for the nth numerator and the nth denominator.

a) $\dfrac{1}{2}, \dfrac{2}{3}, \dfrac{3}{4}, \dfrac{4}{5}$

b) $\dfrac{5}{7}, \dfrac{7}{11}, \dfrac{9}{15}, \dfrac{11}{19}$

BONUS ▶ $\dfrac{3}{5}, \dfrac{3}{4}, \dfrac{9}{11}, \dfrac{12}{14}$

Hint: Change one of the fractions to an equivalent fraction.

10. How many shaded squares and how many unshaded squares would be in Figure 7?

Figure 1   Figure 2   Figure 3

11. Water drains from two tanks at the rate shown in the chart. Describe the pattern in each column. Which tank do you think will empty first?

Minutes	Tank 1	Tank 2
1	500 L	500 L
2	460 L	490 L
3	420 L	470 L
4	380 L	440 L

12. A restaurant has tables shaped as shown. The dots represent chairs.

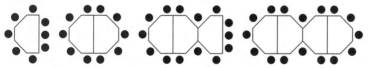

a) Draw pictures to show how many people can sit at 5 and 6 tables. Then fill in the T-table.

b) Describe the pattern in the number of people. How does the gap change?

c) Extend the pattern to find out how many people can sit at 8 tables.

BONUS ▶ Write a formula for the number of people that can sit at an even number of tables. Use your formula to find out how many people can sit at twenty tables. Hint: Make a sequence where the nth term is the number of people at $2n$ tables.

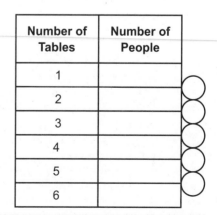

Number of Tables	Number of People
1	
2	
3	
4	
5	
6	

Patterns and Algebra 7-28

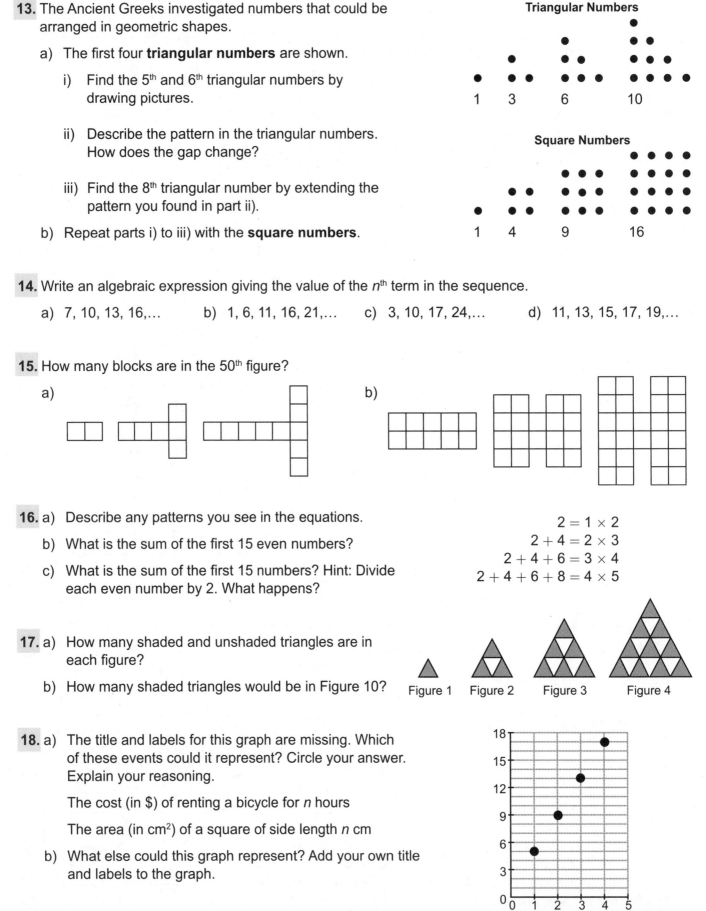

13. The Ancient Greeks investigated numbers that could be arranged in geometric shapes.

Triangular Numbers

    1   3   6   10

a) The first four **triangular numbers** are shown.

   i) Find the 5th and 6th triangular numbers by drawing pictures.

   ii) Describe the pattern in the triangular numbers. How does the gap change?

Square Numbers

   iii) Find the 8th triangular number by extending the pattern you found in part ii).

b) Repeat parts i) to iii) with the **square numbers**.

    1   4   9   16

14. Write an algebraic expression giving the value of the nth term in the sequence.

a) 7, 10, 13, 16,…   b) 1, 6, 11, 16, 21,…   c) 3, 10, 17, 24,…   d) 11, 13, 15, 17, 19,…

15. How many blocks are in the 50th figure?

a)

b)

16. a) Describe any patterns you see in the equations.

   b) What is the sum of the first 15 even numbers?

   c) What is the sum of the first 15 numbers? Hint: Divide each even number by 2. What happens?

$$2 = 1 \times 2$$
$$2 + 4 = 2 \times 3$$
$$2 + 4 + 6 = 3 \times 4$$
$$2 + 4 + 6 + 8 = 4 \times 5$$

17. a) How many shaded and unshaded triangles are in each figure?

   b) How many shaded triangles would be in Figure 10?

Figure 1   Figure 2   Figure 3   Figure 4

18. a) The title and labels for this graph are missing. Which of these events could it represent? Circle your answer. Explain your reasoning.

The cost (in $) of renting a bicycle for n hours

The area (in cm²) of a square of side length n cm

   b) What else could this graph represent? Add your own title and labels to the graph.

Patterns and Algebra 7-28

G7-13 Congruent Triangles

1. Draw any triangle. Draw another triangle that is different in some way. How is
it different? What changed? Draw a third triangle different from the first two.
How is it different? What changed?

To make different triangles, you need to change the lengths of sides or the measures of angles. It
follows that two triangles that have all their **corresponding sides and angles** equal will be exactly
the same. (Corresponding sides and angles match up if you set one shape on top of the other.)

Here is how to mark equal sides and angles in polygons:

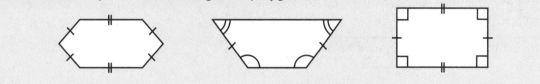

2. Mark the sides and angles in each polygon that look like they are equal.

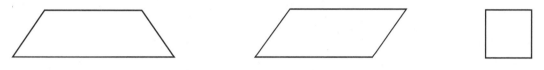

The corresponding sides and angles are marked in these triangles.

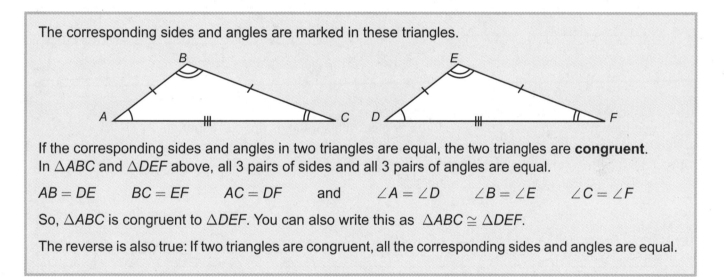

If the corresponding sides and angles in two triangles are equal, the two triangles are **congruent**.
In △ABC and △DEF above, all 3 pairs of sides and all 3 pairs of angles are equal.

AB = DE   BC = EF   AC = DF   and   ∠A = ∠D   ∠B = ∠E   ∠C = ∠F

So, △ABC is congruent to △DEF. You can also write this as △ABC ≅ △DEF.

The reverse is also true: If two triangles are congruent, all the corresponding sides and angles are equal.

3. The two triangles are congruent. Mark the triangles to show the corresponding
equal angles.

a)

b)

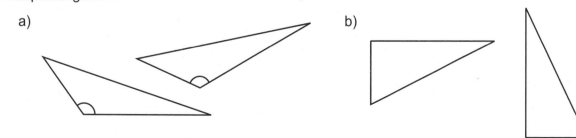

4. Which sides in the pair of triangles are corresponding equal sides?

a) $VW = $ _____ $WX = $ _____ $VX = $ _____   b) $JK = $ _____ $KL = $ _____ $JL = $ _____

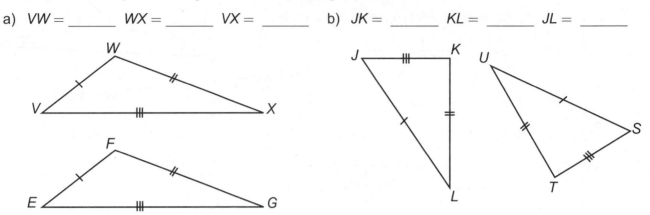

5. Which angles in the pair of triangles are corresponding equal angles?

a) $\angle A = \angle$ _____ $\angle B = \angle$ _____ $\angle C = \angle$ _____   b) $\angle M = \angle$ _____ $\angle N = \angle$ _____ $\angle O = \angle$ _____

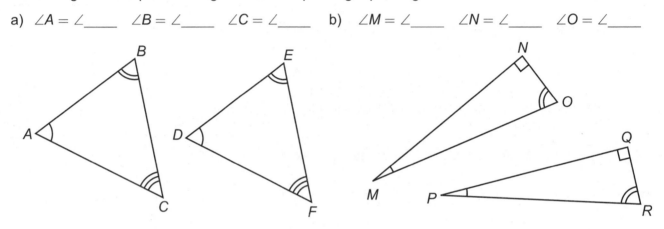

6. These triangles each have the same three angles. Which angles are corresponding equal angles?

$\angle A = \angle$ _____ $= \angle$ _____ $\angle B = \angle$ _____ $= \angle$ _____ $\angle C = \angle$ _____ $= \angle$ _____

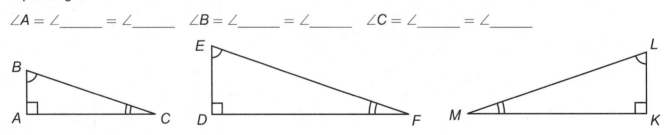

7. a) $\triangle ABC$ is congruent to $\triangle DEF$. Use the side and angle markings to identify the pairs of corresponding equal sides and angles in the two triangles.

$\angle A = \angle \underline{\ D\ }$ $AB = \underline{\ DE\ }$

$\angle B = \angle$ _____ $BC = $ _____

$\angle C = \angle$ _____ $AC = $ _____

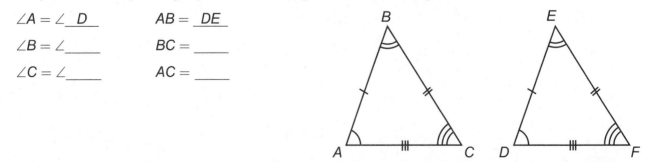

b) △*SRT* is congruent to △*WXY*. Identify the pairs of
corresponding equal sides and angles in the triangles.

∠_____ = ∠_____   ∠_____ = ∠_____

∠_____ = ∠_____

_____ = _____   _____ = _____

_____ = _____

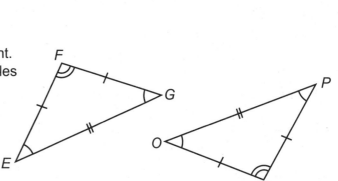

c) Isosceles triangles *ABC* and *KLM* are congruent.
Identify the corresponding equal sides and angles
in the two triangles.

∠_____ = ∠_____   ∠_____ = ∠_____

∠_____ = ∠_____

_____ = _____   _____ = _____

_____ = _____

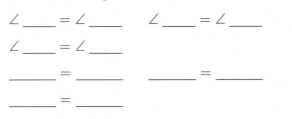

d) Isosceles triangles *EFG* and *NOP* are congruent.
Identify the corresponding equal sides and angles
in the two triangles.

∠_____ = ∠_____   ∠_____ = ∠_____

∠_____ = ∠_____

_____ = _____   _____ = _____

_____ = _____

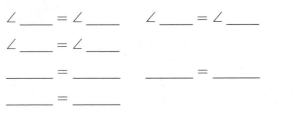

8. Kali notices that there are three equal angles in
these two triangles. She decides that the triangles are
congruent. Is she right? What did she forget to check?

_____

_____

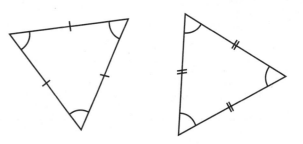

9. These two triangles are congruent. Why do you not
have to mark the third pair of angles to know that they
are equal? (Hint: If you know the measures of two
angles in a triangle, then you know the measure of
the third angle. Why?)

_____

_____

_____

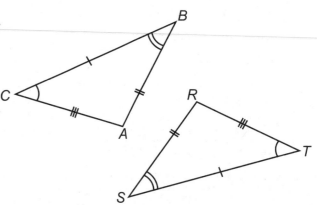

Important: When two triangles are congruent, you have to write the letters that name the vertices in the proper order to show what is equal to what.

Example: The markings show that these two triangles are congruent. To write a correct congruence statement, follow these steps.

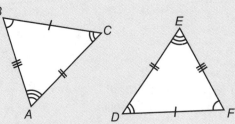

First triangle	Second triangle	Congruence statement
Choose any vertex on one of the triangles, e.g., vertex *A*.	Record the corresponding vertex on the other triangle, e.g., ∠*A* = ∠*E*	△*A* ≅ △*E*
Choose an adjacent vertex, e.g., vertex *B*.	Record the corresponding vertex on the other triangle.	△*AB* ≅ △*EF*
Write the letter of the third vertex.	Write the letter of the third vertex.	△*ABC* ≅ △*EFD*

10. Write a correct congruence statement for the pair of triangles in Question 9.

△ _____ ≅ △ _____

11. There are 2 or more equal angles in these congruent triangles. For each pair of triangles, …

  i) Write the pairs of equal angles.
  ii) Write a congruence statement for the triangles.
  iii) Write a different congruence statement that is also correct.

a)   b)

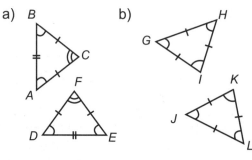

12. A correct congruence statement also tells you which sides are equal. Finish circling the corresponding sides and angles in congruent triangles *PQR* and *KLM*.

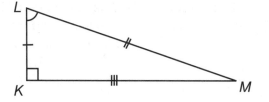

Corresponding sides

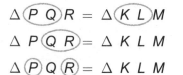

△ P Q R = △ K L M

△ P Q R = △ K L M

Corresponding angles

△ (P) Q R = △ (K) L M

△ P (Q) R = △ K L M

△ P Q R = △ K L M

13. You are told that $\triangle PQR \cong \triangle LKM$. You do not have a diagram of these triangles. Use the order of the vertex names in the congruence statement to complete the list of corresponding sides and angles for these two congruent triangles.

$\underline{PQ} = \underline{LK} \qquad \angle\,\underline{\quad P\quad} = \angle\,\underline{\quad L\quad}$

$\underline{QR} = \underline{KM} \qquad \angle\,\underline{\qquad} = \angle\,\underline{\qquad}$

$\underline{\quad} = \underline{\quad} \qquad \angle\,\underline{\qquad} = \angle\,\underline{\qquad}$

14.

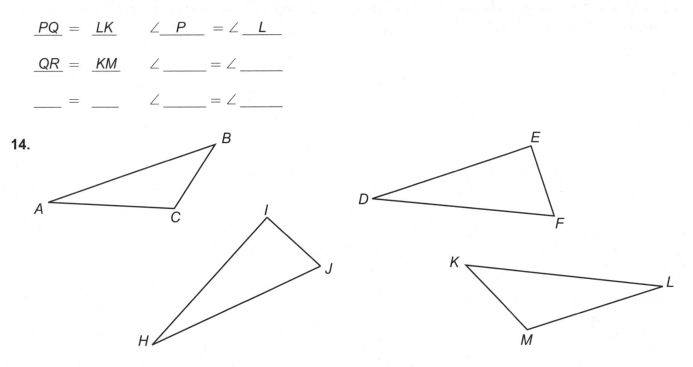

a) Measure all the sides of each triangle to the nearest millimetre. Write the lengths on the triangles.

b) Measure all of the angles in each triangle. Write the angle measures inside each vertex.

c) Name a pair of congruent triangles. _____

d) Using a ruler and a protractor, draw a triangle that is congruent to $\triangle ABC$.

15. Tom looked at these two triangles. He noticed that there are 3 pairs of corresponding equal sides and 3 pairs of corresponding equal angles. He wrote this congruence statement:

$\triangle VWX \cong \triangle ABC$

Then Tom lost his diagram, but he was not worried. He used his congruence statement to list the equal sides and angles. Here is his list:

$VW = AB \quad \angle V = \angle A$
$WX = BC \quad \angle W = \angle B$
$XV = CA \quad \angle X = \angle C$

Compare Tom's list of equal sides and angles with the diagrams. Is his list correct? Put an X beside any statements that are incorrect.

How should Tom have written the congruence statement?

$\triangle\ \underline{\qquad} \cong \triangle\ \underline{\qquad}$

G7-14 Congruency and Area

INVESTIGATION ▶ Can two congruent shapes have different areas?

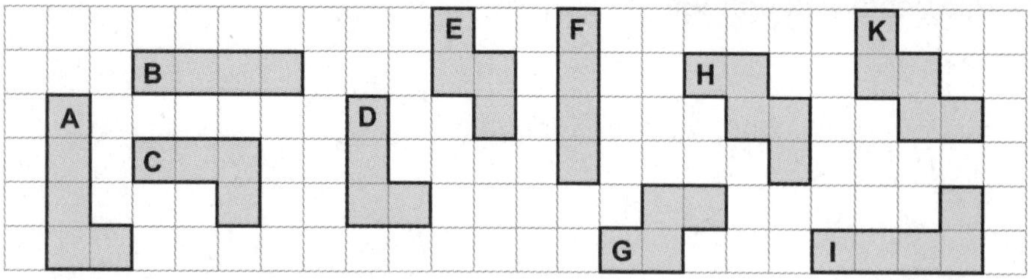

A. Sort the shapes by area.

4 squares: _B,_____   5 squares: _____

B. Sort the shapes into pairs of congruent shapes.

_____, _____, _____, _____, _____

C. Look at each pair of congruent shapes. Do they have the same area? _____

D. Are all shapes with the same area congruent? If yes, explain why. If no, find a counter-example in the shapes above.

_____

E. Can two congruent shapes have different areas? Explain.

_____

1. a) Can two congruent shapes have different corresponding side lengths? Explain.

_____

b) Can two congruent shapes have different perimeters? Explain.

_____

> **REMINDER ▶** Area of triangle = base × height ÷ 2.

2. a) Find the areas of △ABC and △ADC.

Area of △ABC: _____   Area of △ADC: _____

b) Are triangles △ABC and △ADC congruent? Explain your thinking.

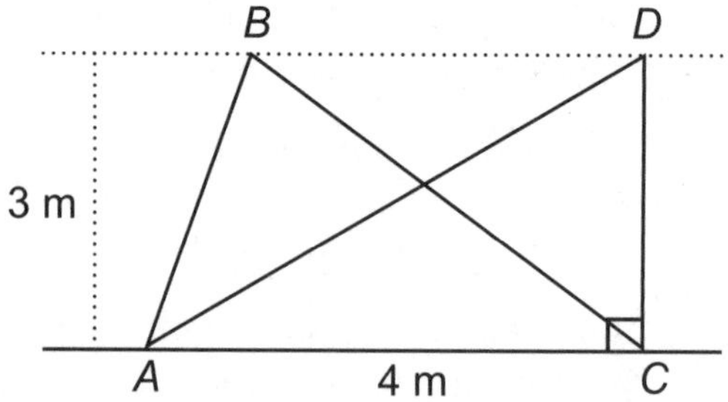

3. Use grid paper.

a) Draw two rectangles with area 12 cm² that are not congruent.
b) Use your rectangles to draw two right triangles with area 6 cm² that are not congruent.

BONUS ▶ Draw an obtuse scalene triangle and an acute scalene triangle, both with area 6 cm².

INVESTIGATION 1 ▶ Do you have to check that all 3 pairs of sides and all 3 pairs of angles are equal to determine if two triangles are congruent?

A. 3 sides

Conjecture: If two triangles have 3 pairs of equal sides, then the triangles are congruent.

a) Test the conjecture: Take 3 straws of different lengths. Make a triangle with them and trace it. See if you can make a different triangle with the same 3 straws. Try with a different set of 3 straws. What did you discover?

_____

b) Do you think this result will be true for all triangles? Explain.

B. 2 sides and the angle between

Conjecture: If two sides and the angle between them in one triangle are equal to two sides and the angle between them in another triangle, the triangles are congruent.

a) Test the conjecture: Draw three triangles, each with one side 3 cm long, one side 5 cm long, and a 45° angle between these sides. What did you discover?

_____

b) Do you think this result will be true for all triangles? Explain.

C. 2 angles and the side between them

Conjecture: If two angles and the side between them in one triangle are equal to two angles and the side between them in another triangle, the triangles are congruent.

a) Test this conjecture: Draw three triangles, each with a 60° angle, a 45° angle, and a 5 cm side between these angles. What did you discover?

_____

b) Do you think this result will be true for all triangles? Explain.

D. 2 angles and then a side

Conjecture: If two angles and a side that is not between them in one triangle are equal to two angles and the corresponding side in another triangle, the triangles are congruent.

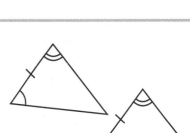

a) Test the conjecture: Draw a 10 cm side, then a 30° angle. Suppose the next angle is a right angle. Use a set square to test if you can make more than one triangle like this. What did you discover?

_____

b) Do you think this result will be true for all triangles? Explain.

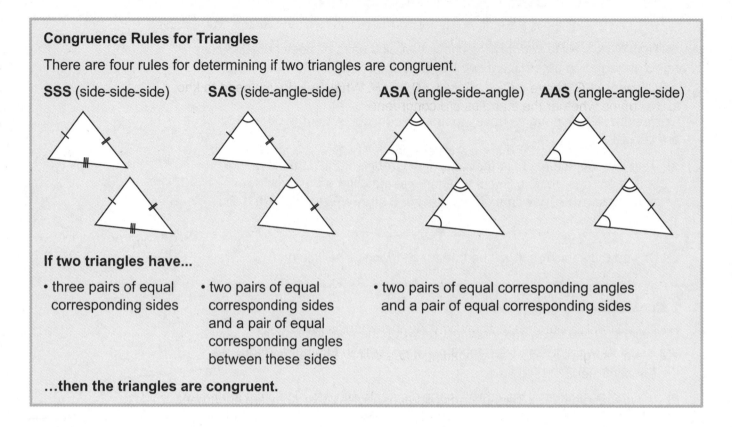

Congruence Rules for Triangles

There are four rules for determining if two triangles are congruent.

SSS (side-side-side) **SAS** (side-angle-side) **ASA** (angle-side-angle) **AAS** (angle-angle-side)

If two triangles have...

- three pairs of equal corresponding sides
- two pairs of equal corresponding sides and a pair of equal corresponding angles between these sides
- two pairs of equal corresponding angles and a pair of equal corresponding sides

...then the triangles are congruent.

1. Which congruence rule tells that the two triangles are congruent? Write the vertex letters in the names of the triangles in the correct order (the order that tells which corresponding parts are equal).

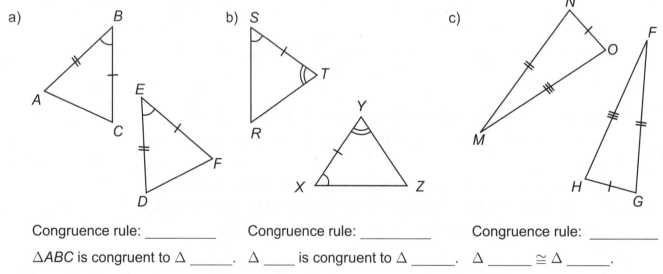

a)   b)   c)

Congruence rule: _____   Congruence rule: _____   Congruence rule: _____

△ABC is congruent to △ _____.   △ _____ is congruent to △ _____.   △ _____ ≅ △ _____.

2. Use each of the four congruence rules to draw a pair of congruent triangles. Name each triangle by choosing a letter for each vertex. Mark each pair of triangles to show the corresponding angles and sides.

3. Draw any triangle. Then draw another triangle that is not congruent to the first triangle. Explain why the triangles are not congruent.

4. △PQR and △XYZ have PQ = XY = 5 cm and QR = YZ = 7 cm. Sketch the triangles. Which pair of angles must be equal for △PQR and △XYZ to be congruent?

5. △BCD and △FGH have ∠C = ∠G and ∠D = ∠H. What else do you need to know to determine whether the triangles are congruent?

6. Joe says △ABC and △DEF are congruent because ∠B = ∠E and CB = EF. For each pair of triangles, explain why Joe is wrong.

a)   b)

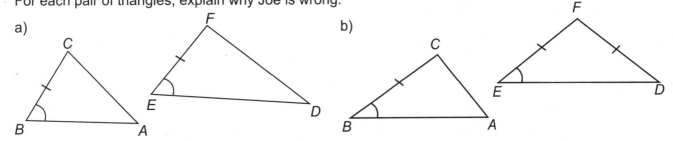

7. Sketch a counter-example to show why the statement is **false**.

a) If two triangles have 2 corresponding sides that are equal, the triangles are congruent.

b) If two triangles have 3 equal parts (sides or angles), then they are congruent.

8. △ABC is congruent to △DEF. △DEF is congruent to △GHI. Is △ABC congruent to △GHI? Sketch the problem. Explain your answer.

9. △ABC and △DEF are both isosceles triangles. ∠A = ∠D and AB = DE. Are △ABC and △DEF always congruent? Explain. Hint: Start by making a sketch that includes all the information you have been given. Try making more than one sketch — there may be more than one answer!

10. There are three ways that a line can divide a shape into two other shapes.

• A **line of symmetry** divides a shape into two congruent parts that are mirror images of each other.

• Some lines divide a shape into two congruent parts that are not mirror images of each other (if you folded the shape along the line, the two parts would not match).

• Other lines divide a shape into two shapes that are not congruent.

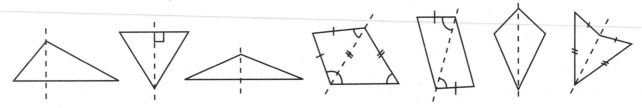

a) Put a check mark beside the lines that **look like** lines of symmetry.

b) Circle the diagrams with lines that you know for sure **are** lines of symmetry. Explain how you know.

INVESTIGATION 2 ▶ Are two triangles that have two pairs of corresponding sides and one pair of corresponding angles always congruent?

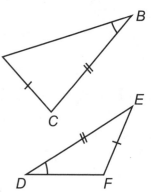

A. What sides and angles in △ABC and △DEF are equal?

_____

B. Can you use the SAS congruence rule? Why or why not?

_____

C. Do triangles △ABC and △DEF look congruent? _____

D. Is **SSA** (side-side-angle) a congruence rule? What about **ASS** (angle-side-side)? Explain.

What about **AAA** (angle-angle-angle) — are triangles with three corresponding equal angles congruent? **No!** Look at these three triangles to see why.

When two triangles have pairs of corresponding angles equal, they are called **similar** triangles, because they have the same shape but not necessarily the same size. You can use AAA as a test for similarity. If the corresponding angles in two triangles are all equal, then the triangles are similar.

---

11. Draw any triangle ABC. Draw a triangle that is congruent to △ABC, and one that is similar to △ABC. Hint: Multiply each side length in △ABC by the same factor.

12. Explain why congruent triangles are always similar, but similar triangles are not always congruent.

13. Use grid paper.

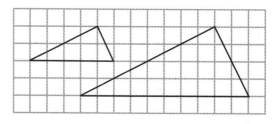

   a) Draw 3 similar right triangles.
   b) Draw 3 similar isosceles triangles.
   c) Draw 3 similar scalene triangles.

14. All sides and all angles in an equilateral triangle are equal.

   a) △EFG and △QRS are both equilateral triangles. FG = RS. Are △EFG and △QRS congruent?

      Start by making a sketch. Explain your answer.

   b) △LMN and △TUV are both equilateral triangles. ∠M = ∠U. Is △LMN ≅ △TUV? Explain.

15. Recall that the sum of the angles in a triangle is 180°. Use this fact to explain why you really only need to know that two pairs of corresponding angles are equal to know that two triangles are similar.

G7-16 Introduction to Constructions

A circle consists of all the possible points that are the same distance from a point called the **centre**. The distance between any point on a circle to the centre of the circle is called the **radius**.

An **arc** is an unbroken part of a circle. The centre of the circle is also called the centre of the arc.

A **compass** is a tool used to construct circles and arcs.

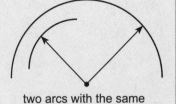

two arcs with the same centre and different radii

1. The centre of an arc is the point where you put the point of the compass to draw the arc. Circle the point that is the centre of the arc.

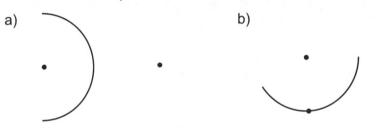

a) b) c)

2. a) Construct a circle with center *O* through point *A*.

   Step 1: Set the compass point on the centre point, *O*.
   Step 2: Adjust the compass width to point *A*.
   Step 3: Draw a circle through point *A*.

   b) Mark any point on the circle and label it *B*.
   Construct *OA* and *OB* using a ruler.

   c) Measure *OA* and *OB*. What do you notice?

   •*A*

   •
   O

3. Construct an arc with center *O* through point *A*.

   a) b)

   A   *B*

   •*O*   •*A*

   •
   O

   •
   B

   Is point *B* on the arc? _____   Is point *B* on the arc? _____

Two lines can intersect at 1 point or 0 points. Two line segments also can intersect at 1 point or 0 points. Two arcs of different circles (or two circles, or an arc and a circle) can intersect at 2, 1, or 0 points.

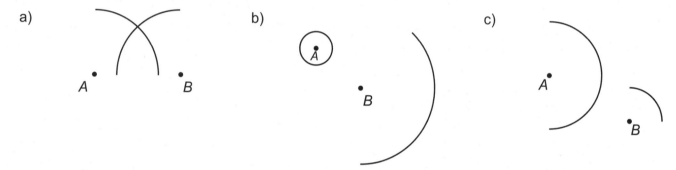

2 points   1 point   0 points

4. The arcs are centred at points *A* and *B*. Use a compass to extend each arc into a circle. How many points of intersection do these circles have?

a)
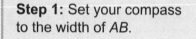

b)
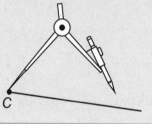

c)
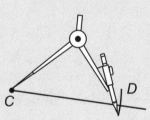

You can use a compass to create a line segment *CD* equal to a line segment *AB*.

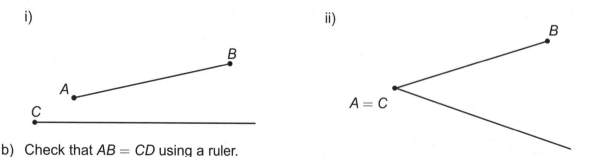

Step 1: Set your compass to the width of *AB*.

Step 2: Without changing the setting of the compass, set the point of the compass at *C*.

Step 3: Construct a little arc intersecting the line. Label the intersection point *D*.

5. a) Use a compass to create a line segment *CD* equal to the line segment *AB* along the given line.

i)
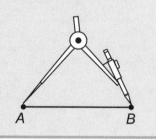

ii)

b) Check that *AB* = *CD* using a ruler.

6. Use a compass to construct two line segments *CD* and *CE* that are equal to *AB*.

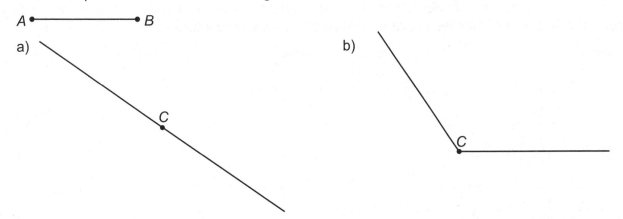

A •————————• B

a)

b)

7. The centre of the arc is at point *C*. Construct a line segment *AB* equal to the radius of the arc.

Step 1: Set the compass to the radius of the arc.
Step 2: Set the point of the compass on *A*.
Step 3: Draw an arc intersecting the line.

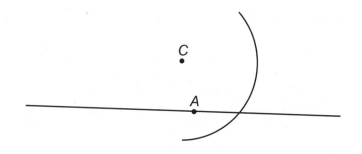

8. The centre of the arc is at point *B*.

a) Construct an arc centred at *C* and with the same radius as the first arc, so that the arcs intersect. Label the intersection point *D*.

b) What do you know about *BD* and *CD*? Check with a ruler.

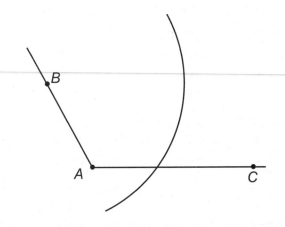

A **straightedge** is any tool used to draw lines and line segments. It is like a ruler without marks. When we say "use a straightedge," you can use a ruler but you cannot use the marks on it.

1. Draw a line from the point to the intersection of the arcs, as shown in part a).

   a)

   b)

   c)

How to construct a triangle with given side lengths *AB*, *BC*, and *AC*, using a compass and a straightedge:

Step 1: Construct a line segment *AC*.

Step 2: Set your compass to the width of *AB*. Construct an arc centred at *A*.

Step 3: Set your compass to the width of *BC*. Construct an arc centred at *C* with radius *BC*, so that it intersects the first arc at one point.

Step 4: Label the intersection point of the arcs *B*. Use a straightedge to join *B* to *A* and *C*.

2. Construct triangles with the following side lengths using a compass and a straightedge.

   Use a ruler to set your compass width to the given lengths:

   a) 3 cm, 4 cm, 5 cm   b) 8 cm, 8 cm, 12 cm   c) 5 cm, 5 cm, 8 cm

   Now set your compass width to the length of these lines:

   d)

   e)

REMINDER ▶ We identify triangles according to the number of equal sides they have and the size of their angles.

number of equal sides:	0 – scalene △	2 – isosceles △	3 – equilateral △
size of angles:	3 acute – acute △	1 right – right △	1 obtuse – obtuse △

3. Are the angles of the triangles you constructed in Question 2 acute, right, or obtuse? Use a protractor or a set square to check. Then name the types of triangles you constructed.

   a) _____scalene right_____   b) _____   c) _____

   d) _____   e) _____

   Which types of triangles could you have identified from the side lengths, without drawing them?

4. *A* and *B* are centres of the circles. Which sides of △*ABC* are equal? How do you know?

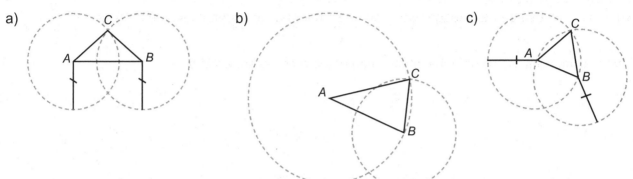

a)

b)

c)

5. In each diagram below, the centres of the two circles are joined by a line.

Join point *C* to the centres of the circles. Then match each pair of circles to the description of a triangle. Some descriptions match more than one picture.

A Isosceles acute triangle   **B** Equilateral triangle   **C** Isosceles obtuse triangle

D Scalene acute triangle   **E** Scalene obtuse triangle

a) _____

b) _____

c) _____

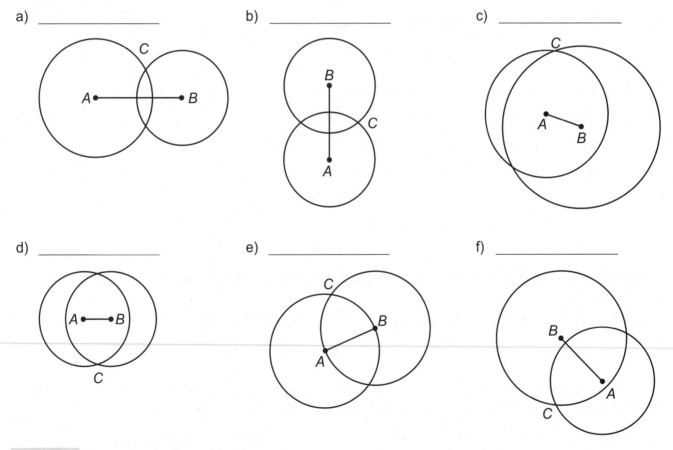

d) _____

e) _____

f) _____

BONUS ▶ Use a compass and a straightedge to construct a diagram that helps you to explain why there is no triangle with side lengths 4 cm, 4 cm, and 9 cm. Explain why such a triangle cannot exist.

Congruence Rules

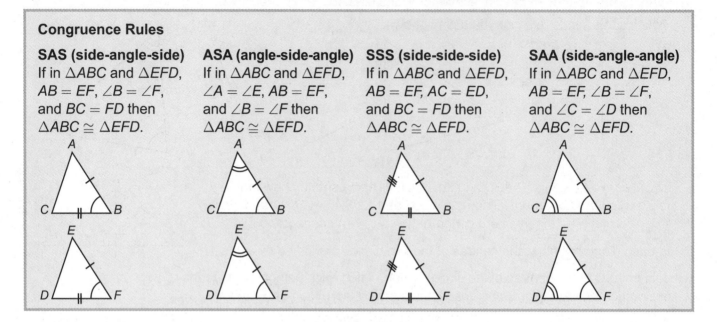

SAS (side-angle-side)
If in △ABC and △EFD,
AB = EF, ∠B = ∠F,
and BC = FD then
△ABC ≅ △EFD.

ASA (angle-side-angle)
If in △ABC and △EFD,
∠A = ∠E, AB = EF,
and ∠B = ∠F then
△ABC ≅ △EFD.

SSS (side-side-side)
If in △ABC and △EFD,
AB = EF, AC = ED,
and BC = FD then
△ABC ≅ △EFD.

SAA (side-angle-angle)
If in △ABC and △EFD,
AB = EF, ∠B = ∠F,
and ∠C = ∠D then
△ABC ≅ △EFD.

1. Match each congruence rule to the pair(s) of triangles you can use it with.

a) Rule SAS: _B_   b) Rule ASA: ____   c) Rule SSS: ____   d) Rule SAA: ____   e) No rule: ____

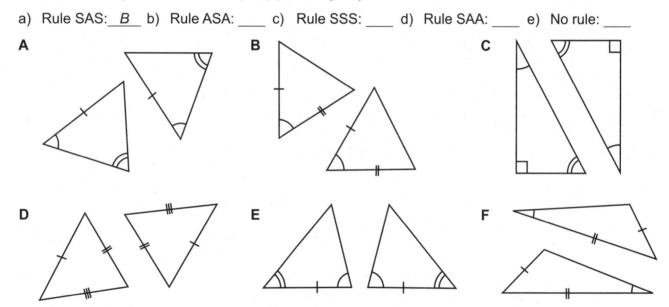

A   B   C

D   E   F

2. Which congruence rule(s) could you use to show that these triangles are congruent?
   For each rule, tell which piece of information you do not need to use.

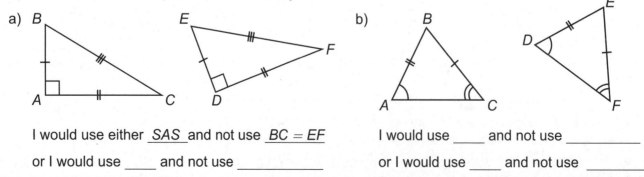

a)

I would use either _SAS_ and not use _BC = EF_

or I would use ____ and not use _____

b)

I would use ____ and not use _____

or I would use ____ and not use _____

3. Which two triangles below are congruent? _____

Which congruence rule can you use to show it? _____

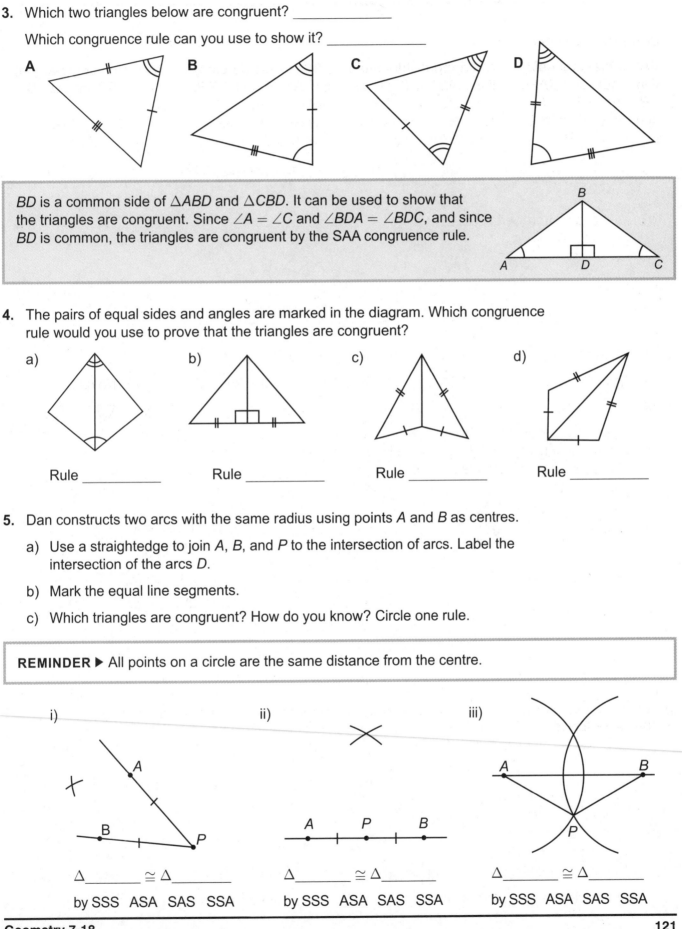

A

B

C

D

BD is a common side of △ABD and △CBD. It can be used to show that the triangles are congruent. Since ∠A = ∠C and ∠BDA = ∠BDC, and since BD is common, the triangles are congruent by the SAA congruence rule.

4. The pairs of equal sides and angles are marked in the diagram. Which congruence rule would you use to prove that the triangles are congruent?

a)

Rule _____

b)

Rule _____

c)

Rule _____

d)

Rule _____

5. Dan constructs two arcs with the same radius using points A and B as centres.

a) Use a straightedge to join A, B, and P to the intersection of arcs. Label the intersection of the arcs D.

b) Mark the equal line segments.

c) Which triangles are congruent? How do you know? Circle one rule.

REMINDER ▶ All points on a circle are the same distance from the centre.

i)

△_____ ≅ △_____

by SSS ASA SAS SSA

ii)

△_____ ≅ △_____

by SSS ASA SAS SSA

iii)

△_____ ≅ △_____

by SSS ASA SAS SSA

G7-19 The Isosceles Triangle Theorem

A **median** of a triangle is a line segment connecting a vertex to the midpoint of the opposite side.

How to draw a median from vertex *A*:

Step 1: Identify the side opposite to *A*.

Step 2: Use a ruler to find the midpoint of the side opposite to *A*.

Step 3: Draw the median.

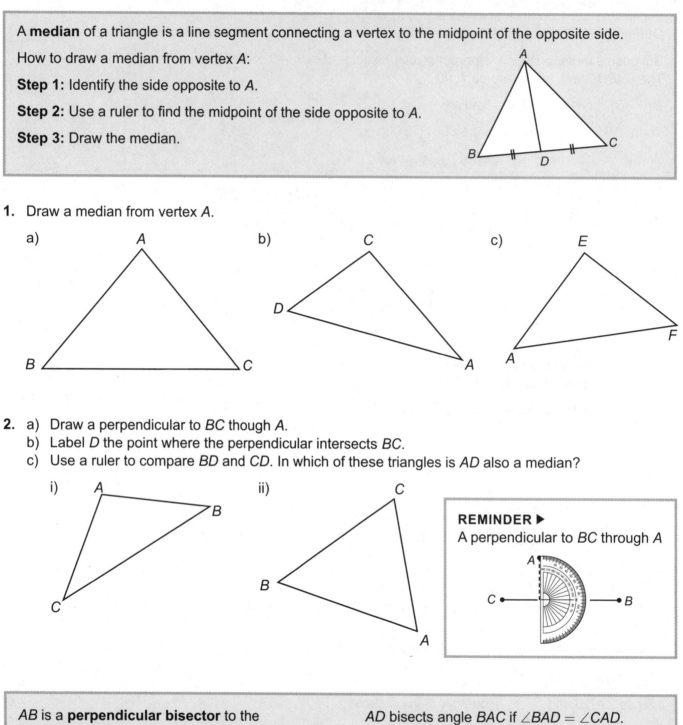

1. Draw a median from vertex *A*.

a)

b)

c)

2. a) Draw a perpendicular to *BC* though *A*.
   b) Label *D* the point where the perpendicular intersects *BC*.
   c) Use a ruler to compare *BD* and *CD*. In which of these triangles is *AD* also a median?

   i)

   ii)

   REMINDER ▶
   A perpendicular to *BC* through *A*

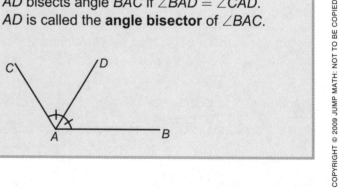

AB is a **perpendicular bisector** to the line segment *CD*. *AB* ⊥ *CD* and *BC* = *BD*

AD bisects angle *BAC* if ∠*BAD* = ∠*CAD*. *AD* is called the **angle bisector** of ∠*BAC*.

If a median is perpendicular to the side it bisects, it is also a perpendicular bisector to that side!
Question: In which types of triangle (if any) will a median be a perpendicular bisector?

Suppose a median *BD* is the perpendicular bisector of side *AC* of △*ABC*.
Then ∠*BDA* and ∠*BDC* are each 90°.

DA = *DC* because *BD* is a median.

Then, △*ABD* is congruent to △*CBD*, by SAS.

So, *AB* = *BC*. This means △*ABC* is isosceles.

We have just proved the following: *If a median in a triangle is a perpendicular bisector, the triangle is isosceles.*

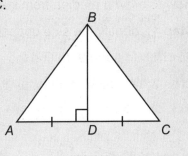

3. Jordan makes a conjecture: In an isosceles triangle, a median is a perpendicular bisector.

   a) Does Jordan's conjecture mean the same as the statement below? _____

      In an isosceles triangle, a median is any perpendicular bisector.

   b) Is Jordan's conjecture true for any median in any isosceles triangle? Draw all the medians in the triangle at right. Check Jordan's conjecture.

   c) How could you improve Jordan's conjecture?

      _____

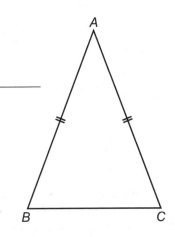

4. Ariel makes a better conjecture than Jordan's: In an isosceles triangle, a median to the unequal side is also the perpendicular bisector.

   Fill in the blanks to prove Ariel's conjecture. Use the information in the diagram at right.

   Assume △*ABC* is isosceles, and *BD* is the median to the unequal side.

   Then *AB* = _____, *AD* = _____, and *BD* is the common side of △*ABD* and △*CBD*.

   Then △*ABD* ≅ △_____, by congruence rule _____.

   This means ∠*ADB* = ∠_____.

   Since ∠*ADB* and _____ together make a straight (180°) angle,

   they must each be _____°. This means *BD* ⊥ *AC*.

   So the median *BD* is also a perpendicular bisector of the side _____.

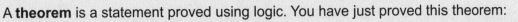

A **theorem** is a statement proved using logic. You have just proved this theorem:

In an isosceles triangle, the median to the unequal side is also the perpendicular bisector.

5. Conjecture: *If a triangle is isosceles, then the median to the unequal side will be an angle bisector.*

Prove the conjecture:

a) Sketch an isosceles triangle *ABC*, so that *AC* is the unequal side. Draw the median to *AC*. Label the median *BD*. Mark the line segments that are equal on your diagram.

b) Which triangles are congruent in your diagram? By which congruence rules?

c) Which angles are equal in △*ABD* and △*CBD*?

d) Which of the three pairs of equal angles in part c) can you use to conclude that *BD* bisects ∠*ABC*?

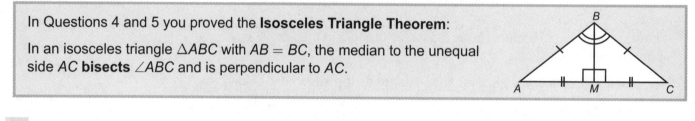

In Questions 4 and 5 you proved the **Isosceles Triangle Theorem**:

In an isosceles triangle △*ABC* with *AB* = *BC*, the median to the unequal side *AC* **bisects** ∠*ABC* and is perpendicular to *AC*.

6. In △*ABC*, *AB* = *BC* and *M* is the midpoint of *AC*. Sketch the triangle and draw *BM*. Cross out the statements that are not true.

BM is a median of △*ABC*

BM is a line of symmetry for △*ABC*

△*BMA* is an isosceles triangle

BM ⊥ *AC*

BM bisects ∠*ABC*

AM = *AB*

BM is a perpendicular bisector of *AC*

△*BMC* is an equilateral triangle

∠*ABM* has to be 45°

BM ∥ *BC*

BM bisects ∠*BAM*

△*ABM* ≅ △*CBM*

7. Which of *DC*, *BE*, *AF* is an angle bisector? How can you check using only a ruler?

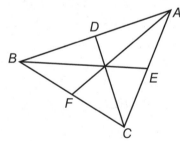

8. Which sides are equal in △*ABC*? Using a ruler only, bisect the angle between the equal sides in △*ABC*. Hint: Use the Isosceles Triangle Theorem.

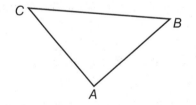

9. Bisect the angle using only a ruler. Hint: Create an isosceles triangle.

a)

b)

c) Extend the short arm first.

10. Explain why your method in Questions 8 and 9 works.

How to construct an **angle bisector**:

Step 1: Construct arc *TS* across each arm of the angle, with arc centre at *Q*, the vertex of the angle.

Step 2: With your compass point at *S*, construct an arc in the interior of the angle as shown.

Step 3: With your compass point at *T* (and without changing the compass setting from Step 2), construct an arc as shown. Label the intersection *U*.

Step 4: Use a straightedge to construct a line from *Q* through *U*. *QU* is the **bisector** of ∠*PQR*.

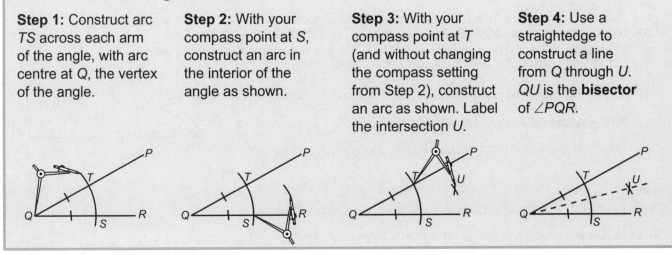

1. The arcs intersecting at *R* have centres *P* and *Q*. They have the same radius.

    a) *QR* = _____   *OP* = _____

    b) Construct the bisector of ∠*QOP*.

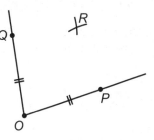

2. a) Use a compass to construct *B* and *D* so that *AB* = *AD*.

    b) Use a compass to construct a point *C* (different from *A*) so that *BC* = *CD*.

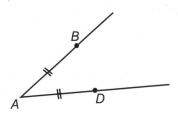

    c) Draw the angle bisector of ∠*A* on the second diagram.

3. Complete Steps 2, 3 and 4 to construct a bisector of ∠*PQR*.

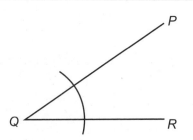

4. Construct a bisector of ∠*PQR*.

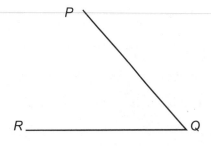

5. Draw one acute and one obtuse angle. Then construct a bisector for each of them, using a compass and a straightedge.

6. a) This diagram is from Step 4 of constructing an angle bisector. Mark the line segments you know are equal.

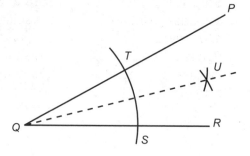

b) Construct *TU* and *SU*. What do you know about them?

_____

c) Which two triangles are congruent? _____

d) Which congruence rule can you use to explain why *QU* is an

angle bisector? _____

REMINDER ▶ The sum of the angles in any triangle is 180°.

---

7. The equal sides are marked. Mark the equal angles. Which triangle is isosceles? Which is equilateral?

a)

b)

8. △*ABC* is an equilateral triangle.

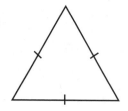

a) What is the angle measure of the angles in ∠*ABC*? _____° ÷ 3 = _____°

b) Construct an angle bisector *AD* of ∠*A* with a compass and a straightedge.

c) Find the measure of the angles: ∠*CAD* = _____, ∠*CDA* = _____

9. To construct two lines that intersect at 60°, Yen constructs an equilateral triangle and extends two of the sides.

a) Explain how could you use Yen's method and angle bisectors to construct two lines that intersect at 30°.

_____

_____

_____

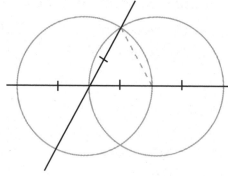

b) Construct two lines that intersect at 30°.

Geometry 7-20

G7-21 Constructing Perpendicular Lines

How to construct a **perpendicular line** through a point on a line:

Step 1: Put your compass point at C and draw arc DE. Points D and E on the line are the same distance from C.

Step 2: Enlarge the settings of your compass (move the arms farther apart). With your compass point at D, mark off a short arc above C.

Step 3: With your compass at E, (keeping it at the same setting as in Step 2), draw a second arc as shown. Label the point of intersection of the arcs F.

Step 4: Using a straightedge, draw a line FC. FC is the **perpendicular** to DE through C.

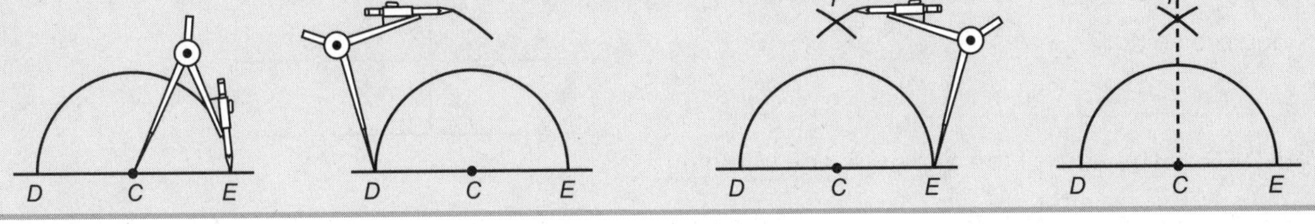

1. Construct a line perpendicular to the given line through C.

a)

b)

INVESTIGATION ▶ Why do the four steps above produce a pair of perpendicular lines?

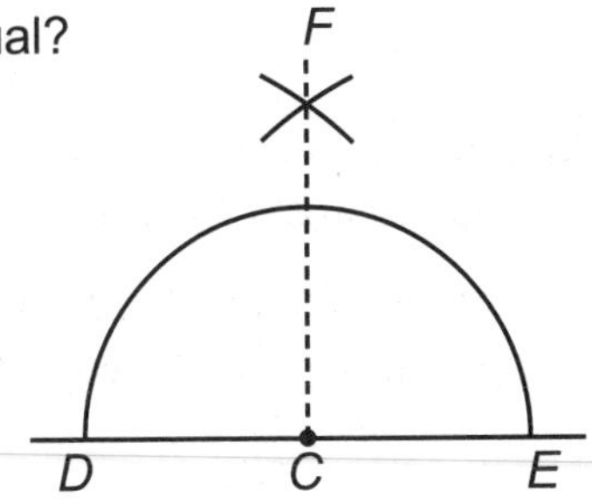

A. This is the diagram from Step 4. Connect D and E to F. You have constructed an isosceles triangle, △DEF.

B. Since △DEF is isosceles, which pair of angles in △DEF do you know are equal? Mark this information on the diagram.

C. Is △DFC congruent to △EFC? _____ If yes, by which congruence rule?

D. What is the sum of ∠DCF + ∠ECF? _____

How do you know? _____

E. Are ∠DCF and ∠ECF equal? _____

How do you know? _____

If ∠DCF and ∠ECF are equal, what do you know about ∠DCF and ∠ECF?

_____

F. Which two line segments in the diagram are perpendicular?

_____

G7-22 Constructing Parallel Lines

Two lines are **parallel** if they are straight and they are the same distance apart everywhere.

Parallel lines never intersect.

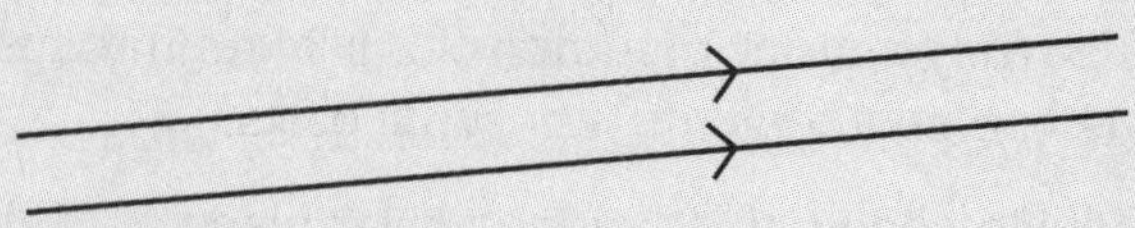

1. Which lines on the diagram look like they are parallel? Mark those lines using the parallel line marks (>, >>).

   a)

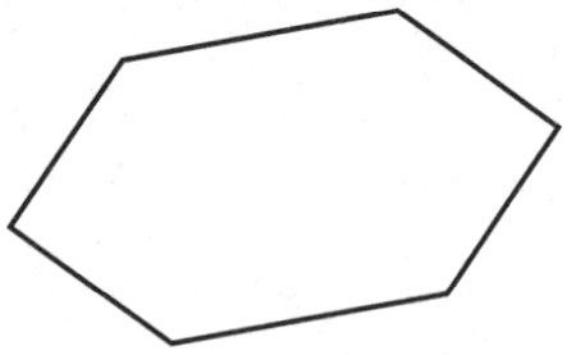

   b)

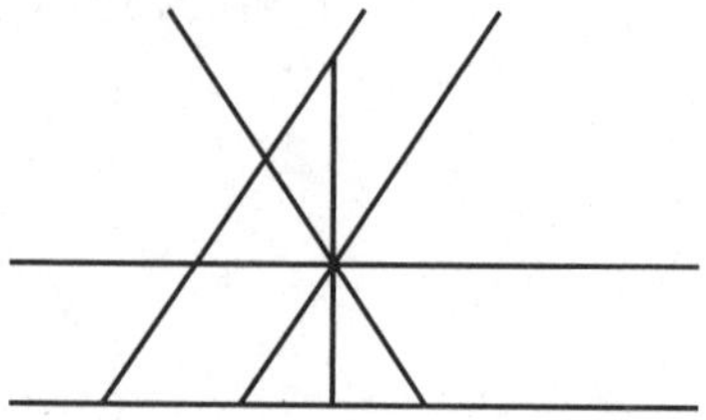

How to construct a line **parallel** to AB:

Step 1: Construct perpendicular CD to AB at any point (using the method described in lesson G7-21).

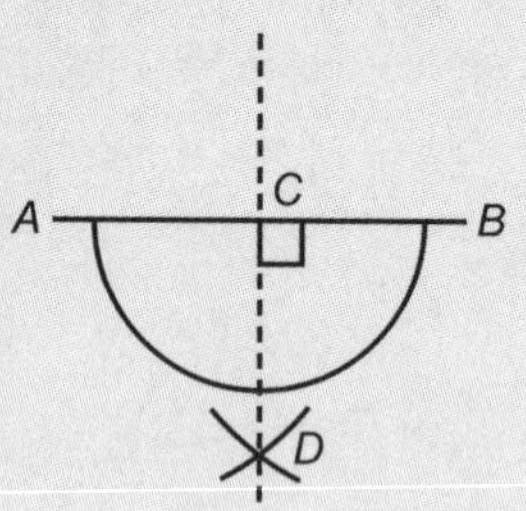

Step 2: Construct perpendicular EF to CD (using the same method). EF is **parallel** to AB.

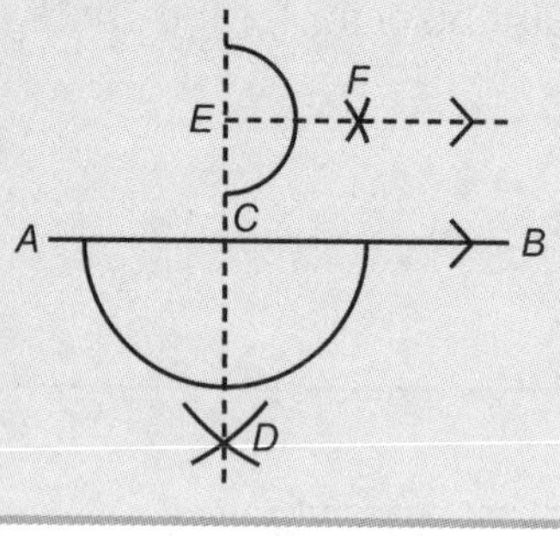

2. Construct a line parallel to the line segment.

   a)

   b)

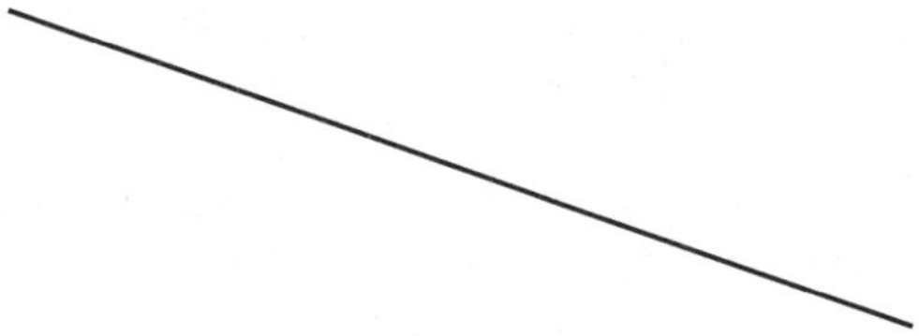

3. a) Ling constructed lines KM and LN using the method above. Mark the right angles on Ling's diagram.

   b) Ling says: "I think KM intersects LN at some point F, only this point is very far away." If Ling is correct, what is the sum of the angles in △KLF?

   $$\underline{\hspace{1.5cm}} + \underline{\hspace{1.5cm}} + \angle KFL = \underline{\hspace{1.5cm}} + \angle KFL$$
   $$\quad\angle KLF \qquad \angle LKF$$

   c) Could there be such a triangle as △KLF? Explain.

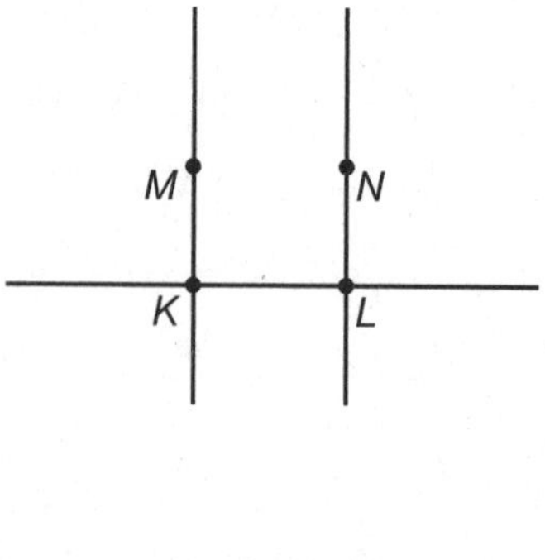

A **perpendicular bisector** of a line segment is a perpendicular that divides the line segment into two equal parts.

How to construct a perpendicular bisector of *AB*:

Step 1: Put your compass point at one end of the line segment. Construct an arc as shown.

Step 2: With your compass at the same radius, construct a second arc centred at *B* as shown.

Step 3: Construct a line ℓ through the intersection points of the two arcs. This is the perpendicular bisector of *AB*.

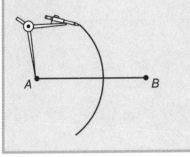

1. Construct a perpendicular bisector for the line segment.

   a)

   b)

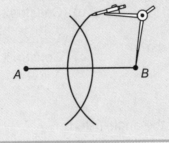

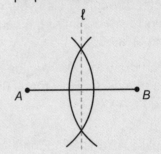

2. ∠*POQ* = 90°. Find the measure of the angles.

   ∠*QOR* _____   ∠*POR* _____

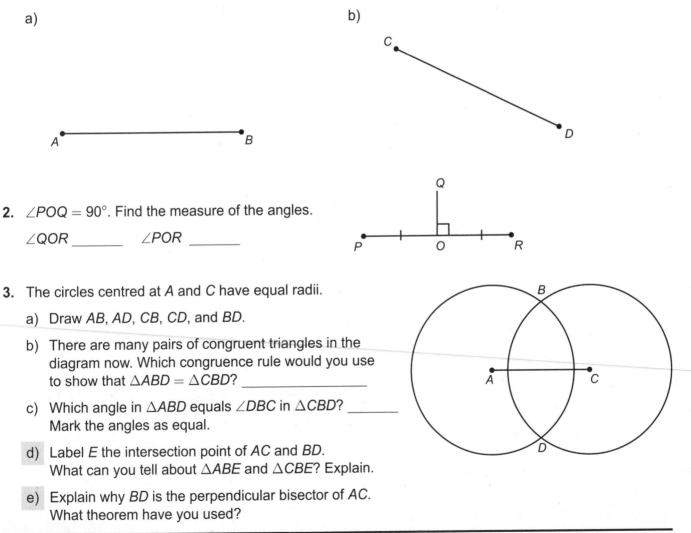

3. The circles centred at *A* and *C* have equal radii.

   a) Draw *AB*, *AD*, *CB*, *CD*, and *BD*.

   b) There are many pairs of congruent triangles in the diagram now. Which congruence rule would you use to show that △*ABD* = △*CBD*? _____

   c) Which angle in △*ABD* equals ∠*DBC* in △*CBD*? _____ Mark the angles as equal.

   d) Label *E* the intersection point of *AC* and *BD*. What can you tell about △*ABE* and △*CBE*? Explain.

   e) Explain why *BD* is the perpendicular bisector of *AC*. What theorem have you used?

A **central angle** is an angle that has its vertex at the centre of a circle.

4. a) Construct a circle. Then construct two
        perpendicular lines passing through its
        centre. Use your diagram to explain why the
        sum of the central angles in a circle is 360°.

    b) Construct a circle with centre *P*. Draw a
        diameter through *P*. Use your diagram to
        explain why the sum of the central angles
        in a circle is 360°.

    c) You can draw four 90° angles through the
        centre of a circle. How many 60° angles
        can you draw?

5. Use a compass and a straightedge. Construct
    a pair of perpendicular lines.

    a) Choose one of the angles you constructed
        and construct an angle bisector for it. What
        is the degree measure of the resulting
        angles?

    b) Construct a pair of lines that intersects at
        a 45° angle.

    c) Construct a triangle with two angles of 45°
        and a side of 6 cm between them.

6. In all cases, ∠*ABC* is 60°. Find the size of the angle listed.

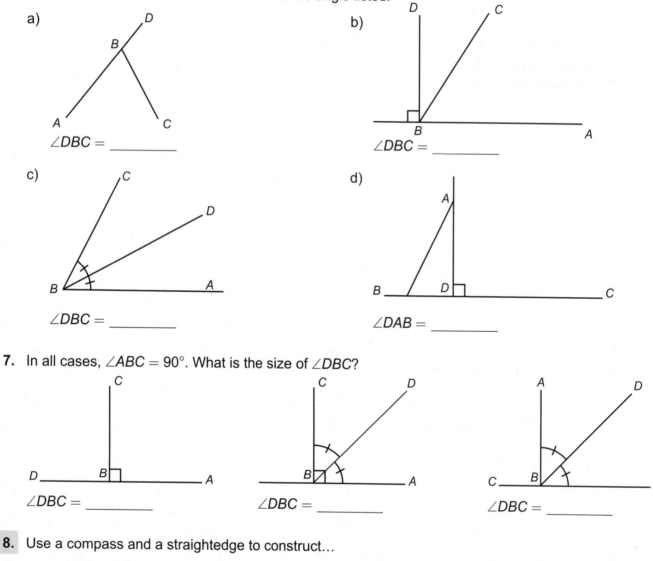

a)

∠*DBC* = _____

b)

∠*DBC* = _____

c)

∠*DBC* = _____

d)

∠*DAB* = _____

7. In all cases, ∠*ABC* = 90°. What is the size of ∠*DBC*?

∠*DBC* = _____

∠*DBC* = _____

∠*DBC* = _____

8. Use a compass and a straightedge to construct...

    a) a line that intersects another line at 120°.

    b) a line that intersects another line at 135°.

G7-24 More Perpendicular and Parallel Lines

1. Sketch two triangles that could be congruent by the following rule.

    a) SAS (side-angle-side)   b) ASA (angle-side-angle)   c) SSS (side-side-side)

2. *CD* is the perpendicular bisector of the line segment *AB*, so that *D* is on *AB*.

    a) Sketch the lines.

    b) What do you know about *AD* and *BD*? _____

    c) What is the degree measure of $\angle ADC$? _____

    d) What is the degree measure of $\angle BDC$? _____

    e) What do you know about $\triangle ADC$ and $\triangle BDC$? Explain.

    f) What can you then say about *AC* and *BC*? _____

    g) Mark another point *E* on the perpendicular bisector of *AB*. What can you say about *AE* and *BE*?

    h) Extend *CD* past *AB*. Does it matter on which side of *AB* the point *E* is? Explain.

    i) Does it matter how far from *AB* the point *E* is?

    j) Look at the triangle $\triangle ABC$. *CD* is a perpendicular bisector of the side *AB*. What are two other names for the line segment *CD* in $\triangle ABC$? _____

> Any point on the perpendicular bisector of a line segment *AB* is the same distance from each endpoint of the line segment. We call such points **equidistant** from points *A* and *B*.

INVESTIGATION ▶ Are **all** points on the perpendicular bisector of *AB* equidistant from *A* and *B*? Could there be a point *C* that is **not** on the perpendicular bisector of *AB* and for which $AC = BC$?

The point *C* is equidistant from *A* and *B*. This means $AC = $ _____

A. What type of triangle is $\triangle ABC$? _____

B. Using a protractor or a square corner, construct a perpendicular from *C* to *AB*. Label the intersection point *D*.

C. Can it be that $CD \perp AB$, but *CD* does not bisect *AB*? Explain.

---

3. $AC = BC = 6$ cm. Point *D* is the midpoint of *AB*. $\angle A = 60°$.

Mark this information on the sketch.

How long is *BD*? How do you know?

_____

_____

_____

1. Write a plus sign (+) if the net result is a gain. Write a minus sign (−) if the net result is a loss.

    a) a gain of $4 ____+____

    b) a loss of $2 _____

    c) a gain of $3_____

    d) a gain of $1 and a loss of $4 ____−____

    e) a gain of $4 and a loss of $2 _____

    f) a loss of $2 and a gain of $3 _____

    g) a loss of $5 and a gain of $1 _____

2. Write each sequence of gains and losses using numbers and signs (+ and −).

    a) a gain of $3 and a loss of $5 ____+ 3 − 5____

    b) a loss of $3 and a gain of $7 ____− 3 + 7____

    c) a loss of $5 and a gain of $4 _____

    d) a gain of $7 and a loss of $6 _____

    e) a loss of $6, a gain of $9, a loss of $3, then a gain of $2 _____− 6 + 9 − 3 + 2_____

    f) a gain of $2, a gain of $4, a loss of $5, then a gain of $1 _____

    g) a loss of $4, a loss of $7, a gain of $9, then a gain of $4 _____

    h) a gain of $3, a loss of $2, a loss of $1, then a gain of $4 _____

3. Decide whether each sequence of gains and losses is a net gain (+) or a net loss (−).

    a) $+ 5 − 3$ ___+___

    b) $+ 3 − 5$ _____

    c) $− 4 + 3$ _____

    d) $− 6 + 1$ _____

    e) $+ 9 − 8$ _____

    f) $+ 6 − 9$ _____

    g) $− 3 + 6$ _____

    h) $− 1 + 34$ _____

    i) $− 8 + 35$ _____

4. How much was gained or lost overall? Use + for a gain, − for a loss, and 0 for no gain or loss.

    a) $+ 6 − 5 =$ ___+ 1___

    b) $− 4 + 3 =$ _____

    c) $+ 5 − 5 =$ _____

    d) $− 6 + 6 =$ _____

    e) $− 3 + 5 =$ _____

    f) $+ 7 − 11 =$ _____

    g) $+ 4 + 2 =$ _____

    h) $− 3 − 1 =$ _____

    i) $− 6 − 2 =$ _____

    j) $− 6 + 2 =$ _____

    k) $+ 6 − 2 =$ _____

    l) $+ 6 + 2 =$ _____

    m) $+ 3 − 8 =$ _____

    n) $− 5 + 2 =$ _____

    o) $+ 9 − 4 =$ _____

    p) $− 5 + 7 =$ _____

    q) $− 3 + 3 =$ _____

    r) $+ 8 − 87 =$ _____

5. Group the gains (+'s) together and the losses (−'s) together. Then write the total gain and the total loss.

    a) $+ 4 − 3 + 2 =$ ____+ 4 + 2 − 3____

        $=$ ____+ 6 − 3____

    b) $− 3 + 4 − 2 =$ _____

        $=$ _____

    c) $− 6 + 8 − 4 =$ _____

        $=$ _____

    d) $+ 9 − 6 + 2 =$ _____

        $=$ _____

BONUS ▶ $− 3 + 4 + 2 − 1 − 5 + 4 + 1 + 2 − 3 =$ _____

$=$ _____

6. Circle all the gains first. Then group the gains (+'s) and losses (−'s). Then say how much was gained or lost overall.

a) $+7-6+2=$ _____

$=$ _____

$=$ _____

b) $+5-7+4=$ _____

$=$ _____

$=$ _____

c) $-5-1\,\boxed{+3}\,-2\,\boxed{+4}\,\boxed{+6}\,-4=$ _$+3+4+6-5-1-2-4$_

$=$ _$+13-12$_

$=$ _$+1$_

d) $+6+3-4-5-8+2-1=$ _____

$=$ _____

$=$ _____

e) $-4+5+6-3-2+8-5+1-4=$ _____

$=$ _____

$=$ _____

> When the same number is gained and lost, the two numbers add 0 to the expression, so we can cancel them.

7. Cancel the numbers that make 0. Then write the total gain or loss.

a) $-\cancel{3}+7+\cancel{3}=$ _$+7$_

b) $-5-2+5=$ _____

c) $+3+4-3=$ _____

d) $-6-4+6=$ _____

e) $-8+7+8=$ _____

f) $-4+4+2=$ _____

g) $+3+5-5=$ _____

h) $-8-6+6=$ _____

i) $-7-8+7=$ _____

j) $+8-3+4+3-4=$ _____

k) $-3+4+2+3-2=$ _____

l) $-8+8-6+7-7=$ _____

m) $-4-3+2+3-2=$ _____

n) $-5-4+4-3+5=$ _____

o) $+6-5-6-2+5=$ _____

p) $-\cancel{3}+\cancel{2}+4-5-\cancel{2}+\cancel{6}+\cancel{3}-\cancel{6}=$ _$+4-5$_

these cancel

$=$ _-1_

q) $-5+2+6-2+3+4+5-3=$ _____

$=$ _____

r) $+8-10-4+7-2+10-7-4=$ _____

$=$ _____

s) $-4-3+2-7+4+2+3=$ _____

$=$ _____

8. Find the mistake in the cancelling. Circle the two numbers that should not have been cancelled.

$-\cancel{3}+\cancel{4}+2+6-\cancel{2}+\cancel{3}+\cancel{4}-\cancel{7}+\cancel{7}=+6$

An **integer** is any one of these numbers: ..., –4, –3, –2, –1, 0, 1, 2, 3, 4, ...

Sometimes the numbers 1, 2, 3, 4, ... are written +1, +2, +3, +4, ...

An integer is **less than** another integer if it is **farther left** on the number line.

←——— smaller   larger ——→

```
 ←—+——+——+——+——+——+——+——+——+——+——+——+——+——+——+——+——→
   –8  –7  –6  –5  –4  –3  –2  –1   0   1   2   3   4   5   6   7   8
```

1. Write three integers that are less than zero. _____   _____   _____

Integers that are **greater than 0** are called **positive**. Integers that are **less than 0** are called **negative**.

2. Circle the integers that are positive.   +5   8   –2   10   +3   +9   –4   –12

3. Circle the least integer in each pair.

   a) –4 or +6   b) –7 or –4   c) 9 or 7   d) –2 or –4
   e) 9 or –4   f) +7 or +2   g) –3 or –4   h) –7 or –5

4. Write < (less than) or > (greater than) in each box.

   a) +2 ☐ +7   b) –6 ☐ +5   c) 5 ☐ –3   d) –2 ☐ –4   e) –4 ☐ –10

5. Write two integers that are between –8 and –3. _____ and _____

6. Mark each integer on the number line with an X and label it with the correct letter.

   A +4   **B** –2   **C** +6   **D** –3   **E** –5

```
 ←—+——+——+——+——+——+——+——+——+——+——+——+——+——+——+——+——→
   –8                           0                            8
```

7. Put the integers into the boxes in **increasing** order.

   + 6   –1   +10   –8   –3   ☐ ☐ ☐ ☐ ☐

8. Put the temperatures into the boxes in order from hottest to coldest.

   14°C   –16°C   27°C   –15°C   –41°C   ☐ ☐ ☐ ☐ ☐

9. a) If $0 < a < b$, mark possible places for a and b on the number line.

   b) Mark $-a$ and $-b$ on the same number line.

   c) Write the correct symbol (< or >) in each box.

```
   ————————————————+————————————————
                    0
```

   If $0 < a < b$, then 0 ☐ $-a$ ☐ $-b$.

A negative integer can represent a loss and a positive integer can represent a gain.

1. Write the gain or loss represented by the integer.

    a) –6 _loss of 6_   b) +4 _____   c) –1 _____   d) +9 _____

> Any sequence of gains and losses can be written as a sum of integers.
>
> Example: $-3 + 4 - 5 = (-3) + (+4) + (-5)$
>
> $\qquad\qquad\quad = (-3) + 4 + (-5).$

2. Write each sequence of gains and losses as a sum of integers.

    a) $+4 - 3 - 5$ _____ $4 + (-3) + (-5)$ _____   b) $-2 + 6 - 3$ _____

    c) $+4 + 2 - 6$ _____   d) $+7 - 5 - 4$ _____

    e) $-3 + 2 + 4$ _____   f) $-3 + 5 - 4$ _____

3. Write each sum of integers as a sequence of gains and losses.

    a) $(+2) + (-7) = $ _$+2 - 7$_ b) $(+2) + (+7) = $ _____ c) $(-2) + (+7) = $ _____ d) $(-2) + (-7) = $ _____

    e) $(+a) + (-b) = $ _____ f) $(+a) + (+b) = $ _____ g) $(-a) + (+b) = $ _____ h) $(-a) + (-b) = $ _____

4. Add the integers by first writing the sum as a sequence of gains and losses.

    a) $(+5) + (-2) = $ _$+5 - 2$_   b) $(-3) + (+4) = $ _____   c) $(-5) + (-4) = $ _____

    $\qquad\qquad\quad = $ _$+3$_ $\qquad\qquad = $ _____ $\qquad\qquad = $ _____

    d) $(+3) + (+4) = $ _____   e) $(-3) + (-8) = $ _____   f) $(-7) + (+9) = $ _____

    $\qquad\qquad = $ _____ $\qquad\qquad = $ _____ $\qquad\qquad = $ _____

    g) $(+5) + (-2) + (+3) = $ _$+5 - 2 + 3$_   h) $(-6) + (+3) + (+5) = $ _____

    $\qquad\qquad\quad = + $ _8_ $ - $ _2_ $ = $ _$+6$_ $\qquad\qquad\quad = + $ ___ $ - $ ___ $ = $ ___

    i) $3 + (-5) + (-2) + 6$ j) $(-2) + (-5) + 4 + 3$ k) $4 + 0 + (-5) + (-3)$ l) $3 + 5 + (-5) + (-3)$

> Integers that add to 0 are called **opposite integers**.
>
> Example: $+3$ and -3 are opposite integers because $(+3) + (-3) = +3 - 3 = 0$.

5. Write the opposite of each integer.

    a) The opposite of $+2$ is _____.   b) The opposite of -5 is _____.

    c) The opposite of 3 is _____.   d) The opposite of -142 is _____.

    BONUS ▶ The opposite of 0 is _____.

6. Add the integers by cancelling the opposite integers.

a) $(+5) + (-5) + (+3) =$ ___+3___ b) $(-5) + 7 + (-7) =$ _____

c) $(+5) + (-4) + (+4) =$ _____ d) $(-4) + (+6) + (-6) =$ _____

e) $(+4) + (-1) + (+1) =$ _____ f) $(+8) + (-8) + (+2) =$ _____

g) $(-6) + 6 + (-3) =$ _____ h) $(+9) + (-9) + (+4) =$ _____

All integers can be written as sums of +1s or –1s.

Examples: $3 = (+1) + (+1) + (+1) = 1 + 1 + 1$ $-3 = (-1) + (-1) + (-1) = -1 - 1 - 1$

7. Write each number as a sum of +1s and –1s. Then find the sum by cancelling pairs of +1s and –1s.

a) $(+4) + (-2) =$ ___+2___
$+1 + 1 + \cancel{1} + \cancel{1} + \cancel{1} - \cancel{1} - \cancel{1}$

b) $(-2) + (-1) =$ _____

c) $(+6) + (-7) =$ _____

d) $(+5) + (-3) =$ _____

e) $(+4) + (+5) =$ _____

f) $(-1) + (-2) =$ _____

g) $(-3) + (-2) =$ _____

h) $(-2) + (+2) =$ _____

Remember: Two losses add to a bigger loss. Example: $-7 - 2 = -9$

A gain and a loss cancel each other. Example: $-8 + 6 = -2$

8. Add the integers mentally. Hint: Start by writing + or – to show whether you have a net gain or a net loss.

a) $(+5) + (-6)$
$= -1$

b) $(+2) + (-6)$
$=$

c) $(+2) + (+4)$
$=$

d) $(-3) + (-5)$
$=$

e) $(-7) + (+10)$
$=$

f) $(-3) + (+3)$
$=$

g) $(-2) + (-8)$
$=$

h) $(-3) + (-4)$
$=$

i) $(-4) + (-8)$
$=$

j) $(-5) + (+3)$
$=$

k) $(-2) + (-3)$
$=$

l) $(-15) + (+20)$
$=$

9. Decide whether each statement is true or false. If you circle false, give a counter-example.

a) The sum of two negative integers is negative.   T   F

b) If you add a negative integer to a positive integer, the result is negative.   T   F

NS7-89 Adding Integers on a Number Line

To add a negative integer, **move left**.

Example: **(+3) + (−4)** = + 3 − 4, so subtract 4 from +3. Start at +3 and move left 4 places.

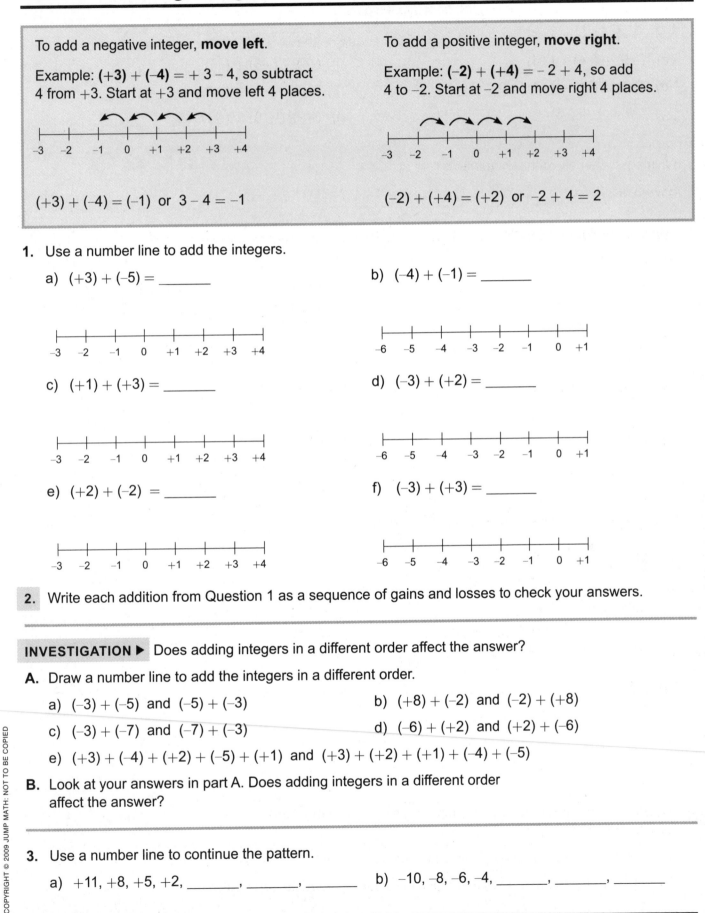

(+3) + (−4) = (−1) or 3 − 4 = −1

To add a positive integer, **move right**.

Example: **(−2) + (+4)** = − 2 + 4, so add 4 to −2. Start at −2 and move right 4 places.

(−2) + (+4) = (+2) or −2 + 4 = 2

1. Use a number line to add the integers.

   a) (+3) + (−5) = _____

   b) (−4) + (−1) = _____

   c) (+1) + (+3) = _____

   d) (−3) + (+2) = _____

   e) (+2) + (−2) = _____

   f) (−3) + (+3) = _____

2. Write each addition from Question 1 as a sequence of gains and losses to check your answers.

INVESTIGATION ▶ Does adding integers in a different order affect the answer?

A. Draw a number line to add the integers in a different order.

   a) (−3) + (−5) and (−5) + (−3)

   b) (+8) + (−2) and (−2) + (+8)

   c) (−3) + (−7) and (−7) + (−3)

   d) (−6) + (+2) and (+2) + (−6)

   e) (+3) + (−4) + (+2) + (−5) + (+1) and (+3) + (+2) + (+1) + (−4) + (−5)

B. Look at your answers in part A. Does adding integers in a different order affect the answer?

3. Use a number line to continue the pattern.

   a) +11, +8, +5, +2, _____, _____, _____

   b) −10, −8, −6, −4, _____, _____, _____

Subtracting Integers on a Number Line

Subtraction undoes addition, so to subtract an integer, do the opposite of what you would do to add the integer.

Example: $(-5) - (-2)$ To add (-2), move ___2___ units to the ___left___.

To subtract (-2), move ___2___ units to the ___right___.

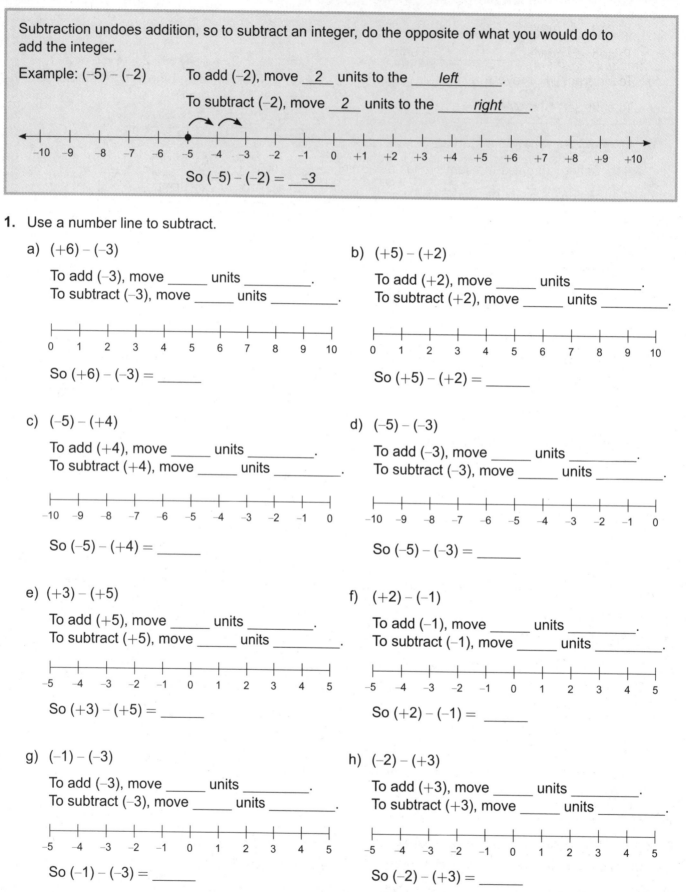

So $(-5) - (-2) = $ ___-3___

1. Use a number line to subtract.

a) $(+6) - (-3)$

To add (-3), move _____ units _____.
To subtract (-3), move _____ units _____.

So $(+6) - (-3) = $ _____

b) $(+5) - (+2)$

To add $(+2)$, move _____ units _____.
To subtract $(+2)$, move _____ units _____.

So $(+5) - (+2) = $ _____

c) $(-5) - (+4)$

To add $(+4)$, move _____ units _____.
To subtract $(+4)$, move _____ units _____.

So $(-5) - (+4) = $ _____

d) $(-5) - (-3)$

To add (-3), move _____ units _____.
To subtract (-3), move _____ units _____.

So $(-5) - (-3) = $ _____

e) $(+3) - (+5)$

To add $(+5)$, move _____ units _____.
To subtract $(+5)$, move _____ units _____.

So $(+3) - (+5) = $ _____

f) $(+2) - (-1)$

To add (-1), move _____ units _____.
To subtract (-1), move _____ units _____.

So $(+2) - (-1) = $ _____

g) $(-1) - (-3)$

To add (-3), move _____ units _____.
To subtract (-3), move _____ units _____.

So $(-1) - (-3) = $ _____

h) $(-2) - (+3)$

To add $(+3)$, move _____ units _____.
To subtract $(+3)$, move _____ units _____.

So $(-2) - (+3) = $ _____

2. a) Would you move **left** or **right** on a number line?

To add +5, move _____ 5 units.

To add –5, move _____ 5 units.

To subtract +5, move _____ 5 units.

To subtract –5, move _____ 5 units.

b) Look at your answers in part a).

Subtracting +5 gives the same result as adding _____ so ☐ – (+5) = ☐ + _____.

Subtracting –5 gives the same result as adding _____ so ☐ – (–5) = ☐ + _____.

3. Write each difference as a sum and then calculate the answer.

a) $(-3) - (-5) = (-3) + \underline{\quad 5 \quad}$
  $= \underline{\quad\quad}$

b) $(+2) - (+5) = (+2) + \underline{\quad\quad}$
  $= \underline{\quad\quad}$

c) $(+4) - (-7) = (+4) + \underline{\quad\quad}$
  $= \underline{\quad\quad}$

d) $(-3) - (+6) = (-3) + \underline{\quad\quad}$
  $= \underline{\quad\quad}$

e) $(-1) - (+6) = (-1) + \underline{\quad\quad}$
  $= \underline{\quad\quad}$

f) $(+3) - (-8) = (+3) + \underline{\quad\quad}$
  $= \underline{\quad\quad}$

4. Write the correct integer in the blank.

a) $x - (-3) = x + \underline{\quad\quad}$

b) $x - (+7) = x + \underline{\quad\quad}$

c) $x - (-25) = x + \underline{\quad\quad}$

5. Subtract by continuing the pattern.

a)
$9 - 4 = \underline{\quad\quad}$
$9 - 3 = \underline{\quad\quad}$
$9 - 2 = \underline{\quad\quad}$
$9 - 1 = \underline{\quad\quad}$
$9 - 0 = \underline{\quad\quad}$
$9 - (-1) = \underline{\quad\quad}$
$9 - (-2) = \underline{\quad\quad}$
$9 - (-3) = \underline{\quad\quad}$
$9 - (-4) = \underline{\quad\quad}$
$9 - (-36) = \underline{\quad\quad}$

b)
$5 - 4 = \underline{\quad\quad}$
$5 - 3 = \underline{\quad\quad}$
$5 - 2 = \underline{\quad\quad}$
$5 - 1 = \underline{\quad\quad}$
$5 - 0 = \underline{\quad\quad}$
$5 - (-1) = \underline{\quad\quad}$
$5 - (-2) = \underline{\quad\quad}$
$5 - (-3) = \underline{\quad\quad}$
$5 - (-4) = \underline{\quad\quad}$
$5 - (-36) = \underline{\quad\quad}$

c)
$12 - 4 = \underline{\quad\quad}$
$12 - 3 = \underline{\quad\quad}$
$12 - 2 = \underline{\quad\quad}$
$12 - 1 = \underline{\quad\quad}$
$12 - 0 = \underline{\quad\quad}$
$12 - (-1) = \underline{\quad\quad}$
$12 - (-2) = \underline{\quad\quad}$
$12 - (-3) = \underline{\quad\quad}$
$12 - (-4) = \underline{\quad\quad}$
$12 - (-36) = \underline{\quad\quad}$

6. Look at the patterns in Question 5. As the number being subtracted decreases by 1, what happens to the difference? How does 17 – (–15) compare to 17 – 0?

What does 2 − 5 mean on a thermometer?

Look at 5 − 2. If the temperature is 5° and drops 2°, the temperature becomes **5 − 2 = 3°.**

Now switch the 2 and the 5. If the temperature is 2° and drops 5°, the temperature becomes **2 − 5 = −3°.**

5°C
4°C
3°C
2°C
1°C
0°C
−1°C
−2°C
−3°C

1. Use the thermometer model to calculate each expression.

   a) If the temperature is 4° and the temperature drops 3°,
      the temperature becomes 4° − 3° = _____°.

      If the temperature is 3° and the temperature drops 4°,
      the temperature becomes 3° − 4° = _____°.

   b) If the temperature is 5° and the temperature drops 1°,
      the temperature becomes 5° − 1° = _____°.

      If the temperature is 1° and the temperature drops 5°,
      the temperature becomes 1° − 5° = _____°.

   c) 6 − 4 = _____   and   4 − 6 = _____

   d) 5 − 4 = _____   and   4 − 5 = _____

   e) 4 − 1 = _____   and   1 − 4 = _____

   f) 6 − 3 = _____   and   3 − 6 = _____

   g) 6 − 2 = _____   and   2 − 6 = _____

6°C
5°C
4°C
3°C
2°C
1°C
0°C
−1°C
−2°C
−3°C
−4°C
−5°C
−6°C
−7°C

2. a) Look at your answers in Question 1. In general, how does $a − b$ compare to $b − a$?

   _____

   b) Use your answer to part a) to predict 98 − 101: _____

   c) Check your prediction on a calculator. Were you correct? _____

3. Use the thermometer model to subtract.

   a) $(−2) − 3 =$ _____   and $(−3) − 2 =$ _____   b) $(−1) − 5 =$ _____   and $(−5) − 1 =$ _____

   c) $(−4) − 2 =$ _____   and $(−2) − 4 =$ _____   d) $(−4) − 3 =$ _____   and $(−3) − 4 =$ _____

4. Look at your answers in Question 3.

   How does $(−a) − b$ compare to $(−b) − a$? _____

   How do both of these compare to $a + b$? _____

5. Use the thermometer model to find the negative integer minus the positive integer. Then change the sign (as you did in Question 2) to find the positive integer minus the negative integer.

a) $(-2) - 3 =$ ___-5___

so $3 - (-2) =$ ___+5___

b) $(-1) - 4 =$ _____

so $4 - (-1) =$ _____

c) $(-5) - 3 =$ _____

so $3 - (-5) =$ _____

d) $(-5) - 4 =$ _____

so $4 - (-5) =$ _____

e) $(-4) - 5 =$ _____

so $5 - (-4) =$ _____

f) $(-6) - 3 =$ _____

so $3 - (-6) =$ _____

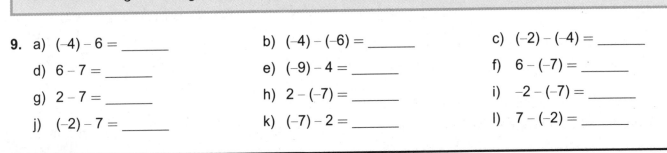

```
0°C
-1°C
-2°C
-3°C
-4°C
-5°C
-6°C
-7°C
-8°C
-9°C
```

6. Copy each answer from Question 5. How can you get the same answer by adding instead of subtracting? Write the correct positive integer in the blank.

a) $3 - (-2) =$ ___+5___

so $3 - (-2) = 3 +$ ___(+2)___

b) $4 - (-1) =$ _____

so $4 - (-1) = 4 +$ _____

c) $3 - (-5) =$ _____

so $3 - (-5) = 3 +$ _____

d) $4 - (-5) =$ _____

so $4 - (-5) = 4 +$ _____

e) $5 - (-4) =$ _____

so $5 - (-4) = 5 +$ _____

f) $3 - (-6) =$ _____

so $3 - (-6) = 3 +$ _____

7. In general, $a - (-b)$ gives the same result as $a +$ _____.

8. Change the subtraction of a negative integer to the addition of a positive integer.

a) $4 - (-2) = 4 +$ ___2___

$= $ ___6___

b) $7 - (-7) = 7 +$ _____

$=$ _____

c) $8 - (-3) = 8 +$ _____

$=$ _____

d) $(-5) - (-1) = (-5) +$ _____

$=$ _____

e) $(-3) - (-4) = -3 +$ _____

$=$ _____

f) $(-2) - (-5) = -2 +$ _____

$=$ _____

To subtract a positive integer, imagine moving down the thermometer.

To subtract a negative integer, add its opposite or move up the thermometer.

9. a) $(-4) - 6 =$ _____

d) $6 - 7 =$ _____

g) $2 - 7 =$ _____

j) $(-2) - 7 =$ _____

b) $(-4) - (-6) =$ _____

e) $(-9) - 4 =$ _____

h) $2 - (-7) =$ _____

k) $(-7) - 2 =$ _____

c) $(-2) - (-4) =$ _____

f) $6 - (-7) =$ _____

i) $-2 - (-7) =$ _____

l) $7 - (-2) =$ _____

NS7-92 Subtraction Using Distance Apart

1. How many units apart are the two whole numbers?

```
├──┼──┼──┼──┼──┼──┼──┼──┼──┼──┼──┼──┼──┼──┼──┼──┼──┼──┼──┼──┤
0  1  2  3  4  5  6  7  8  9  10 11 12 13 14 15 16 17 18 19 20
```

a) 2 and 5 are _____ units apart.

b) 9 and 14 are _____ units apart.

c) 15 and 17 are _____ units apart.

d) 7 and 13 are _____ units apart.

2. Write each statement in Question 1 as a subtraction sentence. Subtract the smaller number from the larger number.

a) ____$5 - 2 = 3$____   b) _____   c) _____   d) _____

3. How many units apart are the two integers?

```
├──┼──┼──┼──┼──┼──┼──┼──┼──┼──┼──┼──┼──┼──┼──┼──┼──┼──┼──┼──┤
-10 -9 -8 -7 -6 -5 -4 -3 -2 -1  0 +1 +2 +3 +4 +5 +6 +7 +8 +9 +10
```

a) −5 and 2 are _____ units apart.

b) −3 and 3 are _____ units apart.

c) −8 and −4 are _____ units apart.

d) −6 and 2 are _____ units apart.

4. Write each statement in Question 3 as a subtraction sentence. Subtract the smaller number from the larger number.

a) ____$2 - (-5) =$____   b) _____   c) _____   d) _____

$a - b$ and $b - a$ are opposite integers because $a - b + b - a = 0$. So to get $a - b$ from $b - a$, just change the sign (from $+$ to $-$ or from $-$ to $+$).

---

5. Subtract the smaller integer from the larger integer by using the distance apart. Then subtract the larger integer from the smaller integer by changing the sign.

a) $4 - (-3) =$ _____

so $(-3) - 4 =$ _____

b) $(-2) - (-9) =$ _____

so $(-9) - (-2) =$ _____

c) $7 - 3 =$ _____

so $3 - 7 =$ _____

d) $6 - (-2) =$ _____

so $(-2) - 6 =$ _____

e) $(-7) - (-10) =$ _____

so $(-10) - (-7) =$ _____

f) $204 - 198 =$ _____

so $198 - 204 =$ _____

6. Write **positive** or **negative**.

a) Circle the answers from Question 5 where a smaller integer is subtracted from a larger integer. When you subtract a smaller integer from a larger integer, the answer is _____.

b) Underline the answers from Question 5 where a larger integer is subtracted from a smaller integer. When you subtract a larger integer from a smaller integer, the answer is _____.

7. Decide which integer is larger and then whether the answer is positive or negative. Then subtract by writing the correct sign in the circle and the distance apart in the blank.

a) $(-5) - (-3) = \bigcirc\!\!\!-\ 2$ ___

b) $9 - (-3) = \bigcirc$ ___

c) $5 - 8 = \bigcirc$ ___

d) $(-6) - (-11) = \bigcirc$ ___

e) $(-4) - 5 = \bigcirc$ ___

f) $12 - 8 = \bigcirc$ ___

Remember: **Sums of integers** can be written as sequences of gains and losses.

$$+5 + (+3) = +5 + 3 \qquad +2 + (-5) = +2 - 5 \qquad -3 + (-2) = -3 - 2$$

Differences of integers may also be written as sequences of gains and losses.

$$+3 - (-5) = +3 + 5 \qquad +2 - (+5) = +2 - 5$$

Taking away a loss gives a gain

Taking away a gain gives a loss

$$+\,(\,+ \quad \longrightarrow \quad +$$
$$+\,(\,- \quad \longrightarrow \quad -$$
$$-\,(\,+ \quad \longrightarrow \quad -$$
$$-\,(\,- \quad \longrightarrow \quad +$$

1. Rewrite each expression as a sequence of gains and losses.

   a) $+3 + (-5)$

   $= +3 - 5$

   b) $-4 - (+2)$

   $=$

   c) $-5 - (-6)$

   $=$

   d) $8 - (+5)$

   $=$

   e) $+3 - (-5) + (-4) + (+2) - (+6)$

   $=$

   f) $(-6) + (-7) - (+3) - (-5) + (+4) - (+8) - (-7)$

   $=$

2. a) Rewrite each algebraic expression as a sequence of gains and losses.

   $a + (+b) = \qquad a + (-b) = \qquad a - (-b) = \qquad a - (+b) =$

   b) Which two expressions are equal to $a + b$? _____ and _____

   c) Which two expressions are equal to $a - b$? _____ and _____

3. Simplify each expression and then add to find the result.

   a) $-5 + (-3)$

   $= -5 - 3$

   $= -8$

   b) $+3 + (+2)$

   $=$

   $=$

   c) $+2 - (+3)$

   $=$

   $=$

   d) $-4 - (-6)$

   $=$

   $=$

   e) $-11 - (-6)$

   f) $+14 + (-8)$

   g) $-3 + (+7)$

   h) $-25 - (-5)$

   i) $-2 + (-3) + (+4)$

   j) $+3 + (-5) + 4$

   k) $-9 - (+8) - (-12)$

   l) $-4 + 5 - (-6) + (-3)$

4. Do you need a gain or a loss to get to +3? How much of a gain or loss do you need?

   a) $-2 \ \underline{+5} = +3$

   b) $+8 \ \underline{} = +3$

   c) $+1 \ \underline{} = +3$

   d) $-12 \ \underline{} = +3$

5. Fill in the missing integer that will make the statement true.

   a) $(-3) + \underline{\ 2\ } = -1$

   b) $+7 - \underline{} = +10$

   c) $(-1) - \underline{} = +3$

   d) $(-6) + \underline{} = -10$

   e) $\underline{} - (-4) = +3$

   f) $\underline{} + (-2) = -6$

   g) $\underline{} - (+5) = -3$

   h) $\underline{} + (+4) = -7$

6. In Question 5, how can you use your answer to part c) to check your answer to part e)? Explain.

NS7-94 Word Problems

1. a) A valley is 300 m below sea level and the top of a mountain is 2 000 m above sea level. Brooke says the difference in height is 2 300 m. Veda says the difference in height is 1 700 m. Who is right? Explain.

   b) Mount Lamlam on the island of Guam is the tallest mountain in the world from below sea level. Its top is 406 m above sea level. Its feet extend to 10 911 m below sea level. How tall is Mount Lamlam?

2. Arrange the temperatures in order from coldest to hottest.

   −19°C   24°C   −18°C   0°C   15°C   3°C   21°C

3. If the temperature is −15°C, what will the temperature be if it...

   a) increases 20°C?   b) increases 15°C?   c) increases 5°C?   d) decreases 10°C?

4. Which temperature is further from −3°C?

   a) −5°C or 5°C   b) 7°C or 10°C   c) 8°C or −15°C   d) 5°C or −10°C

5. Draw a number line from −10 to +10 and mark a number that is...

   A 2 less than 0   **B** 3 less than 4

   C 3 greater than −1   **D** 5 greater than −2

   E halfway between +2 and +6   **F** an equal distance from −8 and −2

   G the same distance from 0 as −9   **H** twice as far from zero as −4

6. Solve the puzzle by placing the same integer in each shape.

   a) 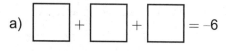   b) $\bigcirc + \bigcirc + \bigcirc = -30$

7. In this square, the integers in each row, column, and two diagonals (these include the centre box) add up to +3.

   Fill in the missing integers.

+5		−3
−2		

8. The chart shows the average temperatures in winter and summer for three Canadian cities.

   Find the range of average temperatures for each city.

City	Average Winter Temp (°C)	Average Summer Temp (°C)	Range
Toronto	−5	20	
Montreal	−10	21	
Vancouver	−3	23	

9. The chart shows the average temperature on 5 planets.

   a) Write the temperatures in order from least to greatest.

   b) What is the difference between the highest and the lowest average temperature?

   c) Which planet has an average temperature 200°C lower than that of Earth?

Earth	+20°C
Venus	+470°C
Saturn	−180°C
Mercury	+120°C
Jupiter	− 50°C

10. When a plane takes off, the temperature on the ground is 10°C. The temperature outside the plane decreases by 5°C for every 1 000 m it climbs above the ground.

    a) What is the temperature outside the plane when it is 3 000 m above the ground?

    b) What will the temperature outside the plane be when it is 3 400 m above the ground?

11. A glass of water has a temperature of +18°C. When Guled adds an ice cube, the temperature decreases by 1°C. Guled writes (+18) + (−7) to find the temperature after adding 7 ice cubes.

    a) How would Guled find the temperature after adding 12 ice cubes?

       (+18) + _____ = _____

    b) Guled's water has 5 ice cubes and a temperature of +13°C. How would Guled find the temperature after **removing** 3 ice cubes? Calculate the new temperature.

12. If you were to spin the spinner twice and add the two results…

    a) what is the highest total you could score? _____

    b) what is the lowest total you could score? _____

    c) what is the largest possible difference between the two scores?

       _____

    d) how could you score zero? _____

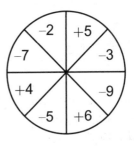

13. How much did the temperature change in the course of each day?

    Monday   _____

    Tuesday   _____

    Wednesday _____

    Thursday   _____

	Daily Low Temp (°C)	Daily High Temp (°C)
Monday	−8	+2
Tuesday	−10	−8
Wednesday	−4	0
Thursday	−17	−5

The position of a point on a coordinate grid is identified by an ordered pair of numbers in a bracket.

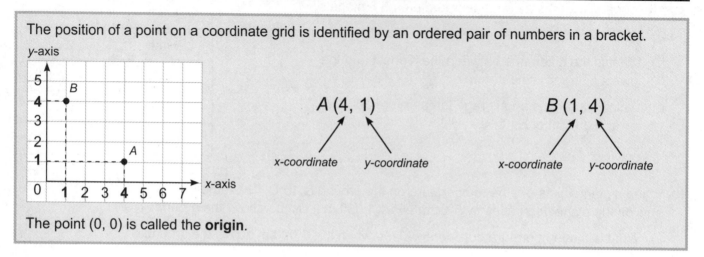

The point (0, 0) is called the **origin**.

1. Fill in the coordinates for the given points.

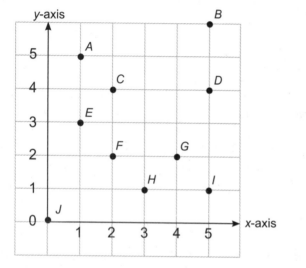

A (_1_ , _5_)   B (__, __)

C (__, __)   D (__, __)

E (__, __)   F (__, __)

G (__, __)   H (__, __)

I (__, __)   J (__, __)

A grid that has been extended to include negative integers is called a **Cartesian coordinate system**.
We use Roman numerals to number the quadrants: 1 = I, 2 = II, 3 = III, 4 = IV.

II		I
Second Quadrant		First Quadrant
III		IV
Third Quadrant		Fourth Quadrant

2. a) Label the origin (O) and the x- and y-axes.

   b) Label the axes with positive and negative integers.

   c) Number the four quadrants (using I, II, III, and IV).

   d) Which quadrants are these points in?

   A (3, 3) _I_   B (−3, −3) ____

   C (−3, 3) ____   D (3, −3) ____

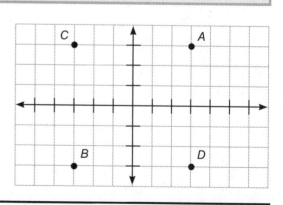

3. In Figure 1, point A (2, 3) is in the first quadrant. Its x- and y-coordinates are both **positive**.

a) Find the coordinates of points…

P (___, ___) Q (___, ___)

R (___, ___) S (___, ___)

b) Plot and label.

B (3, 2) C (1, 4) D (2, 6)

4. In Figure 1, point F (−2, 3) is in the second quadrant. Its x-coordinate is **negative** and its y-coordinate is **positive**.

a) Find the coordinates of points…

K (___, ___) L (___, ___)

M (___, ___) N (___, ___)

b) Plot and label.

G (−3, 2) H (−2, 6) I (−4, 3)

Figure 1

5. In Figure 2, point A (−2, −3) is in the third quadrant. Its x- and y-coordinates are both **negative**.

a) Find the coordinates of points…

K (___, ___) L (___, ___)

M (___, ___) N (___, ___)

b) Plot and label.

B (−3, −4) C (−2, −6) D (−4, −3)

6. In Figure 2, point F (2, −3) is in the fourth quadrant. Its x-coordinate is **positive** and its y-coordinate is **negative**.

a) Find the coordinates of points…

P (___, ___) Q (___, ___)

R (___, ___) S (___, ___)

b) Plot and label.

G (3, −4) H (1, −6)

I (4, −1) J (4, −6)

Figure 2

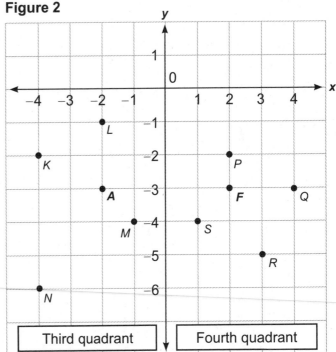

7. In Figure 3, points B (2, 0) and C (−4, 0) are both on the *x*-axis. The *y*-coordinate of any point on the *x*-axis is **zero**.

a) Find the coordinates of points...

   P (___, ___) Q (___, ___)

b) Plot and label.

   A (5, 0) M (−2, 0)

8. In Figure 3, points D (0, 2) and E (0, −3) are both on the *y*-axis. The *x*-coordinate of any point on the *y*-axis is **zero**.

a) Plot and label.

   G (0, 4) H (0, −1)

b) Find the coordinates of points...

   K (___, ___) L (___, ___)

Figure 3

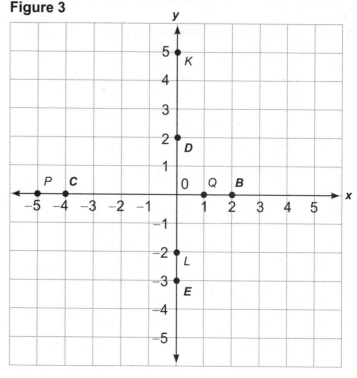

9. a) In Figure 4, find the coordinates of points...

   O (___, ___) P (___, ___) Q (___, ___) R (___, ___) S (___, ___)
   T (___, ___) U (___, ___) V (___, ___) W (___, ___)

b) Plot and label these points in Figure 4.

   A (3, 4) B (5, −2)

   C (−3, −2) D (−4, 1)

   E (3, 0) F (0, 2)

   G (0, 3) H (−5, 0)

c) Sort the points in Figure 4 by location.

   first quadrant: _A, R_____

   second quadrant: _____

   third quadrant: _____

   fourth quadrant: _____

   on the *x*-axis: _____

   on the *y*-axis: _____

   at the origin: _____

Figure 4

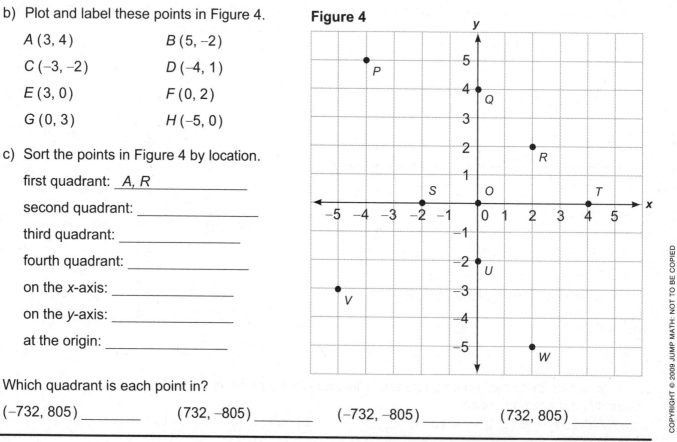

10. Which quadrant is each point in?

   (−732, 805) _____   (732, −805) _____   (−732, −805) _____   (732, 805) _____

G7-26 Coordinate Systems

1. a) Find the coordinates of points…

   A (_−9_ , _5_)   B (__ , __)

   C (__ , __)   D (__ , __)

   E (__ , __)   F (__ , __)

   G (__ , __)   H (__ , __)

   b) Plot and label these points.

   I (8, 4)   J (6, −2)

   K (−3, −2)   L (−4, 1)

   M (3, 0)   N (0, 5)

   O (−5, −7)   P (−7, −3)

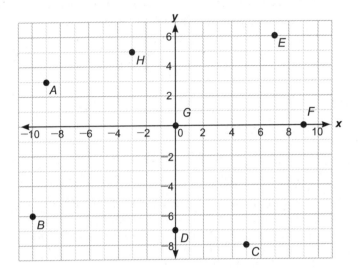

2. a) Plot each set of points on the coordinate system.

   i) (2, −2) (2, −1) (2, 0) (2, 1) (2, 2)

   ii) (−3, −4) (−3, −2) (−3, 0) (−3, 2) (−3, 4)

   iii) (−10, 5) (−5, 5) (0, 5) (5, 5) (10, 5)

   b) Draw a line that joins the points in each set.
      Which axis is each line parallel to?

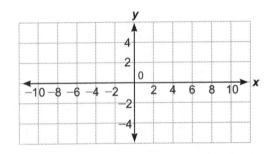

3. Add a point D so that the four points form the vertices of a rectangle.

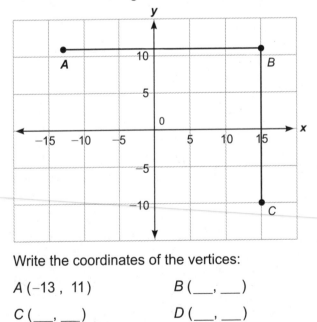

Write the coordinates of the vertices:

A (−13 , 11)   B (__ , __)

C (__ , __)   D (__ , __)

4. Plot and join the points on the grid. Identify the polygon you drew.

A (−24, 28)   B (10, 20)

C (13, −10)   D (−21, −2)

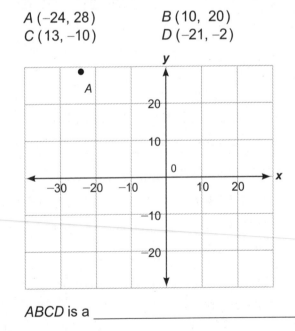

ABCD is a _____

5. Draw a coordinate system on grid paper. Plot and join the points in each group.
Identify the polygon drawn.

   a) A (−2, 2)   B (3, 2)   C (3, 5)

   b) D (1, 1)   E (1, −1)   F (−1, 1)   G (−1, −1)

6. Plot the points $P(3, 2)$ and $Q(3, -1)$. Draw the line PQ.

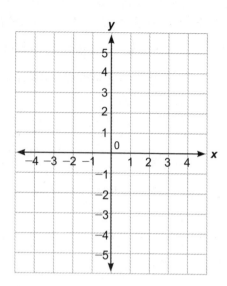

a) Is the line you drew horizontal or vertical? _____

Extend the line and draw three more points on it:

(___, ___)　　(___, ___)　　(___, ___)

Compare the coordinates. What do all points on line PQ

have in common? _____

b) Can any point on the line PQ be in the second quadrant?
Use coordinates to explain your answer.

c) Is the point $(3, 1742)$ on the line PQ? How do you know?

d) Plot three points on line PQ that are below P on the grid.
What can you say about the y-coordinates of any point below
P on the line?

7. Plot the points $P(3, 1)$ and $R(-2, 1)$. Draw the line PR.

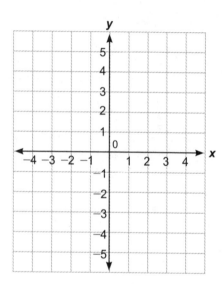

a) Is the line you drew horizontal or vertical? _____

b) Choose three more points on the line you drew:

(___, ___)　　(___, ___)　　(___, ___)

Compare the coordinates. What do all points on the line PR
have in common?

c) Can any point on the line PR be in the fourth quadrant?
Use coordinates to explain your answer.

d) Is the point $(-340, 1)$ on the line PR? How do you know?

e) Plot three points on line PR to the left of P on the grid.
What can you say about the x-coordinates of any point
to the left of P on the line?

8. a) Plot the point $P(3, 2)$ on the grid. Draw a vertical line v through P.

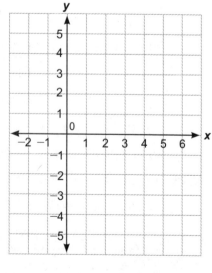

b) Choose three points **to the right** of the line v. Are their
x-coordinates greater than 3, equal to 3, or smaller than 3?

c) Choose one point in each quadrant **to the left** of line v. Are
their x-coordinates greater than 3, equal to 3, or smaller than 3?

d) Without plotting the points, say where the points are relative
to the line v.

i)　$R(2, 2)$ is __to the left of__ the line because __2 is less than 3__

ii)　$T(5, -2)$ is _____ the line because _____

iii)　$S(-2, 3)$ is _____ the line because _____

iv)　$U(3, -3)$ is _____ the line because _____

Then plot the points to check your answer.

9. Plot the point P (2, 3) on the grid. Draw a horizontal line h through P.

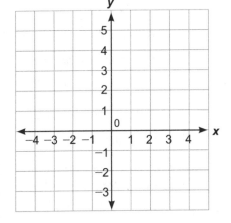

a) Choose three points above the line h.

Are their y-coordinates greater than 3, equal to 3, or smaller than 3?

b) Choose one point in each quadrant below the line h.

Are their y-coordinates greater than 3, equal to 3, or smaller than 3?

c) Without plotting the points, say where the points are relative to the line h.

i) R (4, 5) is ___*above*___ h because ___*5 is greater than 3*___

ii) T (5, –2) is _____ h because _____

iii) S (–2, 4) is _____ h because _____

iv) U (–1, 3) is _____ h because _____

Then plot the points to check your answer.

10. a) Find the coordinates of the vertices of the square.

A (__, __) B (__, __) C (__, __) D (__, __)

b) Describe the location of a point in the square relative to its sides. Use words left, right, above, and below.

Any point inside the square is …

____*right of*____ BC _____ BA

_____ AD _____ CD

c) Use your answers to part b) to fill in the blanks.

Any point on the line BC has __x__-coordinate __–4__ ,

so any point inside the square has __x__-coordinate ___*greater*___ than __–4__ .

Any point on the line BA has _____-coordinate _____ ,

so any point inside the square has _____-coordinate _____ than _____.

Any point on the line CD has _____-coordinate _____ ,

so any point inside the square has _____-coordinate _____ than _____.

Any point on the line AD has _____-coordinate _____ ,

so any point inside the square has _____-coordinate _____ than _____.

d) Any point (x, y) inside the square must have

x-coordinate between _____ and _____ ; y-coordinate between _____ and _____ .

e) Use your answer in part d) to say whether these points are inside or outside of the square. Check your answer by plotting the points.

E (4, 2) F (–2, 6) G (8, 1) H (–6, –10) I (3, –7) J (5, –3)

G7-27 Horizontal and Vertical Distances

1. Use Figure 1 to find the horizontal distance between the points.

Figure 1

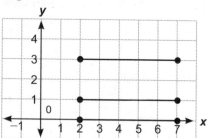

   a) The horizontal distance between (2, 0) and (7, 0) is ____ units.

   b) The horizontal distance between (2, 1) and (7, 1) is ____ units.

   c) The horizontal distance between (2, 3) and (7, 3) is ____ units.

   d) The horizontal distance between (2, y) and (7, y) is ____ units.

2. Use Figure 2 to find the horizontal distance between the points.

Figure 2

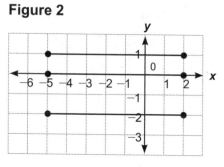

   a) The horizontal distance between (−5, 0) and (2, 0) is ____ units.

   b) The horizontal distance between (−5, 1) and (2, 1) is ____ units.

   c) The horizontal distance between (−5, −2) and (2, −2)

   is ____ units.

   d) The horizontal distance between (−5, y) and (2, y) is ____ units.

3. Look at your answers to Questions 1 and 2. Does the horizontal distance between two points on the same horizontal line depend on the x-coordinate or the y-coordinate?

_____

REMINDER▶

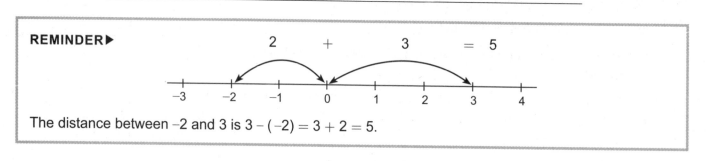

2   +   3   = 5

The distance between −2 and 3 is $3 - (-2) = 3 + 2 = 5$.

4. Subtract the x-coordinates to find the horizontal distance between the points.

   a) (−3, 0) and (1, 0)   ____ units

   b) (5, 0) and (−2, 0)   ____ units

   c) (−1, −10) and (1, −10)   ____ units

   d) (−8, 6) and (−2, 6)   ____ units

Figure 3

5. Use Figure 3 to find the vertical distance between the points.

   a) (0, −2) and (0, 5)   ____ units

   b) (1, −2) and (1, 5)   ____ units

   c) (−2, −2) and (−2, 5)   ____ units

   d) (x, −2) and (x, 5)   ____ units

6. Subtract the y-coordinates to find the vertical distance between the points.

   a) (1, −3) and (1, 2)   ____ units

   b) (1, −5) and (1, 2)   ____ units

   c) (−1, −2) and (−1, 2)   ____ units

   d) (−1, −5) and (−1, −2)   ____ units

   e) (184, −2) and (184, 7)   ____ units

   f) (−51, 2) and (−51, −5)   ____ units

INVESTIGATION ▶ How do coordinates change under translation?

A. A point is moved 4 units right. Find the new coordinates.

i) $(1, -2) \rightarrow (\_\_ , \_\_)$ ii) $(-6, -3) \rightarrow (\_\_ , \_\_)$ iii) $(-1, 1) \rightarrow (\_\_ , \_\_)$ iv) $(3, 0) \rightarrow (\_\_ , \_\_)$

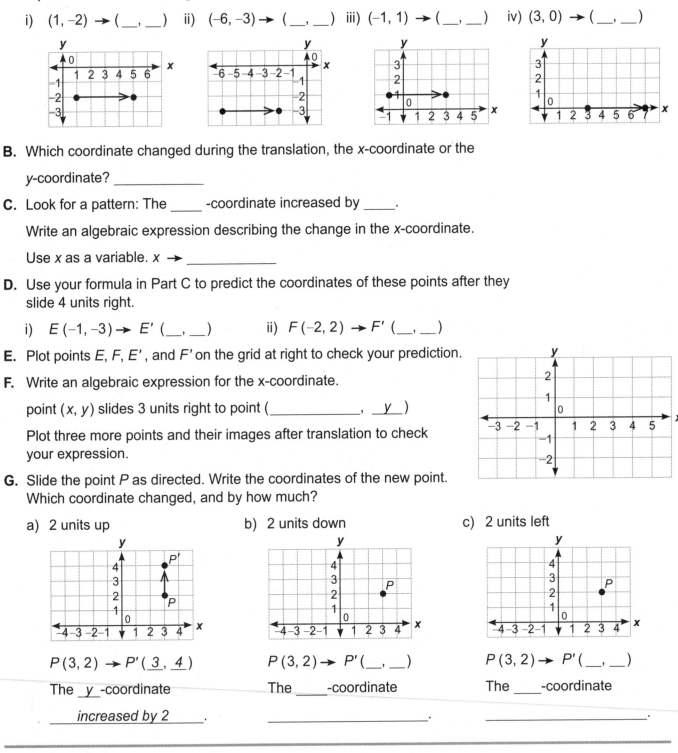

B. Which coordinate changed during the translation, the *x*-coordinate or the

y-coordinate? _____

C. Look for a pattern: The ____ -coordinate increased by ____ .

Write an algebraic expression describing the change in the *x*-coordinate.

Use *x* as a variable. $x \rightarrow$ _____

D. Use your formula in Part C to predict the coordinates of these points after they slide 4 units right.

i) $E(-1, -3) \rightarrow E'(\_\_ , \_\_)$ ii) $F(-2, 2) \rightarrow F'(\_\_ , \_\_)$

E. Plot points *E*, *F*, *E'*, and *F'* on the grid at right to check your prediction.

F. Write an algebraic expression for the x-coordinate.

point (x, y) slides 3 units right to point (_____ , $\underline{\ y\ }$)

Plot three more points and their images after translation to check your expression.

G. Slide the point *P* as directed. Write the coordinates of the new point. Which coordinate changed, and by how much?

a) 2 units up

$P(3, 2) \rightarrow P'(\underline{\ 3\ }, \underline{\ 4\ })$

The $\underline{\ y\ }$-coordinate

_____ *increased by 2* _____ .

b) 2 units down

$P(3, 2) \rightarrow P'(\_\_ , \_\_)$

The ____ -coordinate

_____ .

c) 2 units left

$P(3, 2) \rightarrow P'(\_\_ , \_\_)$

The ____ -coordinate

_____ .

---

7. Point $Q(x, y)$ slid to point Q'. Match the coordinates of Q' to the descriptions of translation.

__D__ $Q'(x + 4, y)$ ____ $Q'(x, y - 4)$ ____ $Q'(x, y + 4)$ ____ $Q'(x - 4, y)$

A 4 units up   **B** 4 units down   **C** 4 units left   **D** 4 units right

G7-28 Translations

1. How many units right or left and how many units up or down did the dot slide from position A to B?

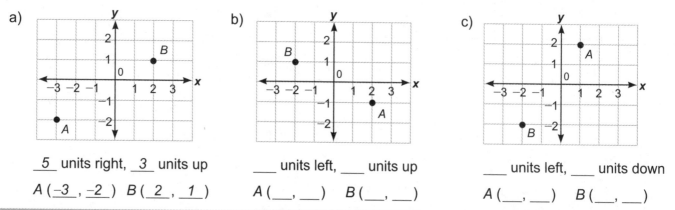

a) __5__ units right, __3__ units up

A (__-3__ , __-2__) B (__2__ , __1__)

b) ___ units left, ___ units up

A (__ , __) B (__ , __)

c) ___ units left, ___ units down

A (__ , __) B (__ , __)

> When a point or a shape is changed by a slide, a translation, or another kind of transformation, the resulting point is called the **image** of the original point.

2. Find the coordinates of the point A. Then predict the coordinates of the point when it slides by the given number of units. Slide the point to check your answer.

a) original point (__ , __)

   6 units right, 3 units down

   image (__ , __)

b) original point (__ , __)

   5 units left, 4 units up

   image (__ , __)

c) original point (__ , __)

   2 units left, 4 units down

   image (__ , __)

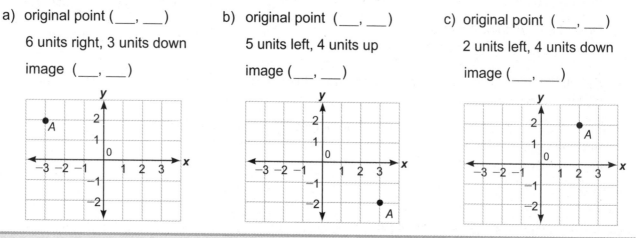

> When the same transformation is performed on several points, it is convenient to use the same letter for each point and its image. To distinguish between the point and the image, add a prime symbol (') or a star (*) to the label of the image. You can use an arrow to show a transformation: A → A' or B → B*.

3. Slide the point P three units down, then copy the shape. Write the coordinates of the point P and its image P'.

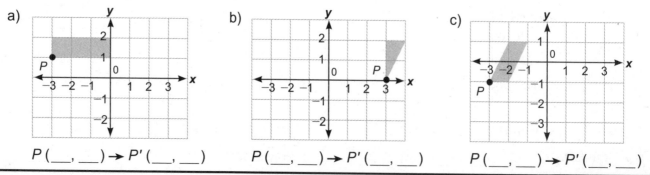

a) P (__ , __) → P' (__ , __)

b) P (__ , __) → P' (__ , __)

c) P (__ , __) → P' (__ , __)

4. Slide each triangle 6 units to the right and 2 units down.

a)

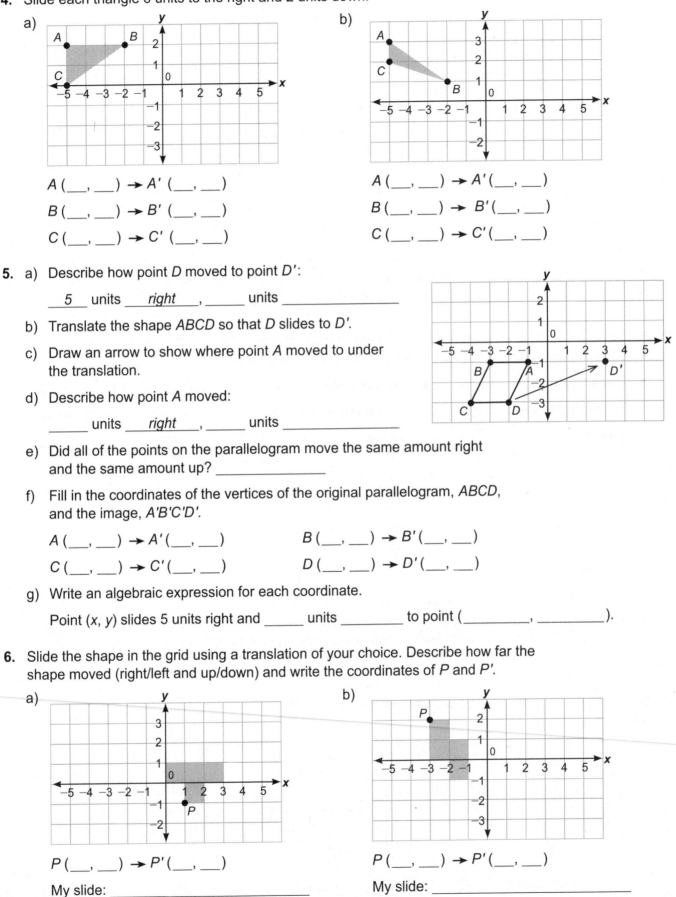

A (__, __) → A' (__, __)

B (__, __) → B' (__, __)

C (__, __) → C' (__, __)

b)

A (__, __) → A' (__, __)

B (__, __) → B' (__, __)

C (__, __) → C' (__, __)

5. a) Describe how point *D* moved to point *D'*:

___5___ units ___*right*___, _____ units _____

b) Translate the shape *ABCD* so that *D* slides to *D'*.

c) Draw an arrow to show where point *A* moved to under the translation.

d) Describe how point *A* moved:

_____ units ___*right*___, _____ units _____

e) Did all of the points on the parallelogram move the same amount right and the same amount up? _____

f) Fill in the coordinates of the vertices of the original parallelogram, *ABCD*, and the image, *A'B'C'D'*.

A (__, __) → A' (__, __)   B (__, __) → B' (__, __)

C (__, __) → C' (__, __)   D (__, __) → D' (__, __)

g) Write an algebraic expression for each coordinate.

Point (*x, y*) slides 5 units right and _____ units _____ to point (_____, _____).

6. Slide the shape in the grid using a translation of your choice. Describe how far the shape moved (right/left and up/down) and write the coordinates of *P* and *P'*.

a)

P (__, __) → P' (__, __)

My slide: _____

b)

P (__, __) → P' (__, __)

My slide: _____

7. Think of "up" as positive and "down" as negative. What is the result of each pair of translations? Write an addition statement using integers to show the result.

a) 3 units up and 5 down

   _+3 + (−5) = −2_ or ___2 units down___

b) 4 units up and 3 units down

   _____ or _____

c) 6 units down and 2 units up

   _____ or _____

d) 7 units down and 11 units down

   _____ or _____

8. Think of "right" as positive and "left" as negative. Write an addition statement using integers to show the result of each pair of translations.

a) 3 units right and 5 left

   _+3 + (−5) = −2_ or ___2 units left___

b) 6 units right and 4 units left

   _____ or _____

c) 7 units left and 2 units right

   _____ or _____

d) 8 units left and 12 units right

   _____ or _____

9. Think of "right" and "up" as positive and "left" and "down" as negative. Write two addition statements using integers to show the result of each pair of translations.

a) 3 units up and 2 units right, then 5 units down and 4 units right

b) 4 units down and 8 units right, then 3 units down and 6 units left

c) 2 units up and 7 units left, then 3 units up and 5 units right

10. a) A rectangle with vertices A (1, 1), B (1, 3), C (4, 3), and D (4, 1) is translated 4 units left and 2 units up.

   i) Predict the coordinates of the vertices of the image.

     A'(__, __) B'(__, __) C'(__, __) D'(__, __)

   ii) Check your answer by drawing both rectangles.

   iii) Translate $A'B'C'D'$ 3 units right and 5 units down.

     A^*(__, __) B^*(__, __) C^*(__, __) D^*(__, __)

     How far did the rectangle $ABCD$ move as the result of the two translations? How could you have predicted this?

b) A trapezoid with vertices A (3, 7), B (2, 4), C (0, 4), and D (2, 7) is translated 4 units right and 3 units down to trapezoid $A'B'C'D'$. The image points are:

   A'(__, __) B'(__, __) C'(__, __) D'(__, __)

Translate $A'B'C'D'$ 2 units right and 7 units up.

How did the original trapezoid $ABCD$ move under the two translations?

_____ units _____ and _____ units _____

Write an integer addition to show your work.

G7-29 Reflections

When a point is **reflected** in a mirror line, the point and the image of the point are the same distance from the mirror line.

The line between the point and the image is **perpendicular** to the mirror line.

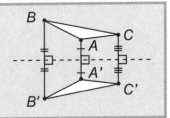

1. Reflect point *P* using the *x*-axis as a mirror line. Label the image point *P'*. Write the coordinates.

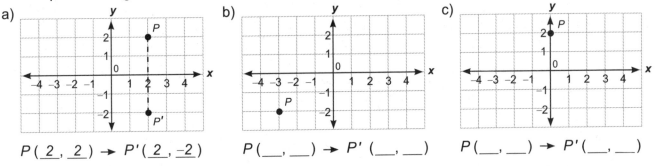

a) $P(\underline{2}, \underline{2}) \rightarrow P'(\underline{2}, \underline{-2})$

b) $P(\underline{}, \underline{}) \rightarrow P'(\underline{}, \underline{})$

c) $P(\underline{}, \underline{}) \rightarrow P'(\underline{}, \underline{})$

2. Reflect points *P*, *Q*, and *R* through the *x*-axis. Label the image points *P'*, *Q'*, and *R'* and write the coordinates. Hint: The image of a point on the *x*-axis through the *x*-axis is the point itself.

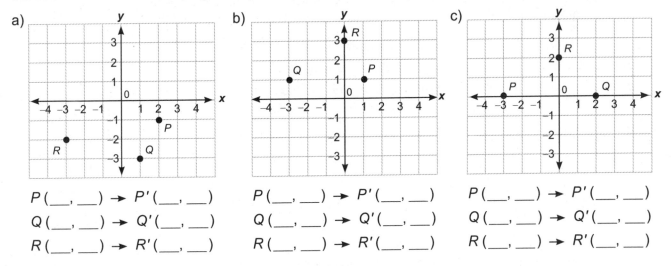

a) $P(\underline{}, \underline{}) \rightarrow P'(\underline{}, \underline{})$
$Q(\underline{}, \underline{}) \rightarrow Q'(\underline{}, \underline{})$
$R(\underline{}, \underline{}) \rightarrow R'(\underline{}, \underline{})$

b) $P(\underline{}, \underline{}) \rightarrow P'(\underline{}, \underline{})$
$Q(\underline{}, \underline{}) \rightarrow Q'(\underline{}, \underline{})$
$R(\underline{}, \underline{}) \rightarrow R'(\underline{}, \underline{})$

c) $P(\underline{}, \underline{}) \rightarrow P'(\underline{}, \underline{})$
$Q(\underline{}, \underline{}) \rightarrow Q'(\underline{}, \underline{})$
$R(\underline{}, \underline{}) \rightarrow R'(\underline{}, \underline{})$

3. Reflect the figure through the *x*-axis by first reflecting the vertices.

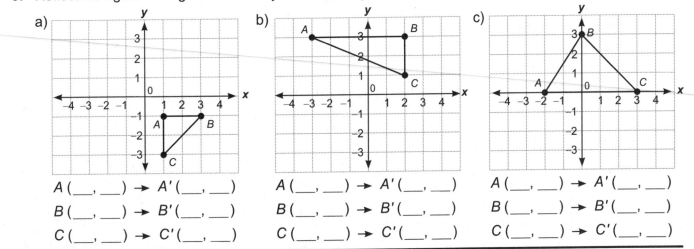

a) $A(\underline{}, \underline{}) \rightarrow A'(\underline{}, \underline{})$
$B(\underline{}, \underline{}) \rightarrow B'(\underline{}, \underline{})$
$C(\underline{}, \underline{}) \rightarrow C'(\underline{}, \underline{})$

b) $A(\underline{}, \underline{}) \rightarrow A'(\underline{}, \underline{})$
$B(\underline{}, \underline{}) \rightarrow B'(\underline{}, \underline{})$
$C(\underline{}, \underline{}) \rightarrow C'(\underline{}, \underline{})$

c) $A(\underline{}, \underline{}) \rightarrow A'(\underline{}, \underline{})$
$B(\underline{}, \underline{}) \rightarrow B'(\underline{}, \underline{})$
$C(\underline{}, \underline{}) \rightarrow C'(\underline{}, \underline{})$

4. Reflect point *P* using the *y*-axis as a mirror line. Label the image point *P'*. Write the coordinates.

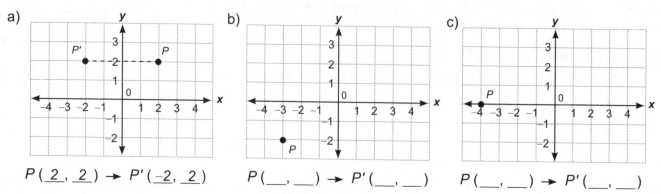

a)

P (_2_ , _2_) → P' (_−2_ , _2_)

b)

P (__ , __) → P' (__ , __)

c)

P (__ , __) → P' (__ , __)

5. Reflect points *P*, *Q*, and *R* through the *y*-axis. Label the image points *P'*, *Q'*, and *R'* and write the coordinates. Hint: The image of a point on the *y*-axis through the *y*-axis is the point itself.

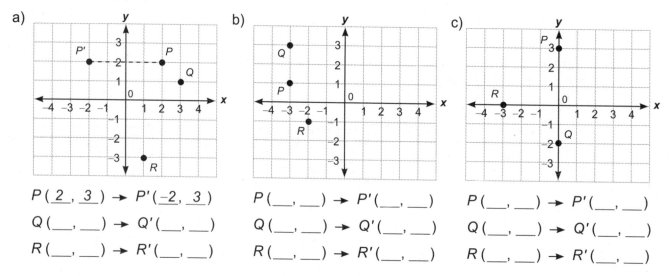

a)

P (_2_ , _3_) → P' (_−2_ , _3_)

Q (__ , __) → Q' (__ , __)

R (__ , __) → R' (__ , __)

b)

P (__ , __) → P' (__ , __)

Q (__ , __) → Q' (__ , __)

R (__ , __) → R' (__ , __)

c)

P (__ , __) → P' (__ , __)

Q (__ , __) → Q' (__ , __)

R (__ , __) → R' (__ , __)

6. Compare the coordinates of the points and the images in Question 5. Which coordinate changes when a point is reflected throughout the *y*-axis? What happens to the other coordinate?

7. Reflect the figure through the *y*-axis by first reflecting the vertices.

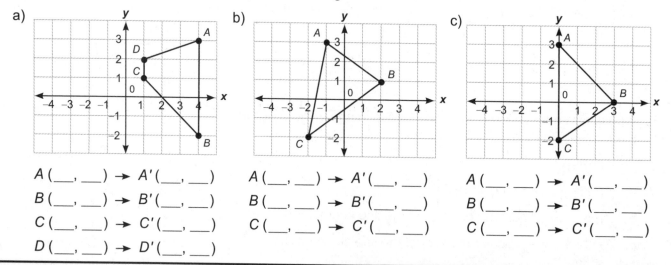

a)

A (__ , __) → A' (__ , __)

B (__ , __) → B' (__ , __)

C (__ , __) → C' (__ , __)

D (__ , __) → D' (__ , __)

b)

A (__ , __) → A' (__ , __)

B (__ , __) → B' (__ , __)

C (__ , __) → C' (__ , __)

c)

A (__ , __) → A' (__ , __)

B (__ , __) → B' (__ , __)

C (__ , __) → C' (__ , __)

G7-30 Reflections — Advanced

INVESTIGATION ▶ What are the distances between points and their reflections in horizontal and vertical lines?

A. a) Which transformation takes △ABC to △A'B'C'?

b) Find the distances between the points. Fill in the table below.

c) Compare the vertical distances in adjacent pairs of columns. What do you notice? Explain.

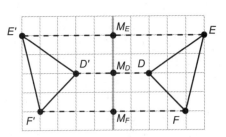

	A and A'	A and M_A	B and B'	B and M_B	C and C'	C and M_C
Distance between...	6	3				

B. a) Which transformation takes △DEF to △D'E'F'?

b) Find the distances between the points. Fill in the table below.

c) Compare the horizontal distances in adjacent pairs of columns. What do you notice? Explain.

	D and D'	D and M_D	E and E'	E and M_E	F and F'	F and M_F
Distance between...	4	2				

C. Compare the results of Part A with those of Part B. What do you notice?

D. Use your findings to draw the mirror line in each picture.

a)   b)   c)

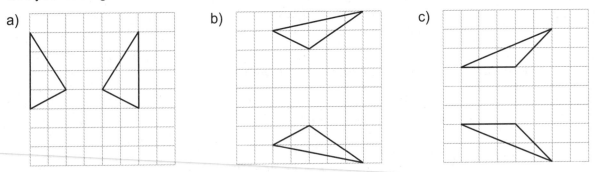

E. A point P is reflected in a line AB. P' is the image under reflection. Sketch the situation.

True or False?

a) AB is parallel to the line PP'. _____

b) AB is a perpendicular bisector of the line segment PP'. _____

c) PP' is a perpendicular bisector of the line segment AB. _____

1. a) Reflect the triangle through the line.

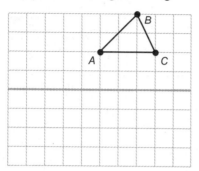

b) Slide the triangle 4 units down.

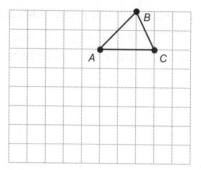

c) Use parts a) and b) to fill in the table with True or False.

	Reflection	Translation
The original figure and the image are congruent.	True	
The original figure and the image face in the same direction.		
The original figure and the image face in the opposite direction.		

2. The pairs of triangles below are related by a reflection (through either a horizontal or a vertical line) or a translation.

Plot the triangles, then say which transformation was used. Identify the mirror lines and draw the translation arrows.

a) △ABC: A (3, 1), B (3, 4), C (5, 2)
△A'B'C': A' (−1, 1), B' (−1, 4), C' (−3, 2)
△A'B'C' was obtained from △ABC by

_____.

b) △DEF: D (3, −3), E (3, −6), F (5, −4)
△D'E'F': D' (−3, −3), E' (−3, −6), F' (−1, −4)
△D'E'F' was obtained from △DEF by

_____.

c) △ABC from part a) and △DEF from part b)
△ABC was obtained from △DEF by

_____.

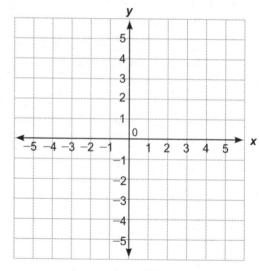

d) Ron thinks that △D'E'F' was obtained by first translating △ABC 2 units down and 6 units left, then reflecting the image in a horizontal line through the points (−2, −2) and (2, −2). Perform the transformations to check if he is correct.

e) Find two transformations that would take △A'B'C' to △D'E'F' if performed one after the other. (There are many possible answers.)

_____

_____

3. a) Reflect △ABC through the x-axis. Label the image △A'B'C'.

b) Reflect △A'B'C' through the y-axis. Label the image △A*B*C*.

c) Ying thinks that △A*B*C* is obtained from △ABC by a translation. Is she correct? Explain why or why not.

_____

_____

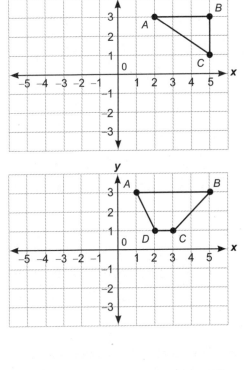

4. a) Reflect ABCD first through the x-axis, then reflect the image through the y-axis.

b) Reflect ABCD first through the y-axis, then reflect the image through the x-axis.

c) What do you notice about the images in a) and b)?

_____

_____

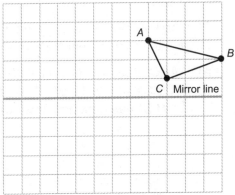

5. a) Reflect △ABC first through the mirror line, then translate the image 5 units left and 1 unit up.

b) Translate △ABC 5 units left and 1 unit **up**, then reflect the image through the mirror line.

Did you get the same result as in a)? _____

c) Translate △ABC 5 units left and 1 unit **down**, then reflect the image through the mirror line.

Did you get the same result as in a)? _____

d) Explain why you have to reverse the vertical direction of the translation to make the triangles coincide.

_____

_____

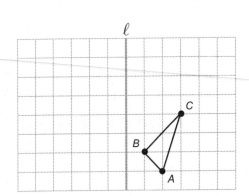

6. a) Reflect △ABC through the mirror line ℓ, then translate the image 2 units right and 3 units up. Label the resulting triangle △A'B'C'.

b) Mark wants to move △ABC onto △A'B'C' using a translation, then reflection in line ℓ. Explain how he can do this.

_____

_____

G7-31 Rotations

1. Draw the arrow after each turn. Start by drawing an arc to show where the final arrow should be.

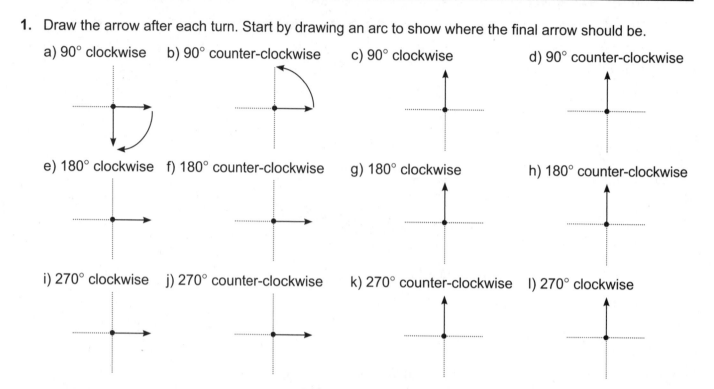

a) 90° clockwise   b) 90° counter-clockwise   c) 90° clockwise   d) 90° counter-clockwise

e) 180° clockwise   f) 180° counter-clockwise   g) 180° clockwise   h) 180° counter-clockwise

i) 270° clockwise   j) 270° counter-clockwise   k) 270° counter-clockwise   l) 270° clockwise

2. Match each rotation in the left column to a rotation in the right column that produces the same result. Hint: Use your answers from Question 1.

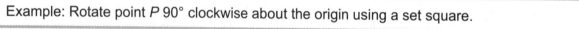

90° clockwise   90° counter-clockwise
180° clockwise   180° counter-clockwise
270° clockwise   270° counter-clockwise

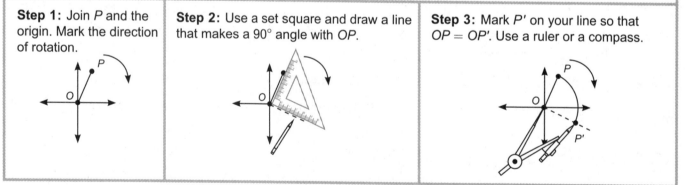

Example: Rotate point P 90° clockwise about the origin using a set square.

Step 1: Join P and the origin. Mark the direction of rotation.

Step 2: Use a set square and draw a line that makes a 90° angle with OP.

Step 3: Mark P' on your line so that $OP = OP'$. Use a ruler or a compass.

3. Using a set square and a circle instead of a compass, rotate P 90° clockwise. Label the image P'. Which quadrants are P and P' in?

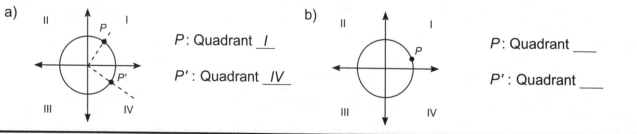

a)

P: Quadrant ___I___

P': Quadrant ___IV___

b)

P: Quadrant ___

P': Quadrant ___

c)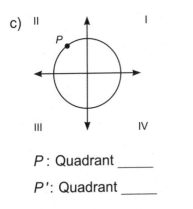

P : Quadrant _____

P' : Quadrant _____

d)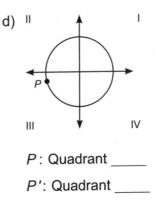

P : Quadrant _____

P' : Quadrant _____

e)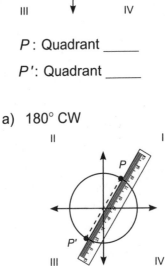

P : Quadrant _____

P' : Quadrant _____

4. Using a set square (or ruler) and a circle, rotate *P* the given amount clockwise (CW) or counter-clockwise (CCW). Label the image *P'*. Which quadrants are *P* and *P'* in?

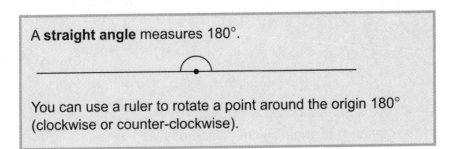

A **straight angle** measures 180°.

You can use a ruler to rotate a point around the origin 180° (clockwise or counter-clockwise).

a) 180° CW

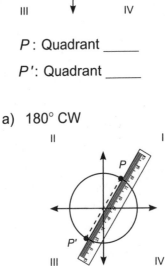

P : Quadrant _I_

P' : Quadrant _III_

b) 180° CW

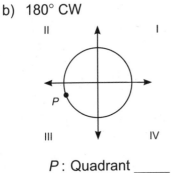

P : Quadrant _____

P' : Quadrant _____

c) 180° CW

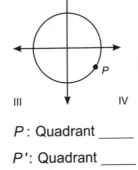

P : Quadrant _____

P' : Quadrant _____

d) 90° CCW

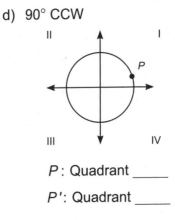

P : Quadrant _____

P' : Quadrant _____

e) 180° CCW

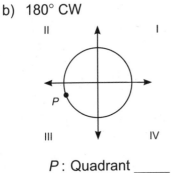

P : Quadrant _____

P' : Quadrant _____

f) 90° CCW

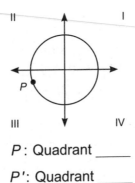

P : Quadrant _____

P' : Quadrant _____

g) 270° CW

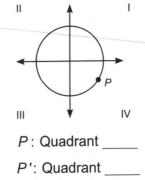

P : Quadrant _____

P' : Quadrant _____

G7-32 Rotations in the Coordinate Plane

1. Rotate the triangle by the given amount. First rotate the dark line, then draw the rest of the triangle.

a) 90° clockwise   b) 90° counter-clockwise   c) 180° clockwise   d) 270° clockwise

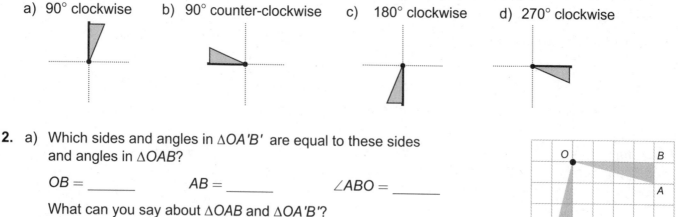

2. a) Which sides and angles in △OA'B' are equal to these sides and angles in △OAB?

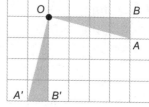

$OB =$ _____ $AB =$ _____ $\angle ABO =$ _____

What can you say about △OAB and △OA'B'?

b) What can you say about ∠AOB and ∠A'OB'?

c) What is the degree measure of ∠BOB'? ∠BOB' = _____

d) What is the degree measure of ∠AOA'? ∠AOA' = _____. Explain.

e) Which transformation takes △OAB to △OA'B'? _____

3. Lina wants to rotate point P (2, 3) 90° clockwise around the origin.

a) Which quadrant is P in? _____

b) Which quadrant will the image P' be in? _____

c) Lina shades a right triangle with hypotenuse OP. Rotate her triangle 90° clockwise around the origin. Label the image P'.

d) The triangle before rotation has horizontal length 2 and vertical length 3.

The image triangle has horizontal length ____ and

vertical length____. P' (__, __).

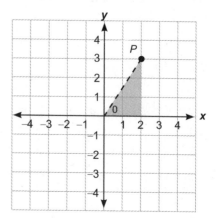

4. Plot the point Q (−8, −2) on the coordinate grid.

a) Use Lina's method to rotate point Q 90° clockwise around the origin. Label the image Q'.

Q is in quadrant ____. Q' is in quadrant ____.

The triangle before rotation has horizontal length __8__ and

vertical length ____.

The image triangle has horizontal length ____ and vertical

length ____. So Q' (__, __).

b) Use Lina's method to rotate a triangle with vertex Q (−8, −2) 90° counter-clockwise around the origin. Label the image Q*. What do you observe?

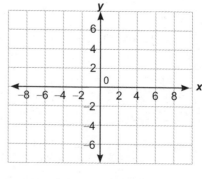

5. Compare the horizontal and the vertical lengths of the image triangles in Question 4.
Are they equal? Are points Q' and $Q*$ the same? Explain.

6. Rotate each point around the origin as given using Lina's method. Write the coordinates of the image.

a) P (3, 2), 90° clockwise; P' (___, ___)

b) P (3, 2), 90° counter-clockwise; $P*$ (___, ___)

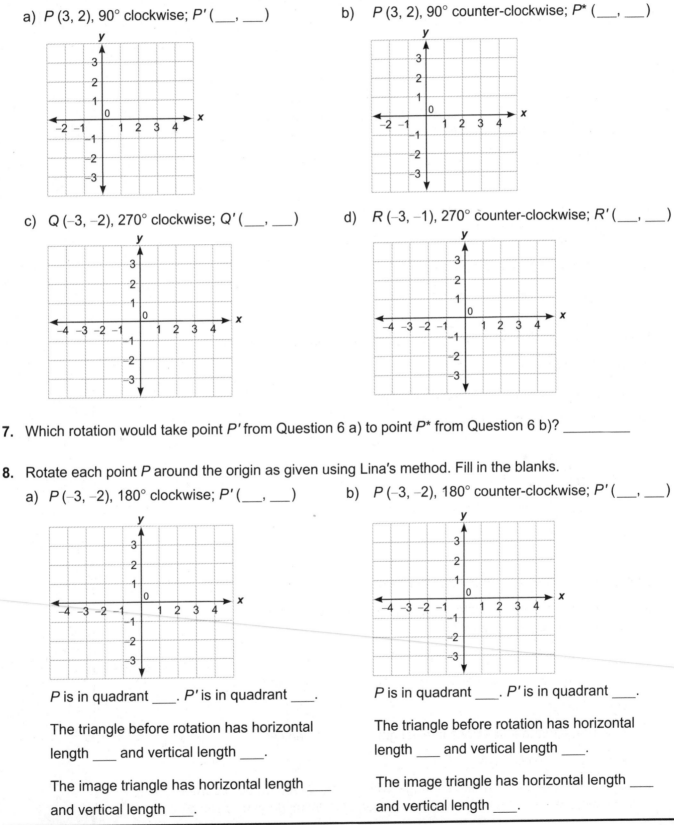

c) Q (–3, –2), 270° clockwise; Q' (___, ___)

d) R (–3, –1), 270° counter-clockwise; R' (___, ___)

7. Which rotation would take point P' from Question 6 a) to point $P*$ from Question 6 b)? _____

8. Rotate each point P around the origin as given using Lina's method. Fill in the blanks.

a) P (–3, –2), 180° clockwise; P' (___, ___)

b) P (–3, –2), 180° counter-clockwise; P' (___, ___)

P is in quadrant ___. P' is in quadrant ___.

The triangle before rotation has horizontal length ___ and vertical length ___.

The image triangle has horizontal length ___ and vertical length ___.

P is in quadrant ___. P' is in quadrant ___.

The triangle before rotation has horizontal length ___ and vertical length ___.

The image triangle has horizontal length ___ and vertical length ___.

9. a) Rotate P 180° clockwise around the origin. P' (___ , ___)

b) Rotate P' 270° clockwise around the origin. P^* (___ , ___)

c) Point P^* can be obtained by rotating point P

$180° + 270° - 360° =$ ___ clockwise around the origin.

Explain where each number in this equation comes from.

_____

_____

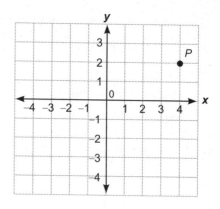

10. Rotate points P, Q, and R around the origin. Label the image points P', Q', and R'.

a) 90° counter-clockwise

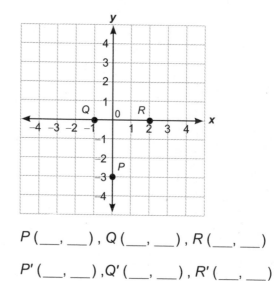

P (___ , ___) , Q (___ , ___) , R (___ , ___)

P' (___ , ___) , Q' (___ , ___) , R' (___ , ___)

b) 270° counter-clockwise

P (___ , ___) , Q (___ , ___) , R (___ , ___)

P' (___ , ___) , Q' (___ , ___) , R' (___ , ___)

c) 180° counter-clockwise

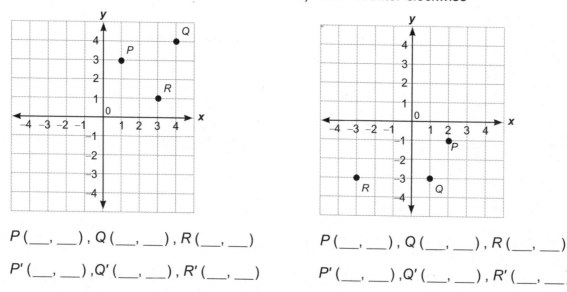

P (___ , ___) , Q (___ , ___) , R (___ , ___)

P' (___ , ___) , Q' (___ , ___) , R' (___ , ___)

d) 270° counter-clockwise

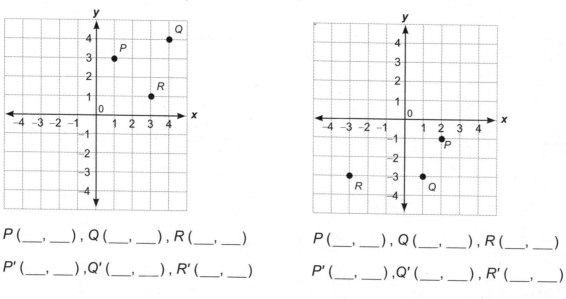

P (___ , ___) , Q (___ , ___) , R (___ , ___)

P' (___ , ___) , Q' (___ , ___) , R' (___ , ___)

11. Rotate the figure around the origin by first rotating the vertices.

a) 90° clockwise

b) 90° clockwise

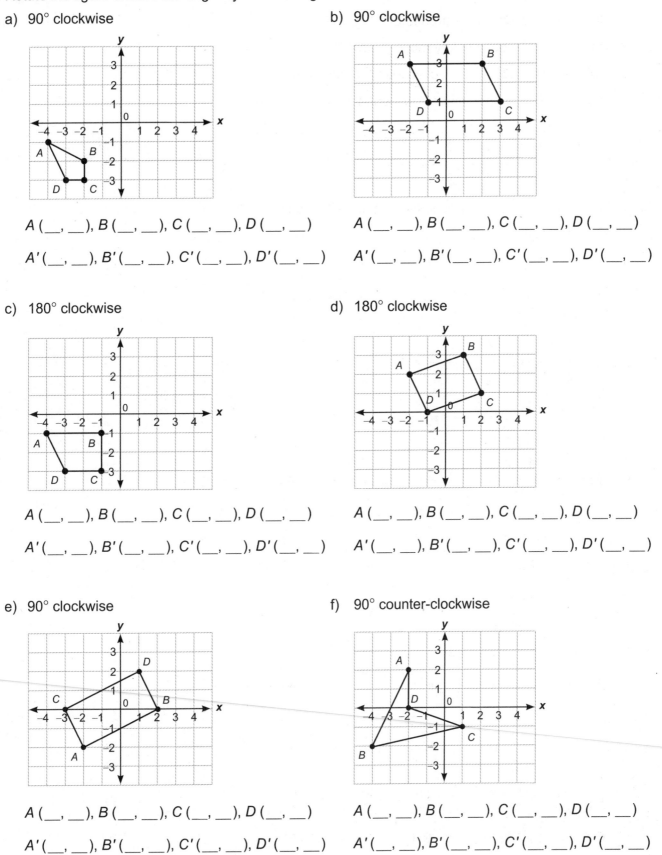

A (__, __), B (__, __), C (__, __), D (__, __)

A' (__, __), B' (__, __), C' (__, __), D' (__, __)

A (__, __), B (__, __), C (__, __), D (__, __)

A' (__, __), B' (__, __), C' (__, __), D' (__, __)

c) 180° clockwise

d) 180° clockwise

A (__, __), B (__, __), C (__, __), D (__, __)

A' (__, __), B' (__, __), C' (__, __), D' (__, __)

A (__, __), B (__, __), C (__, __), D (__, __)

A' (__, __), B' (__, __), C' (__, __), D' (__, __)

e) 90° clockwise

f) 90° counter-clockwise

A (__, __), B (__, __), C (__, __), D (__, __)

A' (__, __), B' (__, __), C' (__, __), D' (__, __)

A (__, __), B (__, __), C (__, __), D (__, __)

A' (__, __), B' (__, __), C' (__, __), D' (__, __)

G7-33 Transformations in the Cartesian Plane

1. Which transformation changes triangle A into...

   triangle B? _____

   triangle C? _____

   triangle D? _____

   Draw the mirror line for the reflection and translation
   arrow for the translation.

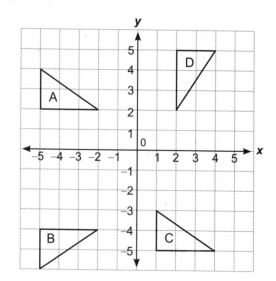

2. a) Find two different points F and G so that △DEF and △DEG
   are congruent to △ABC.

   F (__ , __)   G (__ , __)

   b) Which transformation takes △ABC to △DEF?
      How do you know?

      _____

      _____

   c) Which transformation takes △ABC to △DEG?
      How do you know?

      _____

      _____

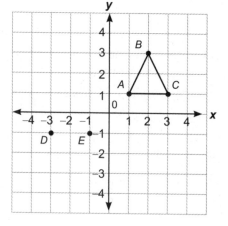

3. Design and perform your own transformations.

   a) I rotate ABCD ____ degrees clockwise.

      A' (__ , __) B' (__ , __) C' (__ , __) D' (__ , __)

   b) I translate A'B'C'D' ____ units _____ (up/down)

      and ____ units _____ (right/left).

      A* (__ , __) B* (__ , __) C* (__ , __) D* (__ , __)

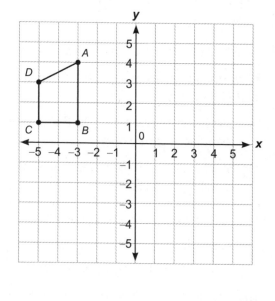

4. Draw a coordinate grid on grid paper. Plot the points
   A (1, 1), B (2, 3), C (3, 3), and D (3, 1).

   a) Join the points. What special quadrilateral is ABCD?

   b) Reflect ABCD first through the x-axis, then reflect the
      image through the y-axis. Label the image A*B*C*D*.

   c) What single transformation takes ABCD to A*B*C*D*?
      How do you know?

5. Draw a coordinate grid on grid paper.

    a) Draw a scalene triangle on your grid.

    b) Reflect the triangle through the x-axis, then reflect the image through the y-axis.

    c) Reflect the original triangle through the y-axis, then reflect the image through the x-axis.

    d) What do you notice about the images in parts b) and c)?

In Question 5, performing the transformations in reverse order did not change the result. Does this happen with any two transformations?

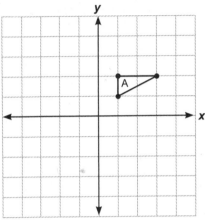

INVESTIGATION 1 ▶ Consider two transformations:

T: Translation 4 units left and 1 unit down.

R: Rotation 90° clockwise around the origin.

How does performing first *T* then *R* compare to performing first *R* then *T*?

A. Start with triangle A. Do *T* first, then perform *R*. Label the resulting triangle B.

B. Start with triangle A. Do *R* first, then perform *T*. Label the resulting triangle C.

C. Do triangles B and C coincide? What transformation would take B to C?

D. Can you obtain B from A by a single rotation around the origin, reflection or translation? Explain.

E. Start with triangle A. Do *R*. Which translation do you need to get triangle B?

INVESTIGATION 2 ▶ Consider two transformations:

F: Reflection through the x-axis.

R: Rotation 90° counter-clockwise around the origin.

How does performing first *F* then *R* compare to performing first *R* then *F*?

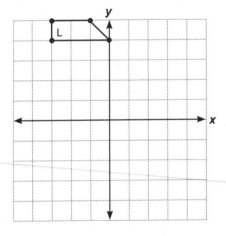

A. Start with trapezoid L. Do *F* first, then perform *R*. Label the resulting trapezoid M.

B. Start with trapezoid L. Do *R* first, then perform *F*. Label the resulting trapezoid N.

C. Do trapezoids M and N coincide? _____

D. Start with trapezoid L. Do *R*. Which reflection do you need to perform to obtain M? How do you know?

BONUS ▶ You can obtain M from L by a single reflection. Find the mirror line.

G7-34 Tessellations and Designs

A **tessellation** is a pattern, made up of one or more shapes, that has no gaps or overlaps and can be extended to cover all of a surface.

Here are some shapes that can be used to tessellate.

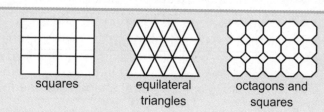

squares   equilateral triangles   octagons and squares

1. Finish the tessellation using the shapes given.

   a) hexagons and triangles

   b) rhombuses

   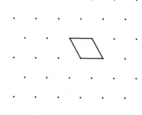

2. Show two different tessellations using the same shape.

   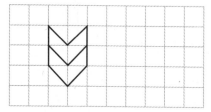

3. How are the tessellations in Question 2 different? Use transformations in your explanation.

4. The picture shows how you can tessellate a grid using an H shape.

   a) Add at least 4 more H shapes to the tessellation.

   b) On grid paper, check which of the shapes below tessellate. Extend your pattern to cover most of a 10 by 10 grid.

   i)   ii)   iii)

   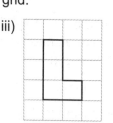

5. a) Which transformation (translation, reflection, or rotation) could you use to move shape A onto…

   i) shape B?   ii) shape C?   iii) shape D?

   b) Philip says: "I can move shape C onto shape B using a 180° rotation and then a translation." Is he correct?

   c) Explain how you could move shape C onto shape D using a reflection and a translation.

6. This is part of the border of a picture frame.

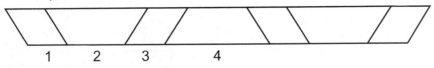

a) How many non-congruent shapes are used in the design?

b) Describe a single transformation that will move the shape in position 1 to position 3.

c) Describe a pair of transformations that will move the shape from position 2 to position 4.

7. Describe a sequence of transformations that would create the design (starting from the shaded figure).

a) b) c)

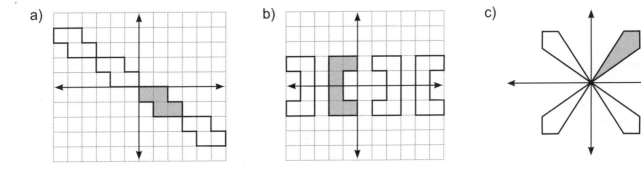

8. a) How many different shapes are in this design? Describe them.

b) Shade one of each different shape in the design. Describe the transformations that take each shaded shape onto the other congruent shapes. Draw and label the mirror lines or centres of rotation.

9. Show how to make a large L shape out of 4 small L shapes like the one shown. Then use 4 large Ls to make an even larger L. Explain how this strategy will allow you to tessellate a grid.

10. The picture shows how you can tessellate a grid using a different L shape.

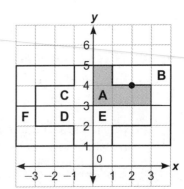

a) Extend the tessellation to cover the entire grid.

b) Which transformation takes shape A onto…

    i) shape B? <u>*180° clockwise (or counter-clockwise) rotation*</u>

                            <u>*around the point (2, 4)*</u>

    ii) shape C?   iii) shape D?

    iv) shape E?   v) shape F?

G7-35 Angles in Polygons and Tessellations

The angles in any triangle add to 180°. Any quadrilateral (4-sided shape) can be divided into two triangles.

Example:
$$\angle A + \angle B + \angle C + \angle D = u + (v + x) + z + (y + w)$$
$$= (u + v + w) + (x + y + z)$$
$$= 180° + 180° = 360°$$

The sum of the **interior angles** in a quadrilateral is **360°**.

1. A pentagon can be divided into three triangles. Find the sum of the angles in each pentagon. Then check your answer by measuring the angles.

   a)

   $$\angle A + \angle B + \angle C + \angle D + \angle E$$
   $$= \underline{\quad (s + u) + (v + x) + z + (y + w + t) + r \quad}$$
   $$= \underline{\hspace{4cm}}$$

   b)

   $$\angle A + \angle B + \angle C + \angle D + \angle E$$
   $$= \underline{\hspace{4cm}}$$
   $$= \underline{\hspace{4cm}}$$

2. Use a protractor to measure the interior angles that are smaller than 180° in this pentagon. Use the sum of the angles in a pentagon (from Question 1) to find the fifth angle.

3. What is the sum of the angles around a point? Use a picture to explain your answer.

4. Sidra divides this pentagon into 5 triangles and adds all the interior angles. How much greater is her total than the sum of the angles in the pentagon alone? How do you know?

5. a) An equilateral triangle has all its angles equal.

   What is the measure of each angle? _____

   b) Six equilateral triangles can fit around a common vertex without gaps or overlaps.

   Why is this possible? _____

   c) How many squares can fit around a common vertex with no gaps or overlaps? How do you know?

   d) Show how you can tessellate using equilateral triangles.

   e) Show how you can tessellate using squares.

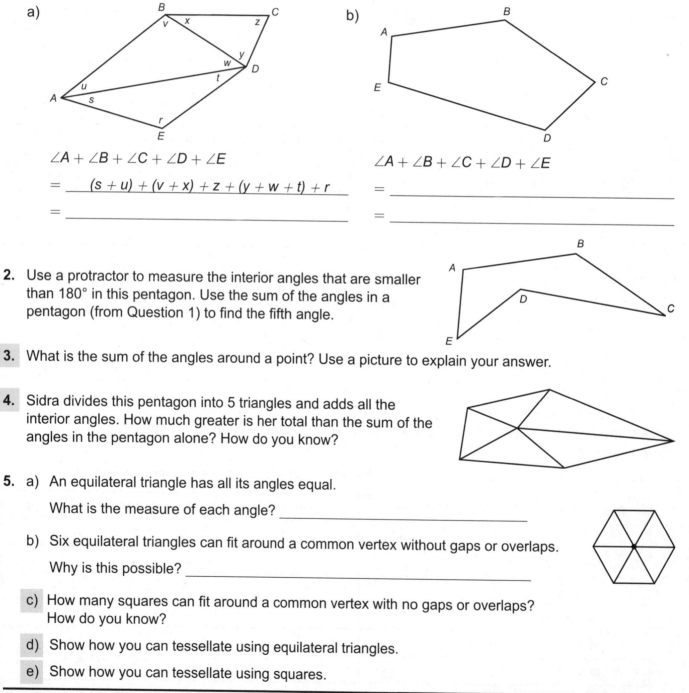

6. Divide each polygon into triangles that all meet at one of the vertices of the polygon.
Then fill in the table and find the sum of the interior angles of each polygon.

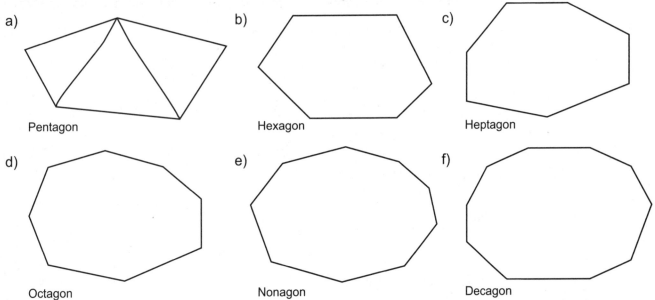

a) Pentagon

b) Hexagon

c) Heptagon

d) Octagon

e) Nonagon

f) Decagon

Polygon	Number of sides	Number of triangles created by diagonals	Expression for the sum of interior angles	Sum of interior angles
Quadrilateral	4	2	180° × 2	360°
Pentagon	5	3	180° ×	
Hexagon				
Heptagon				
Octagon				
Nonagon				
Decagon				
Any polygon	n			

INVESTIGATION ▶ A **regular polygon** has all sides and all angles equal. Which regular polygons tessellate?

A. Use the table from Question 6 to fill in the table. Round to 1 decimal place where necessary.

Regular Polygon	Number of vertices	Sum of interior angles	Measure of one interior angle
Triangle (equilateral)	3	180°	180° ÷ 3 = 60°
Quadrilateral (square)			
Pentagon			
Hexagon			
Heptagon			
Octagon			

B. Look at the numbers in the rightmost column. Does the pattern increase or decrease?

If a regular polygon has more than 8 sides, will each of its angles be greater than 135°? Explain.

C. Imagine several copies of the same regular polygon placed around a common vertex without gaps or overlaps. The polygon has interior angles of size $x°$.

   a) What does $360° \div x°$ tell you?

   b) Explain why $360° \div x°$ must be a whole number for any polygon that tessellates.

D. Use the table in Part A to complete this table.

Regular Polygon	Measure of one interior angle ($x°$)	$360° \div x°$
Triangle (equilateral)	60°	6
Quadrilateral (square)		
Pentagon		
Hexagon		
Heptagon		
Octagon		

E. Use the table in Part D to determine which of the regular polygons listed tessellate. Explain your answer.

F. Use your answer in Part B to explain why no regular polygon with more than 8 sides can tessellate.

---

7. Rectangles are not regular polygons but they tessellate. Use the information about the size of their angles to explain why they can tessellate.

8. Ying wants to create a tessellation using regular octagons and another polygon.

   a) Ying places two octagons so that they share a side. Can she place a third octagon so that it shares a vertex with the first two without creating an overlap? Why or why not?

   b) What is the degree measure of A in the picture? How do you know?

   c) What polygon could Ying use to fill in the gap between the octagons?

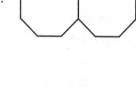

9. a) Use the sum of the angles in a hexagon to find the measure of the angles in these hexagons.

   b) Use the measure of the angles from part a) to predict whether each hexagon tessellates (alone).

   c) Copy the hexagons to a sheet of paper and cut out several copies to check your prediction in part b).

   d) Describe the transformations used to make each tessellation that works.

G7-36 Similarity

Two shapes are similar if their corresponding sides are proportionate and
their corresponding angles are equal.

In △ABC and △DEF, $AB : DE = BC : EF = AC : DF = 1 : 2$
$\angle A = \angle D, \angle B = \angle E, \angle C = \angle F$

We write △ABC ~ △DEF.

1. a) Find the ratio of the corresponding sides of the rectangles.

    $AB : EF$ = ___ : ___

    $BC : FG$ = ___ : ___

    $CD :$ ___ = ___ : ___

    $AD :$ ___ = ___ : ___

    b) Are these rectangles similar? _____

    c) Why is there no need to check equality between the angles
        to decide whether the rectangles are similar?

2. Rectangles A and B are similar. How can you find the
    length of B without a ruler?

    _____

    _____

3. Rectangles A and B are similar. Find the length of B. (Do not forget to include the units!)

    a) width of A: 1 cm   width of B: 2 cm   length of A: 3 cm   length of B: _____

    b) width of A: 2 cm   width of B: 6 cm   length of A: 4 cm   length of B: _____

    c) width of A: 1 cm   width of B: 3 cm   length of A: 5 cm   length of B: _____

4. Rectangles A and B are similar. Draw the rectangles on grid paper.

    a) width of A: 1 unit   b) width of A: 1 unit   c) width of A: 2 units
        length of A: 2 units   length of A: 2 units   length of A: 3 units
        width of B: 2 units   width of B: 3 units   width of B: 4 units

5. A square and a rectangle have the same angles. Are they similar? Explain.

6. Can a trapezoid and a square ever be similar? Explain.

7. A rhombus is a parallelogram with equal sides. Rhombus A has sides 2 cm long.
    Rhombus B has sides 4 cm long.

    a) Are rhombuses A and B necessarily similar?
    b) Draw two pairs of rhombuses A and B so that one pair is similar and the other is not.

8. For each pair of rectangles, say how you know the rectangles are similar or not.

a)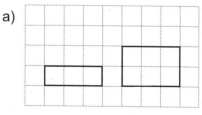

b)

c)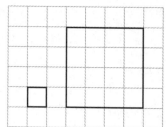

d) 2 cm × 4 cm and 3 cm × 6 cm

e) 1 cm × 2 cm and 2.5 cm × 5.5 cm

9. Draw a trapezoid similar to A with a base that is two times as long as the base of A. Hint: A is 1 unit high. How high should the new figure be?

10. Which of these shapes are similar? How do you know?

_____

_____

_____

11. Which pairs of shapes are congruent? Which are similar? How do you know?

12. Draw a parallelogram on grid paper. Then draw a similar parallelogram that is exactly twice as high as the first. Compare the areas of the figures.

13. a) Measure all angles and all sides of these triangles.

b) Are △ABC and △DEF similar? Explain using both angle measurements and ratios of sides.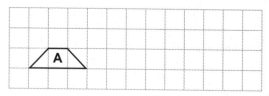

14. These triangles are similar. Find x and y.

a)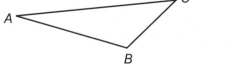

b)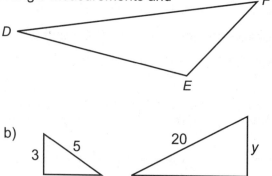

15. a) △KLM has angles 30°, 60°, and 90°.
△POR has angles 35°, 55°, and 90°.
Are the triangles similar? Explain.

b) △GHI has sides 2 cm, 4 cm, and 5 cm.
△UVW has sides 3 cm, 8 cm, and 10 cm.
Are the triangles similar? Explain.

G7-37 Dilatations

1. Find the ratio of the lengths of the line segments.

a)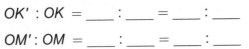

$OA' : OA = $ ___3 : 1___

$OB' : OB = $ ____ : ____

b)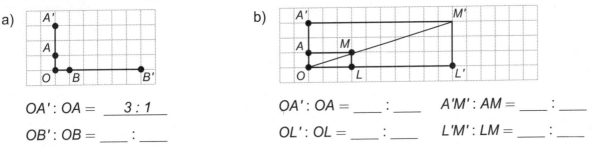

$OA' : OA = $ ____ : ____ $A'M' : AM = $ ____ : ____

$OL' : OL = $ ____ : ____ $L'M' : LM = $ ____ : ____

2. Measure the line segments. Find the ratios of the lengths. Reduce your answers to lowest terms.

$OK' : OK = $ ____ : ____ = ____ : ____

$OM' : OM = $ ____ : ____ = ____ : ____

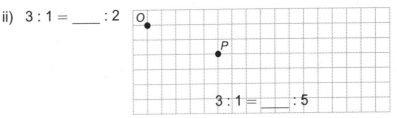

3. Find the equivalent ratios. 3 : 1 = ____ : 2 = 9 : ____ = 12 : ____ = 15 : ____

4. Draw the line OP. Find a point P' on OP so that $OP' : OP = 3 : 1$.
   Hint: OP' is 3 times longer than OP.

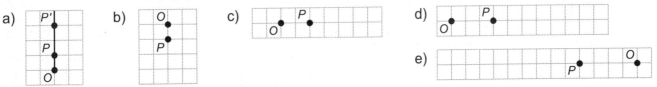

a)   b)   c)   d)

e)

5. a) Find a point P' on OP so that the ratios of the horizontal distances and the vertical distances for $OP' : OP$ are both 3 : 1.

i) 3 : 1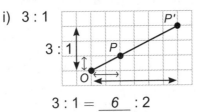

3 : 1

3 : 1 = ___6___ : 2

ii) 3 : 1 = ____ : 2

3 : 1 = ____ : 5

b) Measure the actual lengths of OP and OP'.

Write the ratio $OP' : OP$ in the form ____ : 1. What do you notice?

6. Find point A' on OA, point B' on OB, and point C' on OC, so that
   $OA' : OA = OB' : OB = OC' : OC$ are all equal to...

a) 2 : 1   b) 3 : 2   c) 1 : 3

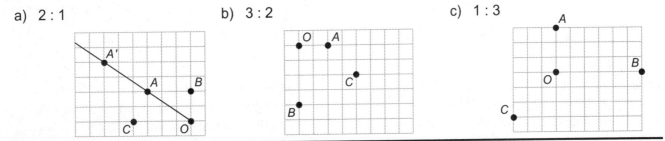

7. a) Draw lines from O through the vertices of $\triangle ABC$.

    b) Find three points A' on OA, B' on OB, and C' on OC, so that
$OA' : OA = OB' : OB = OC' : OC$ are all equal to $3 : 1$.

       Draw triangle $A'B'C'$.

The transformation you performed on $\triangle ABC$ is called a **dilatation**. The point O is the **centre of the dilatation**.

If P is the original point and P' is the image, then the ratio $OP' : OP$ is called the **scale factor of the dilatation**.

The scale factor of the dilatation in Question 7 is $3 : 1$.

INVESTIGATION ▶ How does dilatation affect shapes?

A. Measure the angles of both triangles in Question 7.

    $\angle A =$ ___ $\angle B =$ ___ $\angle C =$ ___ $\angle A' =$ ___ $\angle B' =$ ___ $\angle C' =$ ___

    What do you notice? _____

B. Measure the sides of both triangles.

    $AB =$ ___ $BC =$ ___ $AC =$ ___ $A'B' =$ ___ $B'C' =$ ___ $A'C' =$ ___

C. Find the ratio of the lengths of the corresponding sides of $\triangle ABC$ and $\triangle A'B'C'$.

    $A'B' : AB =$ _____ $B'C' : BC =$ _____ $A'C' : AC =$ _____

    What can you say about $\triangle ABC$ and $\triangle A'B'C'$? _____

---

8. For each statement, say if it is true or false. If it is false, change it to be true.

    a) Dilatation produces congruent shapes.
    b) Rotation produces congruent shapes.
    c) Reflection produces similar but not congruent shapes.
    d) Translation produces congruent shapes.

Example: Perform a dilatation with scale factor $2 : 1$, in which the centre of dilatation is O.

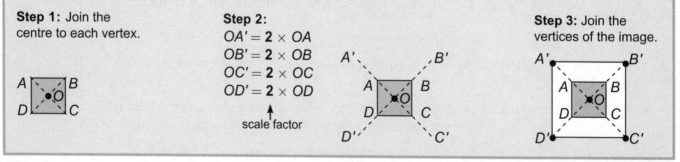

Step 1: Join the centre to each vertex.

Step 2:
$OA' = 2 \times OA$
$OB' = 2 \times OB$
$OC' = 2 \times OC$
$OD' = 2 \times OD$
    ↑
  scale factor

Step 3: Join the vertices of the image.

9. Dilatate the quadrilateral using *O* as the centre and scale factor 2 : 1.

a)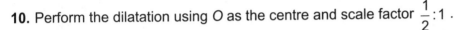

b)

10. Perform the dilatation using *O* as the centre and scale factor $\frac{1}{2}$: 1 .

a)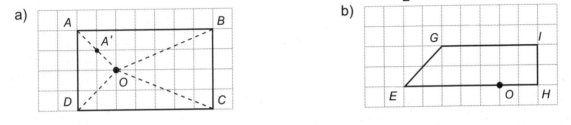

b)

> If the scale factor is a unit rate, we regard the scale factor as a number. Example: 3 instead of 3 : 1.

11. Perform the dilatation using *O* as the centre.

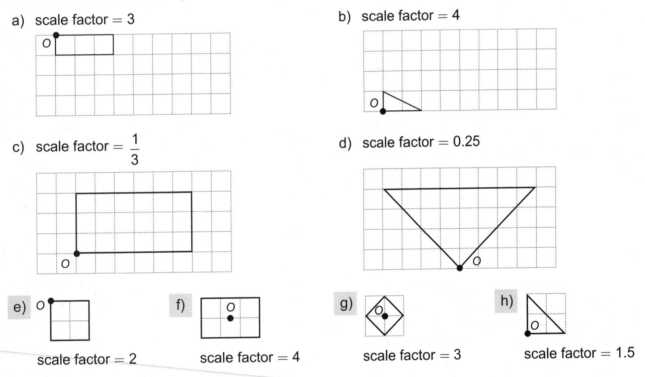

a) scale factor = 3

b) scale factor = 4

c) scale factor = $\frac{1}{3}$

d) scale factor = 0.25

e) scale factor = 2

f) scale factor = 4

g) scale factor = 3

h) scale factor = 1.5

> A dilatation is an **enlargement** if the image is larger than the original, and a **reduction** if the image is smaller than the original.

12. a) For each dilatation in Questions 9, 10, and 11, say whether it is an enlargement or a reduction.

b) Look at the scale factors of the transformations in Questions 9, 10, and 11. How can you tell by looking at the scale factor whether a dilatation is an enlargement or a reduction?

c) What would happen if you perform a dilatation with scale factor 1? Explain.

G7-38 Concepts in Transformations

Reduction

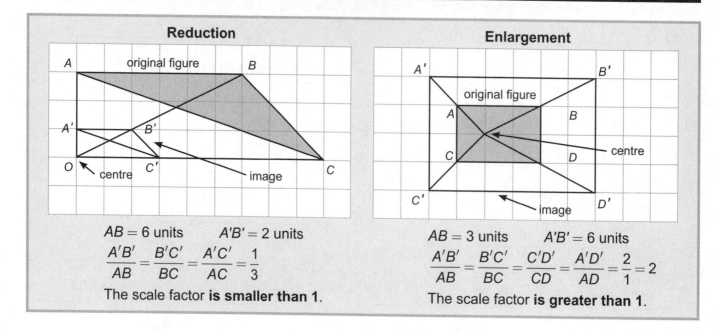

Reduction	Enlargement

$AB = 6$ units $A'B' = 2$ units

$$\frac{A'B'}{AB} = \frac{B'C'}{BC} = \frac{A'C'}{AC} = \frac{1}{3}$$

The scale factor **is smaller than 1**.

Enlargement

$AB = 3$ units $A'B' = 6$ units

$$\frac{A'B'}{AB} = \frac{B'C'}{BC} = \frac{C'D'}{CD} = \frac{A'D'}{AD} = \frac{2}{1} = 2$$

The scale factor **is greater than 1**.

1. Say whether the transformation is an enlargement, a reduction, or neither.

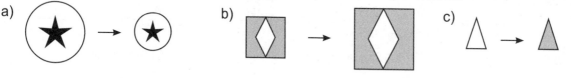

a)   b)   c)

_____   _____   _____

2. Label the vertices of the images (A', B', …). Find the scale factor of the enlargements.

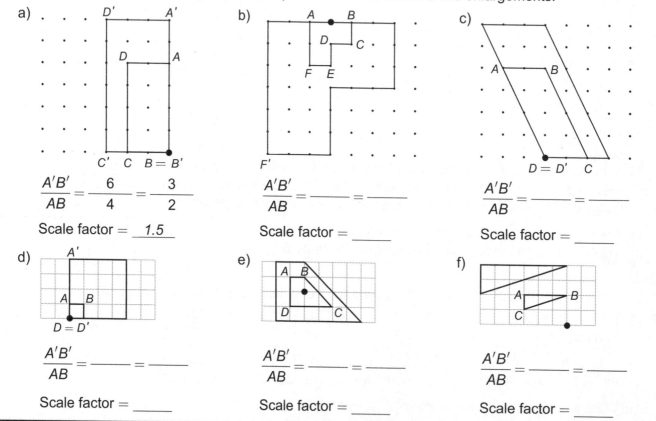

a)

$$\frac{A'B'}{AB} = \frac{6}{4} = \frac{3}{2}$$

Scale factor = ___1.5___

b)

$$\frac{A'B'}{AB} = \frac{}{} = \frac{}{}$$

Scale factor = _____

c)

$$\frac{A'B'}{AB} = \frac{}{} = \frac{}{}$$

Scale factor = _____

d)

$$\frac{A'B'}{AB} = \frac{}{} = \frac{}{}$$

Scale factor = _____

e)

$$\frac{A'B'}{AB} = \frac{}{} = \frac{}{}$$

Scale factor = _____

f)

$$\frac{A'B'}{AB} = \frac{}{} = \frac{}{}$$

Scale factor = _____

3. Label the vertices of the images (A', B', ...). Find the scale factor of the reductions.

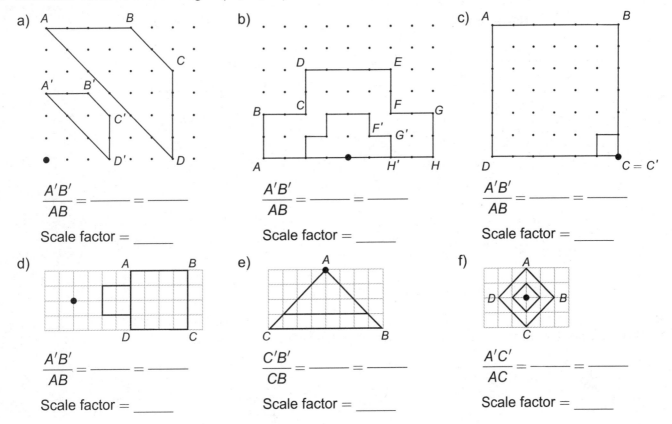

a)

$$\frac{A'B'}{AB} = \underline{\quad} = \underline{\quad}$$

Scale factor = _____

b)

$$\frac{A'B'}{AB} = \underline{\quad} = \underline{\quad}$$

Scale factor = _____

c)

$$\frac{A'B'}{AB} = \underline{\quad} = \underline{\quad}$$

Scale factor = _____

d)

$$\frac{A'B'}{AB} = \underline{\quad} = \underline{\quad}$$

Scale factor = _____

e)

$$\frac{C'B'}{CB} = \underline{\quad} = \underline{\quad}$$

Scale factor = _____

f)

$$\frac{A'C'}{AC} = \underline{\quad} = \underline{\quad}$$

Scale factor = _____

4. Identify the transformation between the shapes as a rotation, reflection, translation, or dilatation.

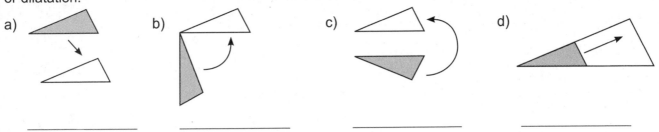

a) _____

b) _____

c) _____

d) _____

5. Ryan thinks that shape B was obtained from shape A by reflection because the shapes point in opposite directions. Ronald thinks that shape B was obtained from shape A by dilatation because shapes are similar and not congruent.

a) Are they correct? Explain why or why not.
b) Which transformations would take shape A to shape B?

6. Identify the transformations needed to obtain each tile in the design from the shaded tile.

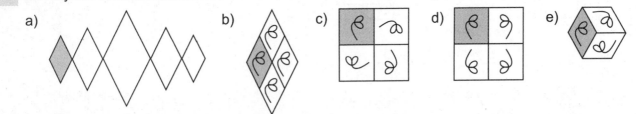

a)

b)

c)

d)

e)

PDM7-17 Theoretical Probability — Review

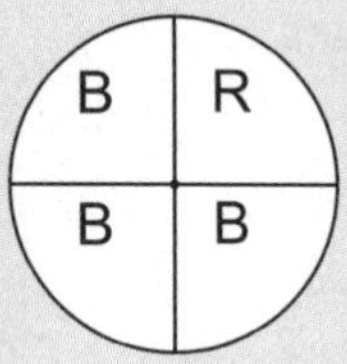

This spinner has 4 regions, so there are 4 **outcomes**.

The spinner will land in 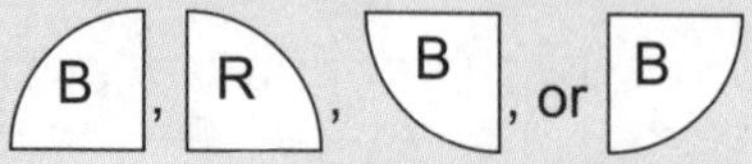 B , R , B , or B

All 4 outcomes are **equally likely** to happen.

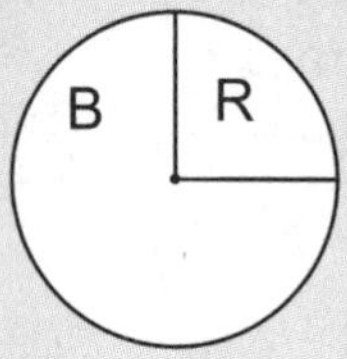

This spinner has 2 regions, so there are 2 **outcomes**.

The spinner will land in 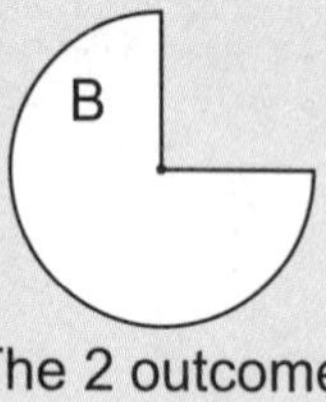 B or R

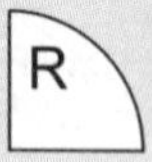

The 2 outcomes are **not** equally likely to happen.

1. How many different outcomes are there when you...

   a) roll a die? _____   b) flip a coin? _____   c) play chess with a friend? _____

2. What are the possible outcomes for these spinners?

   a) 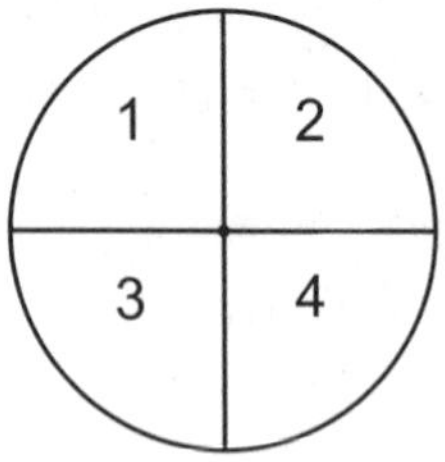 The spinner lands in regions _1_, ___ ___ ___

   There are ____ outcomes.

   b) _____

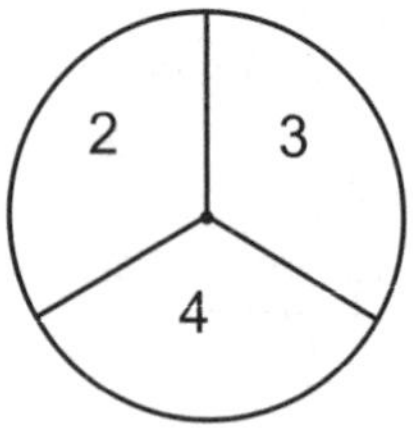

   _____

   There are ____ outcomes.

3. List all the outcomes that are...

   a) even numbers. _____

   b) odd numbers. _____

   c) greater than 9. _____

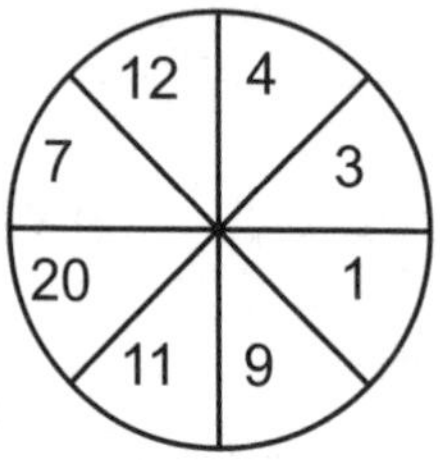

4. You draw a marble from a box. How many different outcomes are there? Are the outcomes equally likely to happen?

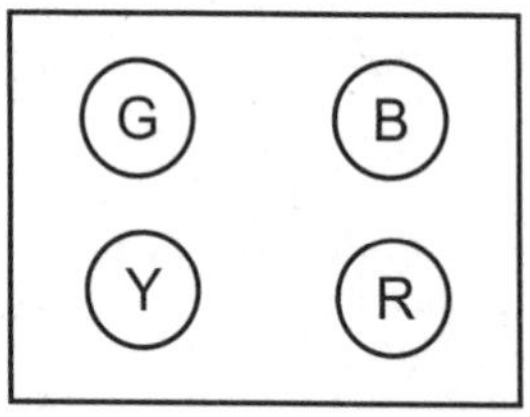

   a) 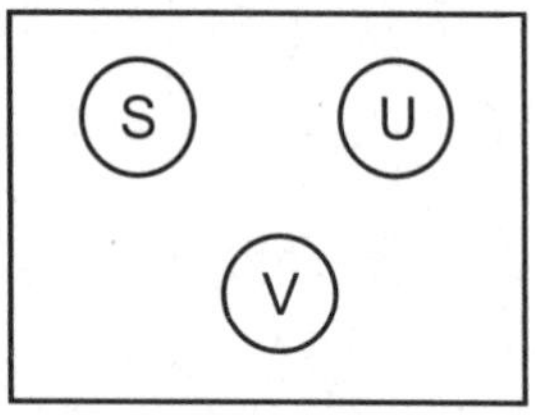 _____ outcomes   b) _____ outcomes

   Equally likely? _yes_   Equally likely? _____

5. You spin a spinner. How many different outcomes are there? Are the outcomes equally likely to happen?

   a) 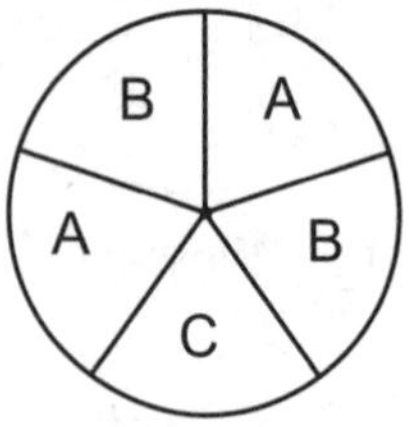 _____ outcomes   b) 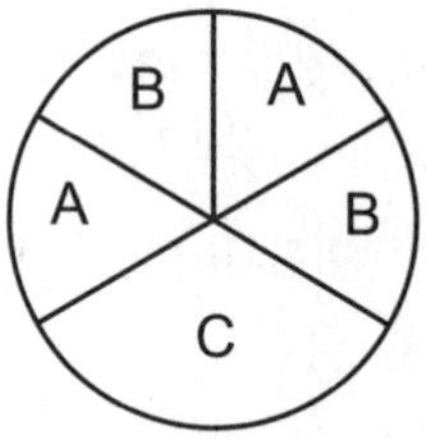 _____ outcomes

   Equally likely? _____   Equally likely? _____

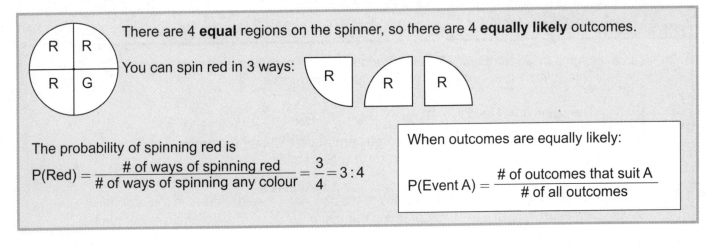

There are 4 **equal** regions on the spinner, so there are 4 **equally likely** outcomes.

You can spin red in 3 ways:

The probability of spinning red is

$$P(Red) = \frac{\text{# of ways of spinning red}}{\text{# of ways of spinning any colour}} = \frac{3}{4} = 3:4$$

When outcomes are equally likely:

$$P(\text{Event A}) = \frac{\text{# of outcomes that suit A}}{\text{# of all outcomes}}$$

6. How many ways are there to…

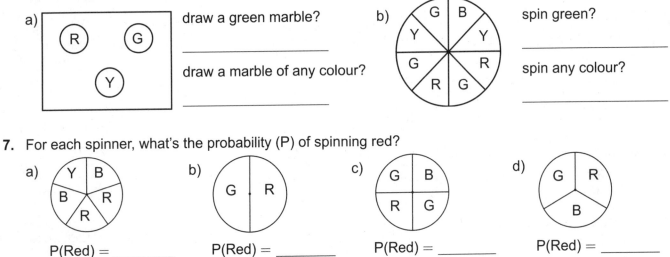

a) draw a green marble?

_____

draw a marble of any colour?

_____

b) spin green?

_____

spin any colour?

_____

7. For each spinner, what's the probability (P) of spinning red?

a) P(Red) = _____

b) P(Red) = _____

c) P(Red) = _____

d) P(Red) = _____

8. If a dart always lands on the board, what is the probability of hitting blue? Reduce your answer if possible.

a)
B	R
G	B

P(Blue) = _____

b)
B	R	G

P(Blue) = _____

c)
B	R	R
G	B	Y

P(Blue) = _____

d)
R	B	R	G
Y	Y	B	B

P(Blue) = _____

9. Cut the spinners into equal parts to make all outcomes equally likely. Find the probability.

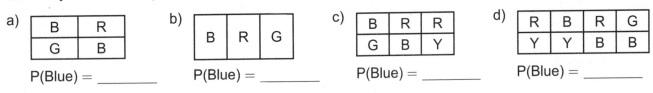

a) P(Blue) = _____

b) P(Red) = _____

c) P(Yellow) = _____

d) P(Green) = _____

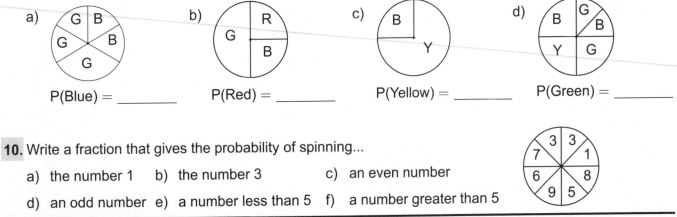

10. Write a fraction that gives the probability of spinning…

a) the number 1   b) the number 3   c) an even number

d) an odd number   e) a number less than 5   f) a number greater than 5

11. a) List the numbers on a regular die. _____

    b) How many outcomes are there when you roll a regular die? _____

12. a) List the numbers on a die that are even.

    b) How many ways can you roll an even number?

    c) What is the probability of rolling an even number?

_____   _____   _____

13. a) List the numbers on a die that are greater than 4.

    b) How many ways can you roll a number greater than 4?

    c) What is the probability of rolling a number greater than 4?

_____   _____   _____

14. Match each net for a die to the correct statement.

A.

	4		
4	5	5	6
	3		

B.

	4		
1	6	4	3
	2		

C.

	4		
2	1	4	6
	4		

D.

	5		
3	2	3	1
	4		

_____ The probability of rolling a 5 is $\frac{1}{6}$.

_____ The probability of rolling a 4 is $\frac{1}{2}$.

_____ The probability of rolling an even number is $\frac{1}{2}$.

_____ The probability of rolling a 1 is the same as the probability of rolling a 3.

15. Write a fraction that gives the probability of spinning...

    a) the letter A   **b)** the letter C

    c) the letter E   **d)** a vowel

    e) a consonant   **f)** a letter that appears in the word "Canada"

16. Clare says the probability of rolling a 1 on a die is $\frac{1}{6}$, so the probability of rolling a 5 is $\frac{5}{6}$. Emma says the probability is $\frac{1}{6}$ for both numbers. Who is right? Explain.

_____

_____

17. Design a spinner on which the probability of spinning red is $\frac{3}{8}$.

18. Design a net for a die on which the probability of rolling an odd number is $\frac{1}{3}$.

PDM7-18 Theoretical Probability

1. Circle the numbers that mean $\frac{3}{4}$.

   34% $\frac{4}{3}$ 0.3 $\frac{30}{40}$ 75% $\frac{3+4}{4+4}$ 3 out of 4 $\frac{3 \times 2}{4 \times 2}$ 9 out of 12 $\frac{75}{100}$ 9 out of 10

2. Express each probability as a fraction, a decimal, and a percentage.

   a) $P(R) = \frac{1}{2} = 0.5 = 50\%$

      $P(B) =$ _____

      $P(any\ colour) =$ _____

   b) $P(R) =$ _____

      $P(B) =$ _____

      $P(G) =$ _____

   c) $P(Y) =$ _____ $P(R) =$ _____

      $P(B) =$ _____ $P(G) =$ _____

3. Circle the numbers that can express probability.

   50% $\frac{1}{3}$ $\frac{3}{1}$ 0.58 $\frac{4}{7}$ $\frac{7}{4}$ 2.64 $2\frac{1}{2}$ 1:6   3

   (−0.2)   1   47.5% $\frac{31}{1000}$ 0.35   (−2)   0   (+0.25)   (+1.37)   2:3

4. Describe an event that has a probability of...

   a) 100%   b) 50%   c) 0%

5. The probability of rain is often given as a percent. For each prediction below, write a fraction giving the probability that it will rain. Reduce your answer to lowest terms.

   a) 60% chance of rain   b) 35% chance of rain   c) 75% chance of rain

6. In baseball, a **batting average** is the ratio of the number of hits to the number of times a player has a turn at bat. Batting averages are decimals that can be changed to fractions out of 1000.

   Example: A batting average of .427 ($= \frac{427}{1000}$) means a player had 427 hits in 1000 times at bat.

   Find the probability of a hit given a player's batting average. Reduce your answers to lowest terms.

   a) .125   b) .300   c) .425   d) .256   e) .324

7. Which player is most likely to have a hit?

   a) Player A: batting average .425   b) Player A: hits one quarter of pitches
      Player B: hits 4 out of 10 pitches   Player B: batting average .230
      Player C: hits 42% of pitches   Player C: hits 23% of pitches

At sports camp, Erin has these choices:

Morning – gymnastics or rowing
Afternoon – volleyball, hockey, or rugby

Erin draws a **tree diagram** so that she can see all the combinations of choices.

Step 1: She writes the name of her two morning choices at the ends of two branches.

Step 2: Under each of her morning choices, she adds three branches—one for each of her afternoon choices.

Step 3: Follow any path along the branches (from the top of the tree to the bottom) to find one of Erin's choices.

gymnastics   rowing

volleyball   hockey   rugby   volleyball   hockey   rugby

Example: The path highlighted by arrows shows gymnastics in the morning and hockey in the afternoon.

1. Follow a path from the top of the tree to a box at the bottom, and write the sports named on the path in the box. Continue until you have filled in all the boxes.

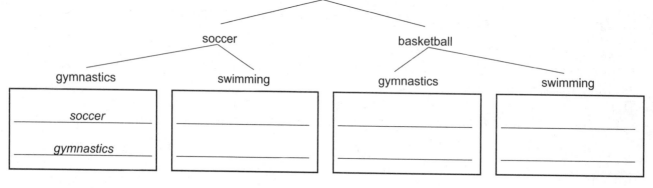

soccer   basketball

gymnastics   swimming   gymnastics   swimming

soccer _____	_____	_____	_____
gymnastics _____	_____	_____	_____

2. Complete the tree diagram to show all of the possible outcomes of flipping a coin twice (H = heads and T = tails).

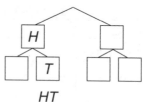

H   ☐

☐ *T*   ☐ ☐

HT

3. Matthew's camp offers the following activities:

Morning – drama or visual arts
Afternoon – dance or creative writing

Draw a tree diagram (like the one in Question 1) to show all the combinations of choices.

4. Complete the tree diagram to show all of the possible outcomes from first flipping a coin (H = heads, T = tails) and then drawing a marble from the box that holds three marbles of different colours: R = red, G = green, Y = yellow.

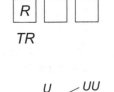

TR

5. Emma is playing a role-playing game and her character is exploring a tunnel in a cave.

   a) Complete the tree diagram that shows all the paths through the cave (U = up, D = down).

   b) How many paths are there through the cave? _____

   c) A monster is waiting at the end of one path. Do you think it is likely or unlikely that Emma's character will meet the monster? Explain.

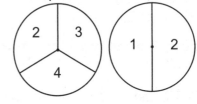

Enter here...
→
If you dare!

6. Draw a tree diagram to show all the combinations of numbers you could spin on the two spinners.

   a) How many pairs of numbers add to four?
   b) How many pairs of numbers have a product of four?

7. A restaurant offers the following choices for breakfast:

   Main Course – eggs, muffins, or pancakes
   Juice – apple, mango, orange, or grape

   Draw a tree diagram to show all the different breakfasts you could order.

8. Make a tree diagram to show all the combinations of points you could get by throwing two darts at this board.

   How many combinations add to 5?

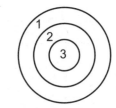

9. a) Look at the tree diagrams you drew above and fill in the table.

Question	# of branches at the 1st level	# of branches at the 2nd level	Total # of paths
4	2	3	6
5			
6			
7			
8			

   b) How can you calculate the total number of paths from the numbers of branches at each level? Explain.

   c) Tegan performs an experiment with a die with 20 faces and a die with 12 faces. She draws a tree diagram to see the possible outcomes. How many paths will her tree diagram have?

PDM7-20 Counting Combinations

Miki wants to know how many outcomes there are for a game with two spinners:

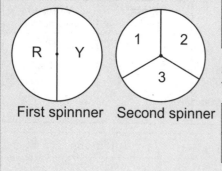

First spinner   Second spinner

Step 1: There are **3 outcomes** on the second spinner, so Miki lists each colour on the first spinner **3 times.**

First Spinner	R	R	R	Y	Y	Y
Second Spinner						

Step 2: Beside each colour, Miki writes the 3 possible outcomes on the second spinner.

First Spinner	R	R	R	Y	Y	Y
Second Spinner	1	2	3	1	2	3

The list shows that there are **6 outcomes** altogether for the game.

For each question below, answer parts a) and b), then write the list of combinations to show all the ways Miki can spin a colour and a number.

1.

First Spinner	
Second Spinner	

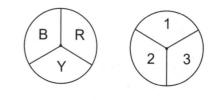

a) How many outcomes are on the second spinner? _____

b) How many times should Miki write B (for blue), Y (for yellow), and R (for red) on his list? _____

c) How many outcomes does this game have altogether? _____

2.

First Spinner	
Second Spinner	

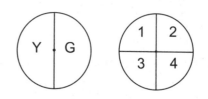

a) How many outcomes are on the second spinner? _____

b) How many times should Miki write Y (for yellow) and G (for green) on his list? _____

c) How many outcomes does this game have altogether? _____

3.

First Spinner	
Second Spinner	

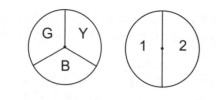

a) How many outcomes are on the second spinner? _____

b) How many times should Miki write G (for green), B (for blue), and Y (for yellow) on his list? _____

c) How many outcomes does this game have altogether? _____

4. If you flip a coin there are two outcomes: heads (H) and tails (T).

List all the outcomes for flipping a coin and spinning the spinner.

Coin	
Spinner	

5. Peter has a quarter (Q) and a dime (D) in his left pocket, and a dime (D) and a nickel (N) in his right pocket. He pulls one coin from each pocket.

List all the combinations of coins that Peter could pull out of his pockets, and their value.

Left pocket	Right pocket	Value of the coins

6. Clare can choose from the following activities at art camp:

Morning: painting or music
Afternoon: drama, pottery, or dance

She makes a chart so she can see all of her choices. She starts by writing each of her morning choices 3 times.

a) Complete the chart to show all of Clare's choices.

b) Why did Clare write each of her morning choices 3 times?

Morning	Afternoon
painting	
painting	
painting	
music	
music	
music	

7. Make a chart to show all the combinations of activities at a camp that offers the following choices:

Morning: swimming or tennis
Afternoon: canoeing, baseball, or hiking

8. a) Record all the scores you could get by throwing two darts at the dart board. (Assume both darts land on the board.)

b) Which combinations give the same score?

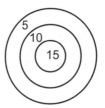

9. A tetrahedral die has 4 vertices numbered from 1 to 4. When you roll this die, there is always a vertex on top. Make a chart to show all the combinations for rolling a pair of tetrahedral dice.

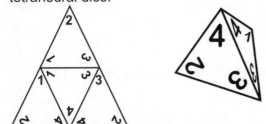

PDM7-21　Compound Events

Jade and Lara have a box of marbles.　(R) (G) (G) (B) (B) (G)

1. Lara draws a marble from the box. She leaves the marble outside the box and draws a second marble. There are five marbles in the box for the second draw.

   a) List all the outcomes of Lara's second draw if on the first draw she draws…

   i)　a green marble　　　　ii) a blue marble　　　　iii) a red marble

   _____R, G, B, B, G_____　　　_____　　　_____

   b) Does the list of possible outcomes of the second draw change with the results of the first? _____

2. Jade draws a marble from the box. She places the marble back and draws a marble again.

   a) List all the outcomes of Jade's second draw, if on the first draw she draws…

   i)　a green marble　　　　ii) a blue marble　　　　iii) a red marble

   _____　　　_____　　　_____

   b) Does the list of possible outcomes of the second draw change with the results of the first? _____

   > Two events are **independent** if the outcomes of one event do <u>not</u> depend on the results of the other event.

3. Whose pair of draws is independent, Jade's or Lara's? _____

4. Are these pairs of events independent? Write yes or no.

   a) Draw a marble from a box and spin a spinner. _____

   b) Toss two coins. _____

   c) Spin two spinners. _____

   d) Spin the same spinner twice. _____

   e) Pull two coins, one after the other (without replacing), from a bag of coins. _____

   f) Pick captains for two teams from a group of students. _____

5. Choose a pair of independent events from Question 4 and explain why they are independent.

6. Bob and Nick each have a box of three marbles, two red and one green. Bob draws a marble, lists the colour, places the marble back in the box, and draws a second marble. Nick draws a marble, lists the colour, and leaves the marble outside the box. Then he draws a second marble.

   a) Draw a tree diagram to show the possible outcomes of each person's draws.
   b) Who has more possible outcomes, Bob or Nick?
   c) Whose way of drawing two marbles is independent, Bob's or Nick's?

7. a) Write a set of ordered pairs to show all the combinations you could spin on the two spinners.

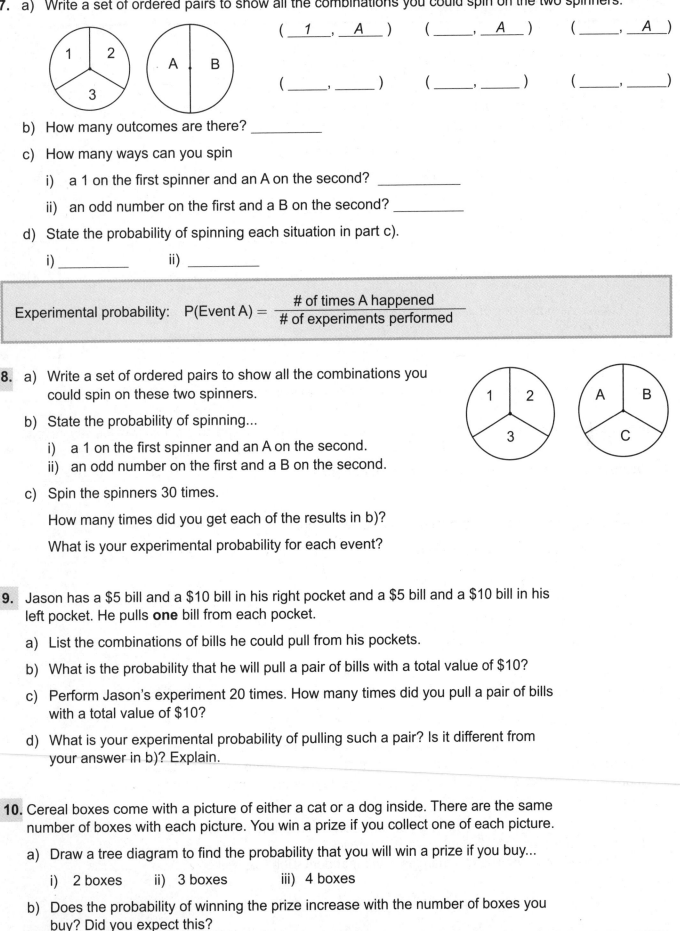

(_1_ , _A_)   (___ , _A_)   (___ , _A_)

(___ , ___)   (___ , ___)   (___ , ___)

   b) How many outcomes are there? _____

   c) How many ways can you spin

      i)   a 1 on the first spinner and an A on the second? _____

      ii) an odd number on the first and a B on the second? _____

   d) State the probability of spinning each situation in part c).

      i) _____   ii) _____

Experimental probability: P(Event A) = $\dfrac{\text{\# of times A happened}}{\text{\# of experiments performed}}$

8. a) Write a set of ordered pairs to show all the combinations you could spin on these two spinners.

   b) State the probability of spinning...

      i)   a 1 on the first spinner and an A on the second.
      ii) an odd number on the first and a B on the second.

   c) Spin the spinners 30 times.

      How many times did you get each of the results in b)?

      What is your experimental probability for each event?

9. Jason has a $5 bill and a $10 bill in his right pocket and a $5 bill and a $10 bill in his left pocket. He pulls **one** bill from each pocket.

   a) List the combinations of bills he could pull from his pockets.

   b) What is the probability that he will pull a pair of bills with a total value of $10?

   c) Perform Jason's experiment 20 times. How many times did you pull a pair of bills with a total value of $10?

   d) What is your experimental probability of pulling such a pair? Is it different from your answer in b)? Explain.

10. Cereal boxes come with a picture of either a cat or a dog inside. There are the same number of boxes with each picture. You win a prize if you collect one of each picture.

   a) Draw a tree diagram to find the probability that you will win a prize if you buy...

      i)   2 boxes   ii) 3 boxes   iii) 4 boxes

   b) Does the probability of winning the prize increase with the number of boxes you buy? Did you expect this?

PDM7-22 Expectation

Kate plans to spin the spinner 15 times to see how many times it will land on yellow.

Since $\frac{1}{3}$ of the spinner is yellow, Kate **expects** to spin yellow $\frac{1}{3}$ of the time.

Kate finds $\frac{1}{3}$ of 15 by dividing by 3: **$15 \div 3 = 5$**

So she expects the spinner to land on yellow 5 times.

1. Divide.

   a) $2\overline{)10}$ b) $2\overline{)12}$ c) $2\overline{)18}$ d) $2\overline{)26}$ e) $2\overline{)68}$ f) $2\overline{)82}$

   g) $3\overline{)27}$ h) $4\overline{)44}$ i) $3\overline{)51}$ j) $3\overline{)63}$ k) $4\overline{)64}$ l) $4\overline{)96}$

2. Using long division, find…

   a) $\frac{1}{2}$ of 38   b) $\frac{1}{2}$ of 56   c) $\frac{1}{3}$ of 39   d) $\frac{1}{3}$ of 42   e) $\frac{1}{4}$ of 56   f) $\frac{1}{4}$ of 76

3. If you flip a coin repeatedly, what fraction of the throws would you expect to be heads? _____

4. How many times would you expect to flip heads if you flipped a coin...

   a) 12 times? _____   b) 40 times? _____   c) 68 times? _____

5. For each spinner below, what **fraction** of your spins would you expect to be red?

   a) *I would expect to spin* _____

   red _____ *of the time* _____

   b) _____

   _____

6. How many times would you expect to spin yellow if you spun the spinner...

   a) 18 times? _____   b) 24 times? _____

   33 times? _____   44 times? _____

   69 times? _____   92 times? _____

7. Sketch a spinner on which you would expect to spin red $\frac{3}{4}$ of the time. What is the probability of spinning a colour that is **not** red? Explain.

8. Find the fractions of the numbers.

   a) $\frac{1}{3}$ of 12 is ___4___, so $\frac{2}{3}$ of 12 is ___8___   b) $\frac{1}{3}$ of 21 is _____, so $\frac{2}{3}$ of 21 is _____

   c) $\frac{2}{3}$ of 39   d) $\frac{2}{3}$ of 42   e) $\frac{2}{3}$ of 75   f) $\frac{3}{4}$ of 48   g) $\frac{3}{4}$ of 56   h) $\frac{3}{5}$ of 75

9. Colour the marbles red and green (or label them R and G) to match the probability of drawing a marble of the given colour.

a) P(Red) = $\frac{3}{4}$

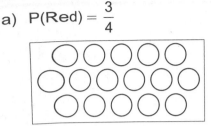

b) P(Green) = $\frac{2}{3}$

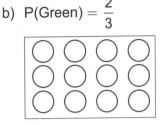

c) P(Red) = $\frac{3}{4}$

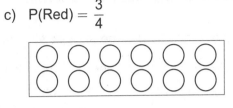

10. How many times would you expect to spin blue if you used the spinner the given number of times? Explain.

a) 60 times

b) 200 times

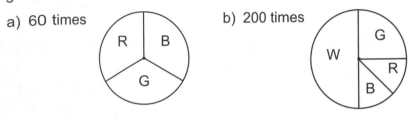

11. The pie diagram shows the fraction of students at a school who walk, ride the bus, bike, or skateboard to school.

a) What fraction of students skateboard to school?

b) If you surveyed 200 students, about how many would you expect to have biked to school?

12. A scientist observes a group of 50 caribou and finds that only 10 of them are male.

a) What is the experimental probability of a caribou in this group being male?

b) What percentage of the group is male?

c) The scientist assumes that the observation represents the ratio of the number of males to the number of females in a larger group of caribou during this time of the year. What fraction of a group of caribou should be males?

d) How many males does the scientist expect to see in a group of 1000 caribou?

13. The chart shows the survival rate (how many birds will survive) under two different environmental protection programs.

If a program could be implemented in only one forest, which one would you choose? Explain.

	Forest A	Forest B
Number of Endangered Birds	5 000	15 000
Survival Rate	80%	2 in 5

14. A batting average of .427 means a baseball player had 427 hits in 1000 times at bat.

a) Express the batting averages below as the probability that a player gets a hit. Reduce your answer to lowest terms.

i) Player A .200

ii) Player B .250

iii) Player C .400

b) Say how many hits, on average, each player is likely to get in 60 times at bat.

1. Tanya and Daniel play a game of chance with the spinner shown.

   If it lands on yellow, Tanya wins. If it lands on red, Daniel wins.

   a) Tanya and Daniel play the game 20 times. How many times would you **expect** the spinner to land on red? _____

   b) When Tanya and Daniel play the game, they get the results shown in the chart. Daniel says the game is not fair. Is he right? Explain.

Green	Red	Yellow
₩	₩	₩ ₩

2. Janet has two dice: one with 4 vertices, marked 1 to 4, and the other with 8 sides, marked 1 to 8.

   a) Make a T-table and list all the outcomes for rolling the two dice.

   b) Circle all the outcomes that add to 5.

   c) What is the probability of rolling a pair of numbers that add to 5?

   d) If you roll the dice 40 times, how many times would you expect to roll a pair of numbers that add to 5?

3. Jo has 3 bills in her pocket: a $5 bill, a $10 bill, and a $50 bill. She pulls out two bills.

   a) What are all the possible combinations of two bills she could pull out?

   b) Would Jo expect to pull a pair of bills that add up to $15? Are the chances likely or unlikely?

   c) How did you solve the problem in part b)? Did you use a list? A picture? A calculation?

4. Simone made an organized list to find all possible outcomes for rolling two regular dice. The table shows **part** of the chart she made.

   Why did Simone write the number 1 six times in her chart? Complete Simone's chart.

First Die	Second Die
1	1
1	2
1	3
1	4
1	5
1	6
2	1
2	2
2	3
2	4
2	5
2	6

5. Suppose you roll 2 regular dice.

   a) What is the probability of rolling a total of...
      i) 4?   ii) 6?   iii) 7?   iv) 11?   v) 12?

   b) What is the probability of rolling...
      i) an even number total?   ii) two even numbers?   iii) two consecutive numbers?

   c) What two totals are you **least likely** to roll?

   d) What total are you **most likely** to roll?

6. Which outcome is more likely: A or B?

   A You roll 2 regular dice and get a total of 12.   **B** You toss a coin 3 times and get 3 heads.